Surviving

Your
Dissertation

3rd Edition

Surviving Your Dissertation
3rd Edition
A Comprehensive Guide to Content and Process

Kjell Erik Rudestam
Fielding Graduate University

Rae R. Newton
California State University, Fullerton

SAGE Publications
Los Angeles • London • New Delhi • Singapore

For information:

 Sage Publications, Inc.
2455 Teller Road
Thousand Oaks, California 91320
E-mail: order@sagepub.com

Sage Publications India Pvt Ltd
B 1/I 1 Mohan Cooperative
Industrial Area
Mathura Road, New Delhi 110 044
India

Sage Publications Ltd.
1 Oliver's Yard
55 City Road
London EC1Y 1SP
United Kingdom

Sage Publications Asia-Pacific Pte Ltd
33 Pekin Street #02-01
Far East Square
Singapore 048763

Library of Congress Cataloging-in-Publication Data

Rudestam, Kjell Erik.
Surviving your dissertation : a comprehensive guide to content and process / Kjell Erik Rudestam, Rae R. Newton. — 3rd ed.
  p. cm.
Includes bibliographical references and indexes.
ISBN 978-1-4129-1678-3 (cloth : alk. paper)
ISBN 978-1-4129-1679-0 (pbk. : alk. paper)
  1. Dissertations, Academic—United States. 2. Report writing.
3. Research—United States. I. Newton, Rae R. II. Title.
LB2369.R83 2007
808'.02—dc22

2006035884

Printed in the United States of America on acid-free paper.

07   08   09   10   11   10   9   8   7   6   5   4   3   2   1

Acquiring Editor:	Lisa Cuevas Shaw
Editorial Assistant:	Karen Margrethe Greene
Production Editor:	Sanford Robinson
Copy Editor:	Cheryl Duksta
Proofreader:	Theresa Kay
Typesetter:	C&M Digitals (P) Ltd.
Indexer:	Maria Sosnowski
Cover Designer:	Michelle Kenny
Marketing Manager:	Stephanie Adams

Contents

Preface   vii

PART I. Getting Started
1. The Research Process   3
2. Selecting a Suitable Topic   9
3. Methods of Inquiry:
    Quantitative and Qualitative Approaches   23

PART II. Working With the Content: The Dissertation Chapters
4. Literature Review and Statement of the Problem   61
5. The Method Chapter: Describing Your Research Plan   87
6. Presenting the Results of Quantitative Studies   117
7. Presenting the Results of Qualitative Research   177
8. Discussion   195

PART III. Working With Process:
What You Need to Know to Make the Dissertation Easier
9. Overcoming Barriers: Becoming an
    Expert While Controlling Your Own Destiny   205
10. Writing   227
    Jody Veroff
11. How to Complete Your Dissertation
    Using Online Data Access and Collection   249
12. Guidelines for the Presentation of Numbers
    in the Dissertation   265
13. Informed Consent and Other Ethical Concerns   275

References   293

Name Index   303

Subject Index   307

About the Authors   317

Preface

W e are obviously pleased that sales of *Surviving Your Dissertation* have warranted a third edition. It is timely to publish an updated edition because the research enterprise is never stagnant and new perspectives, methods, and standards keep proliferating. We know that students still struggle to write a quality dissertation and that they seem to appreciate another resource to help guide them through this process. In fact, the many readers of this book are our best source of inspiration because they frequently remind us of what we have neglected to mention and what they would like to see included.

The content of the third edition has been expanded. The sections on qualitative research approaches have been enriched. Four primary approaches (phenomenology, grounded theory, ethnographic inquiry, and narrative inquiry) have received additional attention, with many more dissertation examples, reflecting a burgeoning interest in these methods among our students. We have also expanded the list of alternative approaches to writing a dissertation, including the mixed method approach, case studies, and action research.

We have attempted to pay more attention to examining the philosophical underpinnings of the various research paradigms and to differentiating between quantitative and qualitative approaches. Within the quantitative arena, we have provided more examples of research designs and have gone into greater detail in describing data analyses and results. We have elaborated on current topics of interest, such as power, confidence intervals, figures and graphs, and alternatives to traditional null hypothesis significance testing. Structurally, we have divided the Results chapter into two chapters, quantitative and qualitative, to accommodate the added content.

An increasing number of students are now using the Internet for data collection, a resource that promises to significantly change the landscape of contemporary social science research. We have introduced a new chapter to discuss this topic. At the same time, many of the software programs and much of the computer guidance we offered in the previous edition now seem outdated. In response, we eliminated the chapter on using a personal computer effectively and interjected suggestions and references for using this important resource throughout the book. Finally, we have updated the chapters on writing and on research ethics to reflect current thinking in the field.

Pedagogically, we have tried to include more examples and more tables and figures to supplement the text. We have also introduced a series of tip boxes to provide the reader with highly accessible and practical advice on a variety of topics. We hope that these changes have resulted in a user-friendly edition while maintaining the breadth and depth of the original text.

We continue to learn from our students and we are deeply grateful for their dissertation experiences, positive and negative. These experiences have provided the inspiration to keep this project moving along much longer than we initially anticipated. We take great satisfaction in the fact that, as co-authors, we continue to share responsibilities and work well together. Along the way, we continue to be grateful for the support of our families, particularly Jan and Kathy, who have learned to gracefully tolerate our intense working sessions. Special thanks go to a host of colleagues at Fielding Graduate University who assisted us with helpful information, content, or feedback: Edward Tronick, Judith Schoenholtz-Read, Sam Osherson, Ruthellen Josselson, Nancy Baker, David Rehorick, Barnett Pearce, Katherine Randazzo, Peggy Collins, and Stefan Kramer. Sage Publications has been a steadfast supporter of this project since its inception, and we want to acknowledge our editor, Lisa Cuevas, and the staff who facilitated the publication of this revision: Karen Greene, Margo Beth Crouppen, Stephanie Adams, and Sanford Robinson. Additional thanks go to reviewers of our second edition, Katherine Randazzo, Alexander Wiseman, Thomas Paradis, Jennifer Devenport, Neal Chalofsky, Steven Aragon, and Elias Avramidis, who provided us with excellent suggestions for the third edition. To these many contributors: We may not have met all of your expectations, but we have appreciated the assistance you have generously given us.

Kjell Erik Rudestam

Rae R. Newton

PART I

Getting Started

1

The Research Process

There is the story of a Zen Buddhist who took a group of monks into the forest, whereupon the group soon lost their way. Presently one of the monks asked the leader where they were going. The wise man answered, "To the deepest, darkest part of the forest so that we can all find our way out together." Doctoral research for the graduate student in the social sciences is often experienced in just that manner—trekking into a forest of impenetrable density and false turns. Over the years, our students have employed various metaphors to describe the dissertation process, metaphors that support the feeling of being lost in the wilderness. One student compared the process to the Sisyphean struggle of reaching the top of a hill, only to discover the presence of an even higher mountain behind it. Another student experienced the task as learning a Martian language, known to the natives who composed her committee but entirely foreign to her. A third student had perhaps the best description when she suggested that it was like waiting patiently in a seemingly interminable line to gain admission to a desirable event, then finally reaching the front only to be told to return to the rear of the line.

One reason that students become more exasperated than necessary on the dissertation journey is that they fail to understand the procedures and practices that form the foundation for contemporary social science research. Many students who are attracted to their field of interest out of an applied concern are apprehensive about making the leap from application to theory, which is an indispensable part of the research enterprise. What may not be so evident is that many of the skills that go into being

3

a consummate practitioner are the same skills that are demanded of a capable researcher. It is well known that curiosity and hypothesis testing are the bedrock of empirical research. In a similar fashion, experienced psychotherapists, to take an example from clinical psychology, are sensitive and keen observers of client behavior. They are persistent hypothesis testers. They are curious about the relationship between family history variables and current functioning. They draw on theory and experience to help select a particular intervention for a particular client problem or moment in therapy.

Dispassionate logic and clear and organized thinking are as necessary for effectiveness in the field as they are for success in research. In fact, the bridge between research and just plain living is much shorter than most people think. All of us gather data about the world around us, wonder what will happen if we or others behave in particular ways, and test our pet hunches through deliberate action. To a large extent, the formal research enterprise consists of thinking systematically about these same issues.

The procedures outlined in this book are intended to assist the doctoral student in planning and writing a research dissertation. The suggestions are equally applicable to writing a master's thesis. There is considerable overlap between these two challenging activities. For most students, the master's thesis is the first rigorous research project they attempt. This means that, in the absence of strong, supportive faculty consultation, the student often concludes the thesis with considerable relief and an awareness of how not to do the study the next time! With a doctoral dissertation, it is generally expected, sometimes as an act of faith, that the student will be a more seasoned and sophisticated researcher. The consensus opinion is that dissertations are generally longer than theses, that they are more original, and that they make a greater contribution to the field.

In most graduate programs, the prelude to conducting a dissertation study is presenting a dissertation proposal. A research proposal is an action plan that justifies and describes the proposed study. We take the completion of a comprehensive proposal as a very important step in the dissertation process. The proposal serves as a contract between the student and his or her dissertation or thesis committee that, when approved by all parties, constitutes an agreement that data may be collected and the study may be completed. As long as the student follows the steps outlined in the proposal, committee members should be discouraged from demanding significant changes to the study after the proposal has been approved. Naturally, it is not uncommon to expect small changes, additions, or deletions down the road because one can never totally envision the unpredictable turns that studies can take.

There is no universally agreed-on format for the research proposal. To our way of thinking, a good proposal contains a review of the relevant literature, a statement of the problem and the associated hypotheses, and a clear delineation of the proposed method and plans for data analysis. In our experience, an approved proposal means that more than half of the work of the dissertation has been completed. This book is intended to help students construct research proposals as well as completed dissertations.

The Research Wheel

One way of thinking about the phases of the research process is with reference to the so-called research wheel (see Figure 1.1). The wheel metaphor suggests that research is not linear but a recursive cycle of steps that are repeated over time. The most common entry point is some form of empirical observation. In other words, the researcher selects a topic from the infinite array of possible topics. The next step is a process of inductive logic that culminates in a proposition. The inductive process serves to relate the specific topic to a broader context and begins with some hunches in the form "I wonder if. . . . " These hunches typically are guided by the values, assumptions, and goals of the researcher that need to be explicated.

Stage 2 of the research wheel is a developed proposition, which is expressed as a statement of an established relationship (e.g., "the early bird is more likely than the late bird to catch the worm"). The proposition

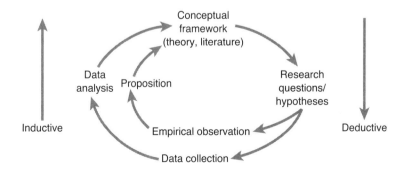

Figure 1.1   The research wheel

exists within a conceptual or theoretical framework. It is the role of the researcher to clarify the relationship between a particular proposition and the broader context of theory and previous research. This is probably the most challenging and creative aspect of the dissertation process. A conceptual framework, which is simply a less-developed form of a theory, consists of statements that link abstract concepts (e.g., motivation, role) to empirical data. Theories and conceptual frameworks are developed to account for or describe abstract phenomena that occur under similar conditions. A theory is the language that allows researchers to move from observation to observation and make sense of similarities and differences. Without placing the study within such a context, the proposed study has a "so what?" quality. This is one of the main objections to the research proposals of novice researchers: The research question may be inherently interesting but ultimately meaningless. For instance, the question "Are there more women than men in graduate school today?" is totally banal as a research question unless the answer to the question has conceptual or theoretical implications that are developed within the study. A study may be worthwhile primarily for its practical implications (e.g., "Should we start recruiting more men into graduate schools?"), but a purely applied study may not be acceptable as a dissertation. Kerlinger and Lee (1999), authors of a highly respected text on research methodology, noted that "the basic purpose of scientific research is theory" (p. 5). Generally speaking, a research dissertation is expected to contribute to the scholarly literature in a field and not merely solve an applied problem. Thus, identifying a conceptual framework for a research study typically involves immersing oneself in the research and theoretical literature of the field.

Having stated our position with regard to the role of theory in dissertation research, it becomes necessary to take a step back. As a psychologist and a sociologist, we are most familiar with research conventions within these two disciplines. Other branches of the social sciences have their own standards of what constitutes an acceptable dissertation topic. We have attempted to keep this book as generalizable as possible and to infuse it with examples from other fields. Ultimately, of course, you will need to follow the rules and conventions that pertain to your discipline as well as to your university and department. For example, a few major universities allow a doctoral student to submit a series of published articles as an equivalent to a dissertation. Many others encourage studies that consist of secondary data analyses derived from national databases, such as census data or the General Social Survey, or data obtained from a larger study. Some fields, notably social work, education, policy evaluation, and professional psychology, may encourage dissertations that solve applied problems rather than make distinct theoretical contributions. Studies that evaluate the effectiveness of programs or interventions are a case in point because they sometimes contribute little in the way of validating a theory. Political science and economics are examples of fields that are diverse enough to accommodate both theoretically based studies and purely applied studies. Within the subspecialty of international relations, for instance, one could imagine a survey and analysis of security agreements of European nations after the unraveling of the North Atlantic Treaty Organization (NATO) that rely on interviews with foreign policy makers and are largely descriptive and applied. In contrast, a study of the role of a commitment to ideology to the success of political parties in the United States, based on an analysis of historical documents and voting records, might be grounded in a theory of how ideology attracts or alienates the voting public.

Moving forward along the research wheel, the researcher uses deductive reasoning to move from the larger context of theory to generate a specific research question. The research question is the precisely stated form of the researcher's intent and may be accompanied by one or more specific hypotheses. The first loop is completed as the researcher seeks to discover or collect the data that will serve to answer the research question. The data collection process is essentially another task of empirical observation, which then initiates another round of the research wheel. Generalizations are made on the basis of the particular data that have been observed (inductive process), and the generalizations are tied to a conceptual framework, which then leads to the elucidation of further research questions and implications for additional study.

The kinds of skills called for at the various points of the research wheel are reminiscent of the thoughts about learning presented by Bertrand Russell many years ago. Russell noted that there are two primary kinds of knowledge acquisition: knowledge by description and knowledge by acquaintance. Knowledge by description is learning in a passive mode, such as reading a book on how to change the oil in one's car or hearing a lecture on Adam Smith's theory of economics. It is the type of learning that is especially well suited for mastering abstract information. Knowledge by acquaintance, on the other hand, is learning by doing, the kind of skill training that comes from practicing a tennis serve, driving an automobile, and playing with a computer. This is concrete knowledge acquisition, oriented to solving problems. The research process demands both skills. First, there is the clear, logical thinking that pertains to working with concepts and ideas and building theories. It is our impression that many graduate students, particularly those who have experience as practitioners in their fields, are weakest in abstract conceptualization, and honing this skill may be the major challenge of the dissertation. Second, there is the practical application of ideas, including the need to plan a study systematically, then collect and analyze data. The ability to focus, problem solve, and make decisions will help bring the study to completion.

2

Selecting a Suitable Topic

The selection of an appropriate topic is the first major challenge in conducting research. In many academic settings, this task is simplified by working with a faculty mentor who is already familiar with an interesting area of study and may even have defined one or more researchable questions. On the other hand, you may not be blessed with a faculty role model who is actively engaged in research in an area of interest to you. There are no simple rules for selecting a topic of interest, but there are some considerations for making a decision as to appropriateness. It is generally unwise to define something as important as a dissertation topic without first obtaining a broad familiarity with the field. This implies a large amount of exploring the literature and talking with the experts. Without this initial exploration you can neither know the range of possibilities of interesting topics nor have a clear idea of what is already known. Most students obtain their research topics from the loose ends they discover in reading within an area, from an interesting observation they have made ("I notice that men shut up when a beautiful woman enters the room; I wonder what the effect of physical attractiveness is on group process?"), or from an applied focus in their lives or professional work ("I have a difficult time treating these alcoholics and want to discover how best to work with them"). Another strategy is to consult with leading scholars in an area of interest and ask them for advice on profitable topics to pursue. Most are happy to talk to and share materials with enthusiastic doctoral students who are obviously familiar with the expert's prior work.

Some Guidelines for Topic Selection

Here are some guidelines for deciding if a topic is appropriate as a dissertation subject.

1. A topic needs to sustain your interest over a long period of time. A suggested study on learning nonsense syllables under two sets of environmental conditions may sound appealing in its simplicity, but remember Finagle's first law of research: If something can go wrong, it will go wrong! Dissertations usually take at least twice as much time as anticipated, and there are few worse fates than slaving hour after hour on a project that you abhor. Remember too that all dissertations are recorded and published with the Library of Congress, and you will always be associated with your particular study.

2. At the other extreme, it is wise to avoid a topic that is overly ambitious and overly challenging. Most students want to graduate, preferably within a reasonable period of time. Grandiose dissertations have a way of never being completed, and even the best dissertations end up being compromises among your own ambition, the wishes of your committee, and practical circumstances. It is not realistic for a dissertation to say everything there is to say about a particular topic (e.g., the European Common Market), and you need to temper your enthusiasm with pragmatism. As one student put it, "There are two types of dissertations: the great ones and those that are completed!" Sometimes it makes sense to select a research topic on the basis of convenience or workability and use the luxury of the postgraduate years to pursue more esoteric topics of personal interest.

3. We suggest that you avoid topics that may be linked too closely with emotional issues in your own life. It always makes sense to choose a topic that is interesting and personally meaningful. Some students, however, try to use a dissertation to resolve an emotional issue or solve a personal problem. For example, even if you think you have successfully overcome the personal impact of the death of your child, this is a topic to be avoided. It will necessarily stir up emotional issues that may easily get in the way of completing the dissertation.

4. A related issue is selecting a topic in which you have a personal ax to grind. Remember that conducting research demands ruthless honesty and objectivity. If you initiate a study to demonstrate that men are no damned good, you will be able neither to allow yourself the sober reflections of

good research nor to acknowledge the possibility that your conclusions may contradict your expectations. It is much better to begin with a hunch ("I've noticed that men don't do very well with housekeeping. I wonder if that has something to do with being pampered as children") and to regard the research as an adventurous exploration to shed light on this topic rather than as a polemical exercise to substantiate your point of view.

5. Finally, you need to select a topic that has the potential to make an original contribution to the field and allow you to demonstrate your independent mastery of subject and method. In other words, the topic must be worth pursuing. At the very least, the study must generate or help validate theoretical understanding in an area or, in those fields where applied dissertations are permissible, contribute to the development of professional practice. Some students are put off when they discover that a literature review contains contradictory or puzzling results or explanations for a phenomenon. Such contradictions should be taken not as setbacks and reasons to steer away from a topic but as opportunities to resolve a mystery. When people disagree or when existing explanations seem inadequate, there is often room for a critical study to be conducted.

From Interesting Idea to Research Question

Let us assume that you have identified a general area of research and that your choice has been based on curiosity and may involve resolving a problem, explaining a phenomenon, uncovering a process by which something occurs, demonstrating the truth of a hidden fact, building on or reevaluating other studies, or testing some theory in your field. To know whether or not the topic is important (significant) you must also be familiar with the literature in the area. Later, we present a number of suggestions for conducting a good review and assessment of the literature. In the meantime, we have noticed that many students have difficulty transforming an interesting idea into a researchable question, and we have designed a simple exercise to help in that endeavor.

Researchable questions almost invariably involve the relationship between two or more variables, phenomena, concepts, or ideas. The nature of that relationship may vary. Research studies generally consist of methods to explicate the nature of the relationship. Research in the social sciences rarely consists of explicating a single construct (e.g., "I will look at everything there is to know about the 'imposter phenomenon'") or a single variable (e.g., voting rates in presidential elections).[1] Even the presence of two variables is apt to be limiting, and oftentimes it is only when a third "connecting" variable is invoked that an idea becomes researchable.

An example might help to demonstrate how the introduction of an additional variable can lead to the birth of a promising study. Let us assume that I am interested in how the elderly are perceived by a younger generation. At this level, a study would be rather mundane and likely to lead to a "so what?" response. So far it implies asking people what they think of the elderly, perhaps using interviews or tests or even behavioral observations. But we really won't learn much about perceptions of the elderly in contemporary society. Introducing a second variable, however, can lead to a set of questions that have promising theoretical (as well as practical) implications: I wonder what the role of the media is in shaping social perceptions of the elderly? I wonder if living with a grandparent makes any difference in how the elderly are viewed? I wonder how specific legislation designed to benefit the elderly has changed our perception of them? I wonder if there is a relationship between how middle-aged adults deal with their aging parents and how they view the elderly? The new variables that were introduced in these potential research questions were, respectively, the slant of the media, presence or absence of a grandparent, type of legislation, and treatment of one's own parents. These variables impart meaning to the research because they offer suggestions as to what accounts for variability in the perception of the elderly.

As an example of generating a research question using three primary variables, let's say that you have inferred that many women lose interest in sexual relations with their husbands after the birth of a child. At this level, the proposed study would consist of checking out this hunch by assessing the sexual interest of women (Variable 1) before and after childbirth (Variable 2). But what would this finding mean? The introduction of a third variable or construct could lead to a much more sophisticated and conceptually meaningful study. An investigator might ask, "I wonder if the husband's involvement in parenting makes a difference? What's the role of his sexual initiative? How about childbirth complications? Father's involvement in the birthing? The length of time they have been married? Time after delivery? Presence of other children in the home?" There is no end to the number of interesting questions that can be raised simply by introducing another variable into the proposed study. This variable would then help to explain the nature of the relationship between the primary variables. In fact, one could brainstorm a whole list of potential third variables that could contribute to a better understanding of the relationship between childbirth and sexuality.

Note that the precise function of the third, or connecting, variable depends on the logic of the conceptual model or theory underlying the study. In this regard, a distinction can be made between two terms, *mediator* and *moderator*, which have often been used interchangeably. A moderator variable pinpoints the conditions under which an independent variable exerts its effects on a dependent variable. Strictly speaking, a moderator effect is an interaction effect in which the influence of one variable depends upon the level of another variable (Frazier, Tix, & Barron, 2004). The most commonly employed moderator variable is undoubtedly gender. The relationship between provocation and aggression, for example, may be very different for men and women. The role of context can also be conceptualized as a moderator variable. The famous Kinsey report on sexual behavior would certainly have generated very different results if the interviews with participants about their sex lives had taken place in the presence of family members. Identification of relevant contextual variables has important implications for the design of a study because such variables will affect the generalizability of research findings.

A mediating variable, on the other hand, tries to describe how or why rather than when or for whom effects will occur by accounting for the relationship between the independent variable (the predictor) and the dependent variable (the criterion). The mediator is the mechanism through which the predictor affects the outcome (Baron & Kenny, 1986). In the health psychology field, social support can be regarded as either a moderating variable or a mediating variable (Quittner, Glueckauf, & Jackson, 1990). Conceptualized as a moderator, social support could be seen to exert beneficial effects on health outcomes only under conditions of high stress (i.e., there is a statistical interaction between stress and social support). Conceptualized as a mediator, social support acts as an intervening variable between stress and health outcomes (i.e., there is an indirect relationship between stress and illness). Arguing from this model, some stressful events might encourage traumatized individuals to shun or exhaust their supportive resources or perceive them as unhelpful, leading, in turn, to increased symptoms of anxiety and depression. The diagram in Figure 2.1 captures the distinction between moderating and mediating variables in a theoretical model. In the case of mediation, the mediating variable (social support) is placed between stress and health outcomes. In the case of moderation, the arrow from social support points to the arrow from stress to health outcomes, indicating that the relationship between stress and health depends on the level of social support. We have illustrated one potential outcome in a classification plot at the bottom of Figure 2.1. Note that under conditions of low stress, there is no difference in health between the low and high social support groups; however, under conditions of high stress, those with high social support, while still illustrating some decrement in health status, fare much better

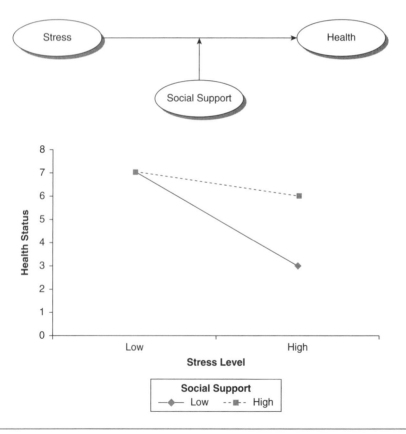

Figure 2.1   The distinction between moderator and mediator variables as represented in causal diagrams

than those with low social support. In other words, social support moderates the relationship between stress and health.

One single research study is not likely to establish and verify all of the important elements of a complex conceptual model. As one of our colleagues puts it, you would need a video camera to capture the entire Grand Canyon on film, whereas the dissertation is more like a snapshot, perhaps of a mule and rider descending one small section of the canyon trail. Yet the proposed model can provide a useful context for current and future research studies. Most ambitious research studies rely heavily on just such theoretical models. For example, Gerald Patterson (Patterson, DeBaryshe, & Ramsey, 1989) spent many years developing and testing a model to explain aggressive and deviant behavior among young males. The model hypothesizes that such antisocial behavior can be causally linked to disrupted parental discipline and poor family management skills. The relationship between these two sets of variables is not direct but mediated by a network of other variables. The process is thought to begin with parents "training" a child to behave aggressively by relying on aversive behaviors in both punishment and negative reinforcement contingencies. The inability of the parents to control coercive exchanges among family members constitutes "training for fighting," which leads, in turn, to aggressive behavior and poor peer relationships. This lack of social skills generalizes to antisocial behavior in the classroom, which makes it next to impossible for the youth to obtain basic academic skills, thus preparing him poorly to cope with life outside school. Ultimately, this leads to high rates of delinquent behavior. An abbreviated summary of one version of the model is shown in Figure 2.2.

As you might imagine, a researcher is in no position to test the entire model in a single study. Indeed, Patterson and his colleagues (Patterson et al., 1989) spent many years testing and elaborating the nature of these relationships. A single study might focus on one particular set of relationships within this complex model. For instance, the investigator might ask whether there is a relationship between physical fighting and poor peer relationships. Each variable would have to be operationalized, probably by obtaining more than one measure of both fighting and peer relationships. In Patterson's work, for instance, he asks mothers, peers, and teachers to rate levels of physical fighting because their perspectives may differ. Likewise, peers, teachers, and self-reports are used to obtain measures of peer relations. The objective of the study—that is, attempting to determine the nature and form of the relationship between the primary variables—determines the research method that is employed.

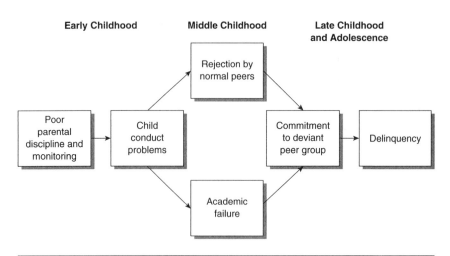

Figure 2.2   A model of antisocial behavior

SOURCE: From Patterson, G. R., DeBaryshe, B. D., & Ramsey, E., "A developmental perspective on antisocial behavior," in *American Psychologist, 44.* Copyright © 1989, American Psychological Association. Reprinted with permission.

A second example of using a comprehensive model as a guide to research comes from Rudolf Moos's ongoing studies of work and family environments (Schaefer & Moos, 1998). Basically, Moos adopted a socio-ecological view of work. The model describes both environmental variables and personal variables and relates them, via a set of cognitive functions and coping variables, to individual adaptation, including morale, job performance, and overall health and well-being (see Figure 2.3). A single study might focus on a small set of environmental system variables and relate them to something else, such as other environmental system variables, personal system variables, coping responses, or health outcomes. For instance, the researcher might explore the contribution of work pressure and supervisory support on innovation in the workplace.

A final example of a research model comes from the recent dissertation of one of our students (MacNulty, 2004). This model was generated from existing research literature and then tested empirically using a number of well-validated self-report scales. The study employed the schema-polarity model of psychological functioning to assess how self-schemas (cognitive representations of self and others) influence the experience of gratitude and forgiveness and whether these latter variables mediate the relationships between self-schemas and physical health and well-being. The model is summarized in Figure 2.4. The plus and minus signs refer to the direction of the hypothesized relationships among the variables.

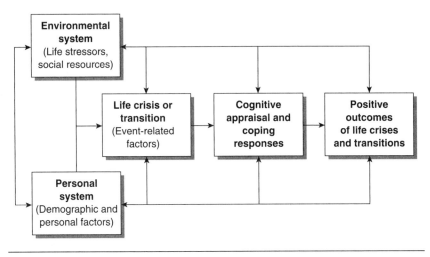

Figure 2.3   A model of work stress and coping

SOURCE: Moos (1985).

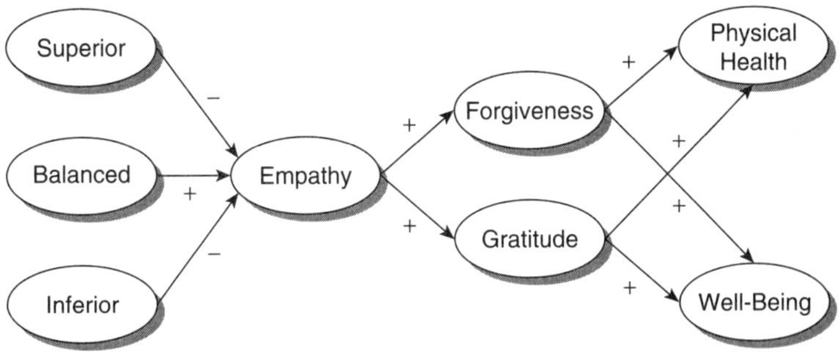

Figure 2.4   A theoretical framework presented as a causal diagram

SOURCE: From *Self-Schemas, Forgiveness, Gratitude, Physical Health, and Subjective Well-Being*, by W. MacNulty, 2004, unpublished doctoral dissertation, Fielding Graduate University, Santa Barbara, CA. Copyright 2004 by W. MacNulty. Reprinted with permission of the author.

Although the results supported most of the initial hypotheses, the proposed model needed to be amended to accommodate the data. This is typical of the research enterprise, in which theories and conceptual models are continually tested and refined to serve as increasingly sophisticated representations of real-life phenomena.

Whether or not a particular dissertation is designed to test a theory or model derived from the research literature, we believe that the creation of a visual model, which shows how the network of relevant variables and constructs may be related to one another, can serve as a powerful research tool for guiding the study. Arranging your ideas spatially helps to organize your thinking, which in turn helps position your proposed study within a larger framework.

Generating Researchable Questions

The exercise that we use to help students generate researchable questions from their interesting ideas is a brainstorming exercise that begins with labeling one or two variables and generating a second or third. Brainstorming consists of openly and noncritically listing all possible ideas in a given period of time. Later you can return to a more critical analysis of each idea and delete those that are uninteresting, not meaningful, or impractical. Ultimately, of course, it is contact with the literature that determines whether or not a research question is viable because the literature houses the tradition of scholarly inquiry that goes beyond the limits of your own knowledge.

We suggest that you do the brainstorming exercise in a small group so that the person receiving the consultation merely serves as a scribe to record the ideas thrown out by the other group members (see Table 2.1). After 5 or 10 minutes, move on to the next person's partially formed research topic. We generally use this exercise in groups of three or four so that group members can frequently shift groups and draw on the spontaneous reactions of a larger number of peers uncontaminated by prior ideas or a particular mindset. The exercise involves suspending critical thinking and allowing new ideas to percolate. It should especially suit divergent thinkers, who will find the demand to be expansive in their thinking exciting and creative. Convergent thinkers may experience the exercise as a bit overwhelming, but they will find fulfillment in other stages of the research process that demand compulsivity, care, and precision. Every chapter of a dissertation contains both divergent and convergent elements.

Note that not all decent research studies focus on three (or more) primary variables. Many studies look at the relationship between two variables or concepts, and a few descriptive studies make do with one variable or construct. This generally occurs in the early stages of research in an area when little is known about a topic. Some investigators are pathfinders in

Table 2.1   Brainstorming Exercise

Begin by defining one or two variables (or constructs) of interest. Then generate a list of additional variables (or constructs) that in some way amplify the original variables or illuminate the relationship between them. The new variables you list may be either independent variables, dependent variables, moderating variables, or even mediating variables in the research questions you eventually select. After brainstorming this list, go back and eliminate those variables that do not interest you or do not seem promising to pursue. Finally, see if you can now define one or more research questions that speak to the relationship among the two or three variables (or constructs) you have specified. Ultimately, each of these variables will need to be operationally defined as you develop your research study.

Here are some examples of the results of this brainstorming exercise applied to topics taken from different disciplines.

Political Science

Begin with an interest in citizen participation in city council meetings. List variables or phenomena that might influence, be influenced by, or be related to this variable. A sample research question is "What is the impact of citizen participation in city council meetings on legislative decision making?"

citizen participation	→	legislative decision making
independent variable		dependent variable

Education

Begin with an interest in single mothers on welfare who return to school. List variables or phenomena that might influence, be influenced by, or be related to this variable. A sample research question is "What is the effect of the availability of child care on single mothers on welfare returning to school?"

child care	→	return to school
independent variable		dependent variable

Criminal Justice

Begin with an interest in the relationship between neighborhood crime watch programs and robbery rates. List variables that might influence or amplify the relationship between these two variables. A sample research question is "What is the effect of neighborhood crime watch programs, in both urban and rural environments, on the rate of burglaries?"

crime watch programs	→	rate of burglaries
	urban/rural environments ↗	
independent variable	moderator variable	dependent variable

(Continued)

Table 2.1 (Continued)

Psychology

Begin with an interest in the relationship between physical attractiveness and self-esteem. List variables that might amplify or influence the relationship between these two variables. A sample research question is "What is the role of body image and physical attractiveness on self-esteem?" Another sample research question is "What is the role of body image in mediating the relationship between physical attractiveness and self-esteem?"

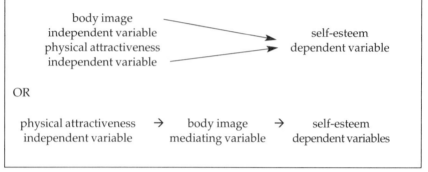

OR

physical attractiveness → body image → self-esteem
independent variable   mediating variable   dependent variables

---

terms of opening up new topics of research by trying to understand as much as possible about a phenomenon and generating more informed hypotheses for others to test in the future. Nevertheless, we believe that most students underestimate what is currently known about most topics and that the most interesting, practical, and theoretically meaningful studies are likely to consider the relationships among several variables.

We conclude this chapter with the outline in Table 2.2, which asks you to look at the kinds of issues that need to be considered and responded to during the course of developing the research proposal. By and large, your dissertation committee will need to be convinced of three things to be comfortable with your proposal:

1. Is the question clear and researchable, and will the answer to the question extend knowledge in your field of study?

2. Have you located your question within a context of previous study that demonstrates that you have mastered and taken into consideration the relevant background literature?

3. Is the proposed method suitable for exploring your question?

Table 2.2   Outline of Issues for a Student Researcher to Complete in the Development of the Research Proposal

---

Review of the Literature

The classic, definitive, or most influential pieces of research in this area are:

The journals that specialize in the kind of research in which I propose to engage are:

The body(ies) of research to which I wish to add is (are):

The experts in the field of my research are:

Statement of the Problem

The intellectual problem(s) I may help solve through this research is (are):

The moral, political, social, or practical problem(s) I may help alleviate through this research is (are):

Method

The method I propose to use to answer my question, prove my point, or gain more detailed and substantive knowledge is:

An alternative way to do it would be:

Three important research studies that have been carried out using the method I propose are:

The reason(s) this method is a good one for my question, proposition, or subject is (are):

Possible weaknesses of this method are:

The skills I will need to use this method are:

Of these skills, I still need to acquire the following:

I propose to acquire these skills by:

Note

1. A *construct* is a concept used for scientific purposes in building theories. Constructs (e.g., self-esteem), like concepts, are abstractions formed by generalizing from specific behaviors or manipulations. When constructs are operationalized in such a way that they can be "scored" to take on different numerical values, they are referred to as *variables*.

BOX 2.1   Student Suggestions

Over the years our students have provided the most useful suggestions for completing a dissertation. Here are some of the suggestions they have offered to one another that pertain to the earliest stages of developing a dissertation. Other suggestions are noted at the appropriate places in subsequent chapters.

1. Start an idea box, a file box to hold index cards or slips of paper where you can store good ideas for future reference. Alternatively, open a file on your computer for the same purpose. Use the idea box for noting books and articles to get from the library, good quotations, inspirations for future studies, half-baked notions that might be useful in the future, and so on.

2. Think of your topic as a large jigsaw puzzle with a piece missing. That is what you want to research, to fill in the gap in your field. To discover which piece is missing, you must read as much of the literature as possible in your field.

3. Before you begin, read several well-written dissertations recommended by your chairperson.

4. As you progress through the dissertation process and your question shrinks in size due to the necessity of maintaining a manageable project for one person, don't lose heart. Even very small questions can serve much larger purposes.

5. To keep the perspective of meaningfulness throughout, keep imagining an audience of individuals who would want to know the results of your work. Even if you can imagine only 25 people in the world who would care, keep that group alive in front of your eyes.

Methods of Inquiry

Quantitative and
Qualitative Approaches

T he principal characteristic of scholarly and scientific inquiry, as opposed to informal, intuitive kinds of inquiry, is the use of rationally grounded procedures to extend knowledge that a community of scholars regards as reliable and valid. The dissertation process is a ritual of socialization into that community of scholars, so it is necessary for you, as a student, to master the scholarly procedures within your discipline. The specific methods chosen to attack a problem will depend on your discipline and the nature of the specific problem. There is no universally accepted approach within the social sciences, although there are rich research traditions that cannot be ignored, as well as a common understanding that chosen methods of inquiry must rest on rational justification. This means that scientific methods differ from more informal methods of inquiry by their reliance on validated public procedures that have been determined to produce reliable knowledge.

Currently there are many disagreements in the social sciences regarding what constitutes knowledge and the procedures for gaining it. One way of thinking about the way in which research generally contributes to the knowledge base of a discipline is by considering the following three-level hierarchy of knowledge, suggested by our colleague Marilyn Freimuth.

Axiologic/Epistemic Level. This is the underlying level of basic world hypotheses that form the foundation for content and method within a field of inquiry. *Epistemology* refers to the study of the nature of knowledge, whereas *axiology* refers to the study of ethics, values, and aesthetics. Examples of constructs at this level include the explanatory principle of cause and effect and the notion of open systems.

Theoretical Level. This is the level of models and theories. Theories are premises to account for data, such as the FIRO theory of interpersonal behavior in groups (Schutz, 1966) or the differential association theory in the study of crime (Sutherland, 1924). The term *model* has been used in many, often confusing ways in the social sciences. Here it refers to a higher order theory, that is, a representational system at a higher level of abstraction that can inform and be informed by alternative theories (close to the framework or worldview that helps guide researchers and has been identified as a "paradigm" by Thomas Kuhn [1962]). Thus, psychoanalysis could be seen as a model, a wide lens with which to view and understand the mysteries of human behavior. Each model carries with it certain sets of assumptions. In the case of psychoanalysis, these assumptions include the unifying importance of causal determinism and unconscious motivation as core constructs. Note that this use of the term *model* differs somewhat from the presentation of working models in Chapter 2.

Empirical Level. In the field of epistemology, *empiricism* refers to a commitment to obtaining knowledge through sense experience (literally, "based on experience" in Greek). Empiricism is frequently contrasted with *rationalism*, which refers to knowledge derived purely through thought and reason, and to more natural philosophical and religious traditions of reaching conclusions. In the present context, the empirical level includes hypotheses and methods and data of scientific research. Hypotheses are tentative answers to questions, generally based on theory.

The primary role of research within this three-level schema is to link the theoretical and the empirical. Theories need the support of data to remain viable, whereas methods carry assumptions that are theoretical in nature. Note that research findings do not contribute directly to the axiologic/epistemic level or even to basic models. Those levels reflect fundamental value commitments and personal preferences that are rarely modified on the basis of additional data, especially the kind of data generated by scholarly research. It is hard to imagine a psychoanalyst becoming a behaviorist or a Republican joining the Democrats without a significant shift in values that goes beyond the accumulated wisdom imparted by a series of research studies. Because most researchers strongly identify with particular values and carry many personal preferences into their work, it becomes especially important to learn to discriminate between beliefs and opinions, on the one hand, and verifiable, data-inspired support for ideas, on the other hand.

A brief look at the history of science is a humbling experience that should put to rest the misguided notion that research discovers truth. Drilling holes in the skull (trephining) used to be an acceptable way of dismissing the demons responsible for mental illness, and it wasn't that long ago that the sun was thought to circle the earth. One wonders what remnants of contemporary scientific truth will be regarded as equally ludicrous tomorrow. Instead, what research contributes is a series of thoughtful observations that support or question the validity of theories, which are in turn based on a set of largely untestable beliefs and assumptions. Every once in a while, at opportunistic moments of scholarly upheaval, a new paradigm appears that seems to do a better job of explaining the available data and guiding further inquiry.

Each social science discipline and set of investigators seems to have its own favored approach to generating knowledge. For instance, public opinion studies usually rely on survey research methods, psychoanalytic studies of infants make use of observational techniques, studies of organizational effectiveness may employ action research methods and case studies, historical investigations of political and social events rely on archival records and content analysis, and laboratory studies of perceptual processes stress experimental manipulation and hypothesis testing. Within your chosen field, it is important to ask how a piece of research acquires legitimacy as reliable knowledge. No doubt part of the answer comes down to underlying epistemological assumptions and values. Certainly research strategies will differ in terms of the problems they address and the outcomes they produce. As we later show, one important distinction in the choice of method seems to be the nature of the relationship between the researcher and the topic of study.

We would argue that researchers in the social sciences have generally been myopic in defining the kinds of studies that might legitimately lend themselves to research dissertations. Most students in the social sciences are taught early on about the difference between independent and dependent variables and how experimental research implies active manipulation of independent variables to observe a subsequent impact on dependent variables. This basic and time-honored strategy has an earthy history in the systematic evaluation of fertilizers for agricultural productivity (Cowles, 2000). It remains a cornerstone in conducting social science research with human subjects. Yet it is certainly not the only way to conduct research.

The only universal in scientific knowledge is a general commitment to using logical argument and evidence to arrive at conclusions that are recognized as tentative and subject to further amendment (Human and Organizational Development Program of Fielding Graduate University, 1998). Good scientists in action often deviate from an "official" philosophy of science and a prescribed methodology. William Bevan (1991), former president of the American Psychological Association, noted,

> If you want to understand what effective science making is about, don't listen to what creative scientists say about their formal belief systems. Watch what they do. When they engage in good, effective science making they don't, as a rule, reflect on their presuppositions; they engage in a practical art form in which their decisions are motivated by the requirements of particular problem solving. (p. 478)

The key to evaluating a completed study is whether or not the selected method is sufficiently rigorous and appropriate to the research question and whether or not the study is conceptually and theoretically grounded. The more familiar you are with the full range of alternative research strategies, the more enlightened and appropriate your choice of a particular method is apt to be. Too often students become so enamored with an approach to research that they choose the method prior to determining the question. Unless the dissertation is designed to illustrate the use of a promising and innovative methodology, this is putting the cart before the horse. In general, the method needs to evolve out of the research question and be determined by it.

Quantitative Methods

The epistemological foundation of most social science inquiry throughout the 20th century was logical positivism, a school of thought that maintains that all knowledge is derived from direct observation and logical inferences based on direct observation. To a great extent, the notion of objectively studying human beings is derived from a love affair social scientists have had with the natural sciences, which sought to understand nature by isolating phenomena, observing them, and formulating mathematical laws to describe patterns in nature. Current research in the social sciences is very steeped in the empirical and quantitative traditions.

Statistical methods are especially useful for looking at relationships and patterns and expressing these patterns with numbers. Descriptive statistics describe these patterns of behavior, whereas inferential statistics draw on probabilistic arguments to generalize findings from samples to populations of interest. Kerlinger (1977) focused on the inferential process when he defined *statistics* as "the theory and method of analyzing quantitative data obtained from samples of observations in order to study and compare sources of variance of phenomena, to help make decisions to accept or reject hypothesized relations between the phenomena, and to aid in making reliable inferences from empirical observations" (p. 185). Note that the focus in the natural science model of research is the study of average or group effects as opposed to the study of individual differences. The kinds of inferential statements that derive from this model of research refer to groups of people or groups of events; that is, they are probabilistic (e.g., "Surveys find that most people believe that police officers use excessive force in dealing with criminals" or "Emotional expressiveness is related to coping effectively with natural disasters").

In experimental research, quantitative research designs are used to determine aggregate differences between groups or classes of subjects. Emphasis is placed on precise measurement and controlling for extraneous sources of error. The purpose, therefore, is to isolate a variable of interest (the independent variable) and manipulate it to observe the impact of the manipulation on a second, or dependent, variable. This procedure is facilitated by the "control" of extraneous variables, thus allowing the researcher to infer a causal relationship between the two (or more) variables of interest.

Methodological control is generally accomplished by two procedures that rely on the principle of randomness. One is random sampling, which uses subjects that have "randomly" been drawn from the potential pool of subjects so that each member of the population has an equal chance or known probability of being selected. Random selection of subjects permits the researcher to generalize the results of the study from the sample to the population in question. The second procedure is randomization, which assigns subjects to groups or experimental conditions in such a way that each subject has an equal chance of being selected for each condition. Subject characteristics are thus randomly distributed in every respect other than the experimental manipulation or treatment, allowing the researcher to infer that resultant differences between the groups must be the result of the isolated variable in question.

Unfortunately, these efforts at experimental control are often impractical in social science research with human subjects. Psychology, for instance, has an honorable tradition of laboratory research using tight experimental designs, but research in the clinical or social arena may not permit the kind of control stipulated by the experimental method. This dilemma is equally prominent in field studies in disciplines such as sociology, education, and political science. Jared Diamond (2005), Pulitzer Prize–winning geographer and biologist, for example, conducted quantitative "natural experiments" to investigate the problem of deforestation on Pacific islands. He and his colleague Barry Rolett numerically graded the extent of deforestation on 81 Pacific islands and statistically predicted this outcome from a combination of nine input variables, such as the amount of rainfall, isolation, and restoration of soil fertility. In a different context, one cannot practically conspire to rear children using two distinct parenting styles, nor ethically proceed to instill child abuse to study its immediate impact in a controlled fashion. Researchers can, however, study analogs of these variables using pure experimental designs (e.g., one can ask parents to use specific interventions at the onset of particular child behaviors). Change studies, in which a treatment or program is being evaluated for its effectiveness, may also lend themselves well to experimental designs. Even so, it may not be possible to randomize subjects into groups that receive a treatment or intervention and those that do not. A number of ingenious solutions have been proposed to deal with the ethics of denying treatment to the needy, including the use of placebos and waiting-list controls (Kazdin, 2002).

More typically, the research method of choice in the social sciences seems to be a quasi-experimental design that compromises some of the rigor of the controlled experiment but maintains the argument and logic of experimental research (Cook & Campbell, 1979). This kind of research has also been called ex post facto research, a systematic empirical approach in which the investigator does not employ experimental manipulation or random assignment of subjects to conditions because events have already occurred or they are inherently not manipulable (Kerlinger & Lee, 1999). So-called causal statements become correlational statements in quasi-experimental research, although it is often possible to infer a sequence of events in causal form. That is one reason why it is crucial to have a theoretical model as a foundation for an empirical study. The model itself helps to inform you in meaningfully interpreting the results of the study.

There is also a need to exercise caution in interpreting the meaning of results whenever subjects assign themselves to groups. A colorful example is the apparent negative correlation that exists between the numbers of mules found in the various states and the number of PhDs living there. The fact that states that have a lot of mules don't have so many PhDs, and vice versa, is an empirical observation that can be statis- tically expressed in the form of a correlation coefficient. A researcher would be hard-pressed to argue a causal relationship between these two variables unless he or she drew on an underlying theoretical model that links the two variables through a third (mediating) variable, such as the degree of urbanization. Note that this simple correlational study could, at least theoretically, be transformed into an experimental study by, for example, flooding some states with mules to see if the PhDs leave or wooing the PhDs across state lines to see if the number of mules increases.

This is not a book on research design, but the adoption of a particular research strategy will affect the final form of the dissertation. Whether or not a study employs a true experimental design, a quasi-experimental design, or a cross-sectional survey design, the most common strategy in the social sciences is a comparison between groups. That is, independent groups of subjects are used for each experimental or control condition. The best known variant of this strategy, the pretest-posttest control group design, uses two equivalent groups of subjects, which both receive pretests and posttests and differ only in the experimental treatment that is given to one group (see Table 3.1).

Table 3.1   Pretest, Posttest, Control Group Design

	Pretest	*Treatment*	*Posttest*
Experimental	yes	yes	yes
Control	yes	no	yes

It becomes possible to evaluate the impact of an intervention because the control group offers a baseline for comparison. One could use this design to evaluate, for example, whether the inclusion of spouses in an after-care program for heart bypass surgery patients will encourage greater compliance with medical regimens. Or one could design a study to evaluate the effect of introducing air bags in automobiles on the rate of physical injury to passengers. Some automobiles of a given make would receive air bags, some would not, and the change in types and rates of injuries would be the dependent measure.

The straightforward pretest–posttest–control group design makes it pos- sible to attribute the effect of experimental interventions to the interventions themselves rather than to some extraneous variable. The interpretation of results of studies using this design may be compromised, however, if the subjects have not been assigned to conditions in a truly random manner. In the proposed air bag study, for example, if automobiles and drivers are not randomly assigned to conditions, it may well be that inherently safer drivers will choose automobiles with better safety features. Because randomization is not always possible, it becomes crucial to argue for the "equivalence" of the two groups, even if they do not derive from the identical population of subjects. One way in which researchers attempt to make this argument is by matching the groups on key variables that are critical to the understanding of the study, such as age, sex, symptomatology, or, in the current example, the previous driving records of the participants.

The basic pretest–posttest–control group design does not adequately control for any effect that the pretest evaluations might themselves have on the subjects. Some assessments can sensitize subjects by making them aware that they are now participating in a study or providing a practice experience that contaminates the validity of posttest results. A simple posttest-only design may get around this difficulty and is probably underused (Campbell & Stanley, 2005). In any case, the choice of a basic research design does not eliminate the need for you to think carefully and creatively about potential sources of error and alternative explanations to account for findings.

Most experimental designs are variants of the treatment and control group format described earlier.[1] Such designs permit the researcher to make causal inferences regarding the relationships among the variables. In contrast, correlational (or observational) studies do not generally enable the researcher to demonstrate causal relationships among variables. Any conclusions regarding causality must be inferred from the underlying theory rather than from the results of the study.

Studies built around experimental or correlational designs generate data that are subsequently analyzed using appropriate inferential statistics. Statistical techniques that are used to evaluate the effectiveness of an intervention or a difference between groups, such as an analysis of variance (ANOVA) or t test, compare the size of between-group differences (e.g., the treatment effect) with the size of within-group differences due to individual variability. They represent the experimental tradition. The logic of the correlational paradigm is quite different (Cronbach, 1975). Correlations depend on comparing two distributions of scores, that is, scores that are broadly dispersed along two dimensions, such as longevity and alcohol use. Statistical techniques that emerged from this tradition, such as multiple regression, are especially popular in social science research that relies on questionnaires, surveys, or scales and the relationship between continuous variables. Because correlational studies typically cannot randomly assign subjects to groups, we have a second major type of control in social science research—statistical control. Statistical control attempts to use complex statistical procedures to remove variability from measures of group difference or relationship that could be attributed to variables other than the major independent variables of interest. Be aware, however, that it is the design of the study and not the choice of statistical method that principally governs the types of statements that can be made about the relationships among the variables.

Both experimental and correlational traditions have a rightful place in the evaluation of quantitative data, and a detailed comparison of them goes beyond the scope of this book. It is important to remember that although statistics is an indispensable tool for scientific inference, the appropriate application of statistics cannot make up for a faulty research design. In many instances statistical methods drawn from both the experimental and correlational paradigms are equally legitimate choices (see Gigerenzer, 1991). In fact, the same data usually can be analyzed in multiple ways. If you are looking at the relationship between locus of control and frequency of medical visits for preventive health, for example, you could express this relationship using a correlation coefficient or by dividing your sample into two or more subgroups on the basis of the personality construct of locus of control and comparing the resulting groups on medical visits. Generally speaking, it is not a good idea to throw away data (you are throwing away data if you have a continuum of locus of control scores but arbitrarily reduce the continuum to two or more discrete values, such as internal or external categories), but these kinds of decisions require statistical expertise and theoretical grounding.

There are two additional points we wish to make regarding the use of quantitative research. One is that there is a tendency in the social sciences to overemphasize the importance of statistically significant findings and to underemphasize the importance of clinically or socially significant findings. In other words, simply because a difference is significant at a certain probability level (typically, .05 or .01) does not mean that the difference will be meaningful in practical terms. For instance, a difference of 5 points on a depression scale might be statistically meaningful but may not be meaningful clinically. Too often students assume that the object of research is to achieve statistical significance rather than to make meaningful inferences about behavior. The primary reason that Jacob Cohen

(1990), the father of power analysis, was drawn to correlational analyses is that they yield an *r*, a measure of effect size. That is, unlike probability (*p*) values, correlation coefficients can straightforwardly indicate the magnitude of the relationship between variables, which may be far more informative than the presence or absence of statistical significance. Cohen (1990) goes on to note that researchers sometimes learn more from what they see than from what they compute, and he argues for an increased use of the graphic display of data, using simple scatter plots and so-called stem-and-leaf diagrams (see Table 3.2) prior to or instead of performing complicated statistical analyses. (We have more to say about this topic in Chapter 6, our discussion of strategies for presenting results.)

Second, as you consider the kinds of designs and controls that are available to the social science researcher, we urge you to be aware of a fundamental dilemma. Good research is a constant balancing act between control and meaningfulness. At one extreme is an emphasis on controlling the observation and measurement of a variable by eliminating the influence of as many confounding variables as possible. What results might be a tight laboratory study in which the findings inspire confidence but are not particularly interesting. At the other extreme is the observation of complex human behavior in the field, without invoking any controls so that the results seem fascinating but are highly unreliable and difficult to replicate. The fashion in social science research has moved back and forth between these poles of emphasizing precision of measurement and generalizability of findings versus emphasizing depth of coverage and description of context. Today the pendulum seems to be swinging in the direction of meaningfulness, hastened by the availability of a greater number of permissible research strategies together with a reevaluation of research epistemology.

Qualitative Methods

The researcher who employs experimental and quasi-experimental designs attempts to control the playing field of the study as much as possible, restrict the focus of attention to a relatively narrow band of behavior (often manipulating experimental conditions to further narrow the object of study to a single variable), and get out of harm's way as a detached and objective observer of the action. A countervailing trend in social science research calls for sidestepping the artificiality and narrowness of experimental studies by promoting methods of inquiry that allow researchers to be more spontaneous and flexible in exploring phenomena in their natural environment. Some of these methods of inquiry challenge the epistemological and

Table 3.2   Stem-and-Leaf Displays

A new graphic display for presenting the distribution of continuously scaled data is the stem-and-leaf display. A stem-and-leaf display presents the data in a manner that highlights characteristics of the distribution that might not be obvious from an examination of the frequency distribution. For example, the table below presents the frequencies of age at first marriage for a sample of 91 U.S. residents selected from the National Opinion Research Center General Social Survey of 1990.

Age at First Marriage	f	Age at First Marriage	f
15	<+>1	26	<+>4
16	<+>2	27	<+>4
17	<+>5	28	<+>2
18	<+>8	29	<+>1
19	10	30	<+>2
20	10	31	<+>1
21	12	32	<+>1
22	<+>8	33	<+>1
23	<+>6	34	<+>0
24	<+>6	35	<+>1
25	<+>5	36	<+>1
		Total	91

In a stem-and-leaf display, the first digit of the variable is broken away from the second digit. The first digit forms a stem and the second a leaf. The stem is placed to the left of a vertical line, and the leaf is placed to the right. In the age at first marriage data, the stems are 10s and the leaves are 1s. Thus, a person married at 21 years of age would be represented by a 2 stem and a 1 leaf. A person married at 25 years would also be represented by the 2 stem but would have a 5 leaf.

The steps in constructing a stem and leaf display from the previous data would be first to select the stems from the frequency distribution, as follows:

Stems

1

2

3

(Continued)

Table 3.2 (Continued)

Then add leaves for each case by observing its second digit and adding that digit to the stem to form the leaf. Thus, in this display, each case is represented by one leaf:

Stems	Leaves
1	56677777888888889999999999
2	0000000000111111111111122222222233333334444445555566667777889
3	0012356

When working with data that are not ordered, the leaves can be added and then ordered in a final step. The above figure indicates that most persons in this sample were married in their early twenties or late teens. Though there is nothing particularly surprising about this, more complex displays can present a large amount of data in an efficient and descriptive figure that allows the reader to view the distribution in a manner that a simple frequency table does not. Chapter 2 of Hamilton's (1990) *Modern Data Analysis* presents detailed instructions on the construction of complex stem-and-leaf displays.

Methods of "Control": Comparison Groups, Control Groups, and Statistics

Technique	Type of Control	Example
Randomization	Methodological	Assigns cases randomly to experimental and control groups
Precision matching (pairwise matching)	Methodological	Pairs subjects on treatment relevant variables and assigns randomly to treatment conditions
Frequency distribution matching	Methodological	Average values of E and C groups are matched on treatment relevant variables
Comparison group	Methodological	Compares two similar groups without random assignment or matching
Hierarchical regression	Statistical	Removes variability due to potential confounding prior to assessing main study variables
Analysis of covariance	Statistical	Removes variability due to the "covariate" prior to assessing main and interaction effects

philosophical foundations of traditional social science research, which is more compatible with a research culture that maintains a belief in a knowable world, universal properties of social behavior, and the attainment of truth through method (Gergen, 2001). The commitment to a logical empirical approach to research is not necessarily seamless with a postmodern worldview, which challenges the sanctity of the scientific method as a vehicle for attaining truth and promotes an awareness that beliefs and apparent "realities" are socially constituted rather than given and, therefore, can show up differently in different cultures, times, and circumstances (Neimeyer, 1993). The term *constructivism* is a name for the epistemology associated with the view that what people may consider objective knowledge and truth are a result of perspective. For the constructivist, knowledge is not "found" or "discovered" from existing facts but constructed as the invention of an active, engaging mind.

There are many flavors of constructivism, but they all focus on how humans create systems of meaning to understand their world and their experience. The term *social constructionism* is usually used to refer to the fact that meaning is typically created not by individual cognitive processes but as part of a social exchange process. A focus on the isolated knower is replaced by an emphasis on the social context in which linguistics and relationships create reality. Knowledge is relative: Describing a person or an event is not mirroring "what is out there" but understanding how meaning is socially constructed within a specific community (Crotty, 1998).

Qualitative methods are usually linked to a constructivist theory of knowledge because qualitative methods tend to focus on understanding experiences from the point of view of those who live them. But that is not necessarily the case. The world of qualitative research is rich with alternative perspectives. At one extreme are those who, in their questioning of the validity of a logical positivistic science applied to human behavior and social systems, take issue with the ideal or even the possibility of having a neutral, disengaged investigator (see Feyerabend, 1981; Popper, 1965; Toulmin, 1972). Taking their hint from modern physics, they suggest that the presence of an observer inevitably alters that which is being observed, that, in fact, one cannot separate the investigator from the object of inquiry. Feminist theorists have other reasons for criticizing the traditional experimental method, claiming that it creates a hierarchy of power in which the omnipotent researcher, often a male, instructs, observes, records, and sometimes deceives the subjects (Peplau & Conrad, 1989). It should be noted, however, that whether a study uses experimental or nonexperimental methods does not necessarily imply anything about the researcher's commitment to nonsexist research.

The impact of these developments in the philosophy of science on method is far from clear. Researchers are experiencing a continually evolving foray into the application of alternate research paradigms to the pursuit of research itself. The labels given to these approaches include "phenomenological," "hermeneutic," "naturalistic," "experiential," "dialectical," and so on. The generic label most commonly used to incorporate these diverse research strategies is "qualitative research." Crotty (1998) maintains that the fundamental distinction between quantitative research and qualitative research takes place at the level of method, rather than the level of theory or epistemology. Moreover, qualitative researchers do not possess a distinct set of methods that are all their own (Denzin & Lincoln, 1998). They can make use of interviews, text analysis, surveys, participant observation, even statistics. Over time, different research traditions have evolved that bring to bear particular perspectives from which to investigate particular topics, such as psychoanalytic studies of children and ethnographic studies of cultures. Within these domains the researcher may draw on many specific methods, such as the ethnographer who employs both interviews and observational descriptions. In general, qualitative research implies an emphasis on processes and meanings over measures of quantity, intensity, and frequency (Denzin & Lincoln, 1998). As suggested earlier, the newer generation of qualitative researchers emphasizes the socially constructed nature of reality, a close relationship between the researcher and the object of study, and the context that influences the inquiry.

The boundaries between quantitative research and qualitative research have become increasingly fuzzy as various disciplines have adopted their own perspectives on adapting methodologies to serve their needs. At the risk of overgeneralization, we are listing eight distinctions between quantitative and qualitative research that are often highlighted. Much of this discussion is inspired by the contributions of Jody Veroff (1993).

The most obvious distinction is that data in quantitative studies are expressed in numbers, where numbers are a metric for measuring, describing, testing, and generalizing about variables of interest to the researcher. In qualitative research, the currency of choice is words. However, in some qualitative (or hybrid) studies, those words may be coded, categorized, expressed in numerical form and analyzed quantitatively.

Second, quantitative research tends to use the hypothetico-deductive approach to research design that prescribes specification of variables and hypotheses prior to data collection. Counterexamples include survey research methods and factor analytic studies that are more exploratory and rely on inductive rather than deductive procedures to interpret findings. In contrast, qualitative research begins with specific observations and moves toward the development of general patterns that emerge from the cases under study. The researcher does not impose much of an organizing structure or make assumptions about the interrelationships among the data prior to making the observations. This is not to imply, however, that the study is not thoroughly planned.

Third, the quantitative researcher usually tries to control the site and context of the study to focus on a limited number of variables. This is particularly true in experimental laboratory research and, to a lesser extent, quasi-experimental studies. The qualitative researcher, on the other hand, is intent on understanding phenomena in their naturally occurring context with all of its inherent complexity. Just because a study is conducted in the field, however, does not mean that it is necessarily qualitative in form.

Fourth, quantitative research seeks to define a narrow set of variables operationally and isolate them for observation and study. This contrasts with qualitative research, which is more holistic and aims for a psychologically rich, in-depth understanding of a person, program, or situation by exploring a phenomenon in its entirety.

Fifth, quantitative research seeks objectivity, by standardizing the procedures and measures as much as possible and by distancing the researcher from the participants. The qualitative researcher values the subjectivity of the participants and sees their unique characteristics not as "error" to be removed or minimized but as valued aspects of the research situation.

Sixth, the aim of quantitative studies is prediction, control, or explanation or theory testing, or all three. Predicting under what circumstances events lead to other events or variables are associated with other variables helps to explain important phenomena in the social sciences. In qualitative studies, the goal is more with description, exploration, search for meaning, or theory building. It tends to be a discovery-oriented approach.

Seventh, the stance of the researcher is different in qualitative research than in quantitative research. The quantitative researcher drives the study by manipulating and controlling the conditions of the study as well as the information provided to the research participants. The qualitative researcher usually invites the subject to participate, sometimes as a formal collaborator, by contributing knowledge about unobservable aspects of his or her experience that are not accessible to the researcher in other ways.

Finally, quantitative research relies on statistical analysis to analyze data. This includes the use of descriptive and inferential statistics to determine the relationship between variables or the significance of group differences or the effect of an intervention. In qualitative research, some kind of text analysis is employed to categorize responses and identify themes that are evaluated subjectively to shed light on a phenomenon of interest. Although individual differences may be explored to further understanding about the phenomenon, those differences between individuals or groups are usually not the focus of the study. They are used to build theory or add to theory development.

The appropriate selection of methods of inquiry is contextual and depends to a large extent on learning the standards used in your own discipline. For example, qualitative methods have an especially comfortable home in the ethnographic and field study traditions of anthropology and sociology that emerged in the 19th century. Psychologists and psychiatrists also developed detailed case histories of their patients at about that time. Today, qualitative dissertations are widespread, although any classification of qualitative methods is apt to be a simplification. The following approaches are frequently adopted in contemporary social science dissertations: phenomenological research, ethnographic inquiry, grounded theory, and narrative research. They are described in more detail throughout the book. As Crotty (1998) clarified, all methodologies and methods (methodologies can be regarded as the strategies, action plans, or designs that inform the choice of specific methods, that is, procedures and techniques for data collection and analysis) flow from

Table 3.3   Common Differences Between Quantitative and Qualitative Research Strategies

Quantitative	*Qualitative*
1. Data expressed in numbers	1. Data expressed in words
2. Hypothetico-deductive	2. Inductive
3. Controlled research situations	3. Naturally occurring and contextual
4. Isolation of operationally defined variables	4. Holistic view of phenomena
5. Seeks objectivity	5. Interested in subjectivity
6. Emphasis on prediction and explanation	6. Emphasis on description, exploration, search for meaning
7. Researcher directs, manipulates, controls	7. Researcher participates and collaborates
8. Statistical analysis	8. Text analysis

philosophical positions that provide a theoretical context for the choice of methodology. Theories and methods need to be logically linked. However, it is also possible for different theoretical perspectives to employ very similar methods. For instance, case studies have a rich tradition in the literature as a method of collecting data. But there are big differences between observing a well-known political figure to learn about campaign tactics, interviewing the Dalai Lama about the role of spirituality in world affairs, and measuring the social behavior of an autistic child before and after a treatment intervention. All of these examples can formally be described as case studies, but they emanate from different perspectives on research. We remind you to be tolerant of overlapping categorizations because there is considerable inbreeding among research paradigms (Lincoln & Guba, 2000). And we urge you again to select methods, regardless of their source, based on their sensitivity and application to the research questions you are asking.

Phenomenology

Phenomenologists take issue with positivist science and maintain that the scientific world is not the "lived" world that we experience on a daily basis. Edmund Husserl (1970), the reputed founder of phenomenology, argued that traditional science distances people from the world of everyday experiences. As Crotty (1998) noted, the phenomenological movement was inspired by the declaration "Back to the things themselves!" This implies making sense of phenomena directly and immediately.

The reader who seeks a historical perspective of the philosophical basis of phenomenology is referred to analyses by Crotty (1998) and by Gubrium and Holstein (1997). Crotty, in particular, maintained that the practice of phenomenological research, especially in North America, has evolved to the point that the everyday experiences of participants are accepted much more subjectively and uncritically than the theory of phenomenology would suggest. Gubrium and Holstein (1997) discussed how phenomenology has become a philosophical basis for interpretive research strategies that include ethnomethodology (the study of the meaning of ordinary talk and social interactions) and conversational analysis (the study of the structure of such talk and interactions).

As it is most commonly understood, the focus of phenomenological research is on what the person experiences and its expression in language that is as loyal to the lived experience as possible (Polkinghorne, 1989). Thus, phenomenological inquiry attempts to describe and elucidate the meanings of human experience. More than other forms of inquiry, phenomenology attempts to get beneath how people describe their experience to the structures that underlie consciousness, that is, to the essential nature of ideas. Phenomenologically oriented researchers typically use interviews or extended conversations as the source of their data. Important skills for the researcher include listening, observing, and forming an empathic alliance with the subject. The investigator remains watchful of themes that are presented but resists any temptation to structure or analyze the meanings of an observation prematurely. Once the basic observations are recorded, the data may be reduced, reconstructed, and analyzed as a public document.

Moustakas (1994) distinguishes between two main trends in phenomenological research. One has been called "empirical" phenomenological research and is represented by a tradition of studies from Duquesne University starting with van Kaam's (1966) study of "feeling understood." Giorgi's (1985) ongoing work is illustrative: The researcher collects naïve descriptions of a phenomenon from open-ended questions and dialogue with a participant and then uses reflective analysis and interpretation of the participant's story to describe the structure of the experience. Moustakas's (1994) own version of phenomenological inquiry is called heuristic research, meaning "to discover" or "to find." The process begins with a question or a problem that the researcher seeks to illuminate or answer, which is personally meaningful in terms of understanding the relationship between oneself and world. Moustakas's (1994) early study of loneliness serves as an example. According to Moustakas, heuristic research has a somewhat different flavor from the Duquesne approach: The process maintains closer contact with the individual stories of the participants than does structural analysis. At the same time, it is broader in scope than a single situation in the life of a participant and may go beyond narrative description to include stories, self-dialogues, journals, diaries, and artwork as sources of data.

Several of our doctoral students have developed dissertations based on phenomenologically oriented qualitative interviews. In one dissertation study, a student interviewed families shortly after a reunion with an adult member who had been released from prison (Wardell, 1985). The objective of the interviews was to get as close as possible to the experience of the transition between prison and family life from the perspective of the reuniting family. Three major categories of experience (temporality, emotionality, and togetherness) emerged from a larger number of themes. A second student explored how people make meaning from experiences of unanticipated mortal danger (Clark, 1997). Clark conducted open-ended interviews with

10 participants who had experienced life-threatening events in the arena of sports. Her analysis of and reflection on these interviews, presented in both prose and prose trope, a form of narrative poetry, revealed how the events forced participants to experience multiple realities and get to a deeper understanding of the layered human experience. Finally, Sharon Sherman (1995) completed a largely phenomenological dissertation on the meaning of living with asthma. Her interviews with asthmatic adults led to the development of a conceptual model by which to understand this experience.

Ethnographic Inquiry

The ethnographic paradigm includes anthropological descriptions, naturalistic research, field research, and participant observations (Hoshmand, 1989). Ethnographers attempt to capture and understand specific aspects of the life of a particular group by observing their patterns of behavior, customs, and lifestyles. The focus is on obtaining full and detailed descriptions from informants. There is a strong emphasis on exploring the nature of a specific social phenomenon rather than testing hypotheses (Atkinson & Hammersley, 1994). Ethnographers tend to work with uncoded, unstructured data to produce explicit interpretations of the meanings of human actions.

Ethnographic inquiry can be found on a continuum ranging from relatively pure description to more theoretically guided explanations of cultural, social, and organizational life. On the more inductive end of the continuum, the researcher develops theory out of the descriptive and interpretive process; on the deductive end of the continuum, the researcher builds a study out of an established theoretical framework. Typically, the ethnographer initiates prolonged contact and immersion in a setting of interest, while maintaining as much detachment as possible from the subject matter. The naturalistic setting could be the mental hospital explored in the work of Erving Goffman (1961) or the street corner populated by unemployed Black men in a classic study by Liebow (1968). A more traditional anthropological example would be a study of health practices among Native Americans living on a reservation or the early immersion in non-Western cultures by Mead, Malinowski, or Franz Boas, the renowned ethnographer who advanced social relativism as the prevailing form of American anthropology. The investigator might obtain some preliminary understanding of the history of the culture by referring to archival records and artifacts in preparation for living among the informants for several months. During that time, the researcher would keep field notes of all observations and interactions and perhaps follow up the observations with intensive, qualitative interviews. The data are recorded verbatim, if possible, using the language of the participant, and then reduced for analysis and presentation. We give further consideration to the description of methods and presentation of qualitative results in Chapters 5 and 6.

When conducting ethnographic studies, there is a fundamental tension between being an objective, detached observer and an emotionally involved participant (Mertens, 2005). It is the tension between adopting two roles while trying to understand the actions, beliefs, and knowledge of a particular group of people (the insider perspective is called emic, and the outsider perspective is called etic). George Herbert Mead (1934), a social psychologist and philosopher from the late 19th and early 20th centuries, argued that to "enter the attitudes of the community" one must "take the role of others" and this adoption of the perspective of others found its way into ethnographic inquiry. Today, ethnography is being transformed by an infusion of critical inquiry, which means going beyond trying to understand a culture to addressing political dimensions within it (Crotty, 1998). Another extension of ethnographic inquiry is called autoethnography, whereby the researcher becomes the object of study. Stacy Holman Jones (2005) showed how a qualitative researcher might subject his or her own gender, class, and cultural beliefs and behaviors to the same study as those of other participants.

Ethnographic inquiry was the basis of Sarah MacDougall's (2005) creative dissertation on the transformational capacity of a contemporary group process called PeerSpirit circling. MacDougall drew on evidence from ancient and contemporary indigenous cultures indicating the efficacy of circle council as a means to effective problem solving and used focus groups, participant observation, interviews, and autoethnography to demonstrate how the practice fosters personal transformative experiences that lead to collaborative social action.

Grounded Theory

One of the more prominent types of qualitative research is referred to as grounded theory. In Crotty's (1998) opinion, grounded theory is a form of ethnographic inquiry that relies on a clearly formulated series of procedures for developing theory. When researchers use the term *grounded theory*, they are usually referring to those analytical steps (which are described in Chapter 7), but the term can also apply to a method of inquiry itself. As such, grounded theory has its roots in the theory of symbolic interaction, which also influenced ethnographic inquiry (Crotty, 1998). Symbolic interaction evolved as a pragmatic approach to the study of social interactions through the original contributions of George Herbert Mead. The theory argues that every person is a social construction, that people become persons through their interactions with society, using the vehicles of language, communication, and community. From the social interactionist perspective, the researcher must put himself or herself in the role of the other person to view the world from that person's perspective and understand the meaning of his or her actions (Crotty, 1998).

As a research methodology, the grounded theory approach is a way of conceptualizing the similarities of experience of an aggregate of individuals. It is a discovery-oriented approach to research, which offers a set of procedures for collecting data and building theory. The researcher has a research question but rarely a set of theoretical propositions or hypotheses to color the interpretation of findings that emerge from the study. Grounded theory became popular as a research methodology through a successful 1967 book by Glaser and Strauss. A few years thereafter the authors ended their collaboration and published independently, Strauss with his colleague Juliette Corbin (Strauss & Corbin, 1990) and Glaser (1998) on his own. The nuance of differences between their approaches makes for interesting reading (see, e.g., Rennie, 1998). One of the key differences is the extent to which theory is truly discovered, without the preconceptions of the researcher, as opposed to verified, which is more the case in the traditional hypothetico-deductive paradigm. To make matters even more complicated, whereas most authorities view Strauss and especially Glaser as quite positivistic and objective in their orientations to research, recent writers are more explicitly constructivist and postmodern. A good example is Charmaz (2005), who very clearly focused on interpreting a phenomenon rather than reporting it or verifying it. She made the point that, in contrast to her orientation, grounded theory methodology originally gave researchers a way of doing qualitative studies with positivist approval. As a student, it may not matter so much which approach to grounded theory methodology you adopt, as long as you have a good understanding of what you are doing, why you are doing it, and that you are doing it consistently.

A dissertation by Virginia Hedges (2003) used a grounded theory approach to examine the success stories of Latino students who were unusually successful in navigating the public school system. Data from one-on-one, open-ended interviews were analyzed using the constant comparative method (see Chapter 7). A grounded theory consisting of the conceptual categories of encouragement, *familia*, meaningful relationships, and goal-orientation emerged that describes a process by which Latino students enhance their cultural identity. Another grounded theory dissertation by Candice Knight (2005) explored significant training experiences that contributed to the perceived competency development of exceptional humanistic psychotherapists. Transcribed data from videotaped interviews with 14 participants from throughout the United States and Canada led to the emergence of a multivariate theoretical training model.

Narrative Inquiry

We have added narrative inquiry as a fourth major qualitative methodology, in part because of its increasing visibility in the research literature and also because many of our students seem to be employing this model for their dissertations. Simply put, narrative inquiry can be regarded as a qualitative methodology that deals with biographic data as narrated by the person who has lived them (Chase, 2005). Forerunners of narrative inquiry include the life history method espoused by sociologists and anthropologists early in the 20th century. Life histories are often based on extensive autobiographies from noteworthy cultures or subgroups. Lewis's (1961) well-known study of a Mexican family, published as *Children of Sanchez*, introduced the culture of poverty as a concept. More recent influences on the development of narrative inquiry include sociolinguists who have studied oral narratives of everyday experience and feminists who have addressed the distinctiveness of women's narratives, such as Belenky, Clinchy, Goldberger, and Tarule's (1986) honored study *Women's Ways of Knowing*.

According to Chase (2005), a narrative may be oral or written and derived from naturally occurring conversation, an interview, or fieldwork. It can be a story that refers to a specific event, such as a job interview or a romantic liaison; it can be a story that reflects on an important life issue, such as athletics or dying; it can even be a story about one's entire life. What is distinct about the contemporary narrative approach to research is the focus on meaning making, as opposed to merely documenting a history or an experience. Narrative researchers need considerable training in interviewing skills, drawing out and listening to the thoughts, feelings, and interpretations of the narrator as he or she constructs and organizes previous life experiences. Each person's narrative is unique, not only because of the uniqueness of that person's thought processes but also because of the uniqueness of the setting in which it is produced. Chase (2005, p. 657) referred to narratives as "socially situated interactive performances" to capture the notion that narratives are a product of a narrator and the listener coming together at a specific time and place for a specific purpose. In the final stages of narrative inquiry, researchers also become narrators, as they interpret and make sense of the narratives they have elicited. In this endeavor, the subjectivity of the researcher and of those who are studied is part of the research process. The researcher's reflections, including how he or she makes interpretations and judgments, become part of the data pool and are also documented. This turning back and reflecting on oneself is known as reflexivity (Turner, 1988) and has become a fundamental construct in contemporary narrative research.

Specific approaches to narrative research may differ somewhat depending on the academic discipline (Chase, 2005). Psychologists tend to emphasize the content of stories and may be interested in the relationship between life stories and the quality of psychological development (i.e., the life and the story differ from, but may impact, one another). For example, a dissertation by Denise Humphrey (2003) used a narrative approach to explore the intricate relationships of women who had been adopted in a closed adoption system with their adoptive mothers, birth mothers, and biological children. Humphrey interpreted the interview narratives of these women through the lens of Kohut's concepts of self-object needs and functions. Humphrey concluded that becoming a mother serves a restorative function for the adoptee that helps overcome deficiencies in the adoptive process. A second student, Ellen Schecter (2004), observed that little is known about how women in general, and lesbians in particular, negotiate sexual fluidity in terms of their sexual identity. Through in-depth, qualitative interviews, she examined the experience of long-time lesbians who, in midlife, became intimately partnered with a man. Common themes in the narratives were found, leading to a new conceptual model that shows how social and personal constructions are used to create idiosyncratic sexual identities that fit the individual.

In contrast to these psychological studies, sociologists may focus on how participants construct their experience within specific institutional or organizational contexts (i.e., narratives as lived experience) or how they understand certain aspects of their lives. An example is David Riessman's (1990) classic study of men's and women's divorce stories. The link between narrative inquiry and ethnography has been captured best by anthropologists who become involved with one or more members of a community over time and construct narratives about those encounters.

Dissertation Implications of Qualitative Research

The distinctiveness of qualitative research has implications for the write-up of the research proposal and dissertation. Qualitative research designs typically are not intended to prove or test a theory, and it is more likely that the theory will emerge once the data are collected (an inductive approach rather than a traditional deductive approach). This does not mean, however, that the researcher can ignore the theoretical perspectives of previous work cited in the literature review. We are in general agreement with Miles and Huberman (1994), who take a moderate position on the role of theory in naturalistic studies. They view a conceptual framework as the "current version of the researcher's map of the territory being investigated" (p. 20). This means that the framework may change as the study evolves. The amount of prestructuring depends on what is known from the literature about the phenomenon being studied, the measures or instruments that are available, and the time allotted for the study. Very loose designs imply the collection of great amounts of data that may initially look important but turn out to be tangential or irrelevant, along with great amounts of time to sift through these data. At the very least, a conceptual framework allows different investigators who are exploring a similar phenomenon to communicate with one another and compare experiences and results.

Adopting a tentative conceptual framework allows the researcher to focus and bound the study with regard to who and what will and will not be studied. Miles and Huberman (1994) chose to express their conceptual frameworks in terms of graphic "bins" that consist of labels for events, settings, processes, and theoretical constructs. They reason that the researcher will come to the study with some ideas about the content of these bins. For instance, a qualitative study on prison behavior could reflect working decisions focusing on current behavior rather than prior history (events), high-security prisons (settings), interactions among prisoners and between prisoners and guards (processes), and authority relations and organizational norms (theoretical constructs). These choices and distinctions are, of course, informed by the theoretical and empirical literature.

Research questions can then be formulated as a way of explicating any theoretical assumptions and orienting the investigator (and the student's committee) to the primary goals and tasks of the study. One cannot study every aspect of prison life—the issues adopted by the researcher and expressed as research questions have direct implications for the choice of methodology. A focus such as "how prisoners and guards negotiate conflict and express power in relationships" has implications for the behavioral events that will be sampled and the research tools that will be used to obtain information (e.g., field notes, interview transcripts, diaries, prison documents). Research questions in qualitative research can be revised or reformulated as the study proceeds.

Students selecting a qualitative design need to convince their committees that they understand the role of the qualitative researcher. This includes experience with the sensitive kind of interviewing found in naturalistic studies, whereby the investigator enters the world of the participant subject without a fixed agenda and maintains sufficient scientific rigor in the process. Because the researcher is regarded as a person who comes to the scene with his or her own operative reality, rather than as a totally detached scientific observer, it becomes vital to understand, acknowledge, and share one's own underlying values, assumptions, and expectations. This perspective should become clear in the "Review of the Literature" and "Method" chapters of the dissertation. Moreover, researcher subjectivity can be reduced by a variety of data-handling procedures. Will there be audio- or videotaping to augment written field notes? How will these materials be reduced in scope? Will process notes be included that describe the researcher's reactions at various points of the study? Will pilot studies be used to test the suitability of procedures? Will conclusions be provided to informants for verification prior to publication (member checking)? Specification of these ingredients can be convincing documentation of the rigor of the proposed study without compromising the necessary open contract of the proposal.

Because qualitative data may consist of detailed descriptions of events, situations, and behaviors, as well as direct quotations from people about their experiences and beliefs, the "Results" chapter of the dissertation will be directly influenced as well. We found that students often have the mistaken belief that a qualitative study might be easier to conduct because there are no specific hypotheses and no statistical tests to perform. However, the sifting and resifting of transcripts with huge amounts of open-ended responses into a coherent pattern generally takes as much effort and leads to as much frustration as the statistics that were being avoided. Good research is always taxing in some way.

Other Possible Approaches to the Dissertation

Hermeneutics

Hermeneutics has been described as the interpretation of texts or transcribed meanings (Polkinghorne, 1983). One engages in a hermeneutic approach to data to derive a better understanding of the context that gives it meaning. It can be argued that hermeneutics is more of a theoretical perspective than a particular research methodology (Crotty, 1998). Hermeneutics, as a specialized field of study, was pioneered by biblical scholars in the 17th century who used textual analysis and interpretation to elicit the meanings of religious text. More recently, researchers in the social sciences, as well as scholars in the field of literary criticism, have extended the application of hermeneutics to the interpretation of secular texts.

There is ongoing debate within the field of hermeneutics between the objectivists, who consider the text to contain meaning independent of the interpreter, and others who view active interpretation as primary to all understanding, a position quite similar to modern constructivist thinking in the philosophy of science (Winograd & Flores, 1986). From this latter orientation, understanding is the fusion of the perspective of the phenomenon and the perspective of the interpreter. Everyone brings life experiences and expectations to the task of interpretation, but because even people's self-understanding is limited and only partially expressible, interaction with the meaning of the text can help produce a deeper understanding of both the observer and the observed. As Mahoney (1990) put it, "New or changed meanings arise from the active encounter of the text and its reader" (p. 93).

Texts from ancient cultures, for instance, may be analyzed in their historical context with the notion of applying their meanings to current issues. This understanding, which must show the meaning of a phenomenon in a way that is both comprehensible to the research consumer and loyal to the frame of reference of the subject, may then lead to more formal research questions. In hermeneutics, the data are given to the researcher, whereas in a standard phenomenological study the researcher helps to create the transcribed narrative that has usually been obtained by interviewing the participant(s) (Hoshmand, 1989). Phenomenological research can have a hermeneutic basis that is more interpretive than descriptive. A good example of a dissertation taking this approach is Smith's (1998) study of family/divorce mediators and how they remain internally balanced and focused while trying to resolve challenging disputes between separating partners. Smith conducted three in-depth interviews with seven different nationally recognized mediators and performed an inductive analysis of interview transcripts that revealed layers of voices existing within the mediators' consciousness. Hermeneutic phenomenology, as a research method, can also make use of data sources such as literature, poetry, visual arts, and video, while retaining the participants' oral or written descriptions of their experiences (Hein & Austin, 2001).

A hermeneutically informed approach to research is quite complex. Because language is regarded as the core of understanding, the researcher needs to return repeatedly to the source of data, setting up a dialogue with it, so to speak, asking what it means to its creator and trying to integrate that with its meaning to the researcher. Although we are all hermeneutically inclined whenever we seek to learn the contexts of things, ideas, and feelings, hermeneutic inquiry is relatively rare as a formal approach to research in the social sciences. Ambitious, well-known examples of hermeneutic studies are psychodynamically guided biographies, such as Erik Erikson's *Young Man Luther*, and the work of Carl Jung, who used an archetypal, mythic perspective to describe contemporary problems.

According to Martin Packer (1985), the hermeneutic approach is applicable to the study of all human action, where the action is treated as though it has a textual structure. The investigator studies what people do when they are engaged in everyday, practical activities. What sets hermeneutics apart from more empirical or rational orientations to the study of human behavior is the belief that a particular activity can be understood only in conjunction with understanding the context in which it occurs rather than as an abstraction or a set of causal relationships. As Packer put it, "The difference between a rationalist or empiricist explanation and a hermeneutic interpretation is a little like the difference between a map of a city and an account of that city by someone who lives in it and walks its streets" (p. 1091). The mapmaker's product is formal and abstract; the inhabitant's map is personal and biased. At the dissertation level, the hermeneutic approach is further exemplified by Elliott's (1997) study of five Renewal of Canada conferences, in which the materials that were studied included videotapes, formal and informal papers and reports, press releases, and media coverage of the conference workshops and meetings. The outcome is an understanding of the conditions that contribute to or hinder the quality of the communicative interaction in a discursive attempt to bridge differences.

Case Studies

The term *case studies* usually refers to studies that focus on a single individual, organization, event, program, or process, or what Stake (2000, p. 436) called a "specific, unique bounded system." Many academic departments are wary of supporting case studies as dissertations because departments are dubious of the likelihood of learning much of conceptual value from a single instance or example. On the other hand, case studies are frequently found in practice-oriented disciplines, such as education, social work, management science, urban planning, and public administration, in addition to some traditional social science disciplines (Yin, 2002). Indeed, there are many ways of thinking about case studies from both quantitative and qualitative perspectives. A quantitative approach in the classic experimental tradition could include what has been called a single-subject or $N = 1$ design. It is an empirical approach associated with specific statistical procedures (see Kazdin, 1982; Kennedy, 2004). Single-subject quantitative studies can be used to assess changes in a phenomenon over time through the use of repeated measures or to assess the impact of a particular treatment by removing or reversing the intervention and evaluating differences in the dependent variable. Single-subject research strategies are especially appropriate in developing or refining novel interventions and in closely examining the behavior of individual subjects.

Case studies, however, are more commonly associated with qualitative designs, in which there is an intensive effort to understand a single unit of study within a complex context. The research questions may vary, but the goal is to obtain a comprehensive understanding of the case. As Stake (2005) advised, "place your best intellect into the thick of what is going on" (p. 449) and use your observational and reflective skills to excavate meanings. How important is generalizing to a larger population? It depends. Stake (2000) described the intrinsic case study as one where generalization is irrelevant because the attraction is understanding the unique (or even typical) person, group, or event. He described the instrumental case study as one that is intended to shed light on an issue or test a generalization rather than focus on the case per se. In our opinion, a purely descriptive or exploratory case study does not fulfill the expectations of a doctoral dissertation unless it includes an explanatory element with theoretical implications. This means that the researcher needs to generalize to the world of theory as opposed to other possible cases. It also means that the research question is more apt to be of the "how" or "why" category than the descriptive "who," "what," and "where" questions that pertain, for example, to survey research and many other applied endeavors. However, we are aware that this is not a universal standard. The interested reader is referred to authors on case studies such as Stake (2000) and Yin (1994) who discussed these and related issues from somewhat different perspectives.

Finally, it should be said that any number of specific data collection methods might be included in a good case study. This would include interviews, behavioral observations, participant observation (as in ethnographic research), documentation, and the examination of archival records. Classic case studies include the sociological description of Middletown, a small Midwestern town (Lynd & Lynd, 1929); W. F. Whyte's (1955) *Street Corner Society;* and Freud's (1997) *Dora: An Analysis of a Case of Hysteria.* Thus, it is better not to think of your potential dissertation as using the case study method but rather to think of applying a method to a single case. Among case study dissertations at our own institution is a psychobiography of Richard Price, cofounder of the Esalen Institute, which used the theoretical perspective of intersubjectivity theory and drew from archival documents, personal histories, and interviews with colleagues, friends, and family members to identify the recurring themes and patterns in Price's subjective world so as to illuminate their influence on his contributions to Gestalt theory and practice and the evolution of Esalen (Erickson, 2003). A very different case study dissertation comes from Paula Holtz (2003), who conducted an ex post facto study of three brief psychodynamic psychotherapies that investigated the self- and interactive regulation and coordination of the timing of vocal behaviors of therapist and patient throughout the course of each therapy session. The study used a repeated single-case design, computerized scoring of the vocal behaviors, and time-series analyses. Among other findings, the analyses provided substantial evidence in support of the psychoanalytic dyadic systems view that each therapist or patient self-regulates the timing of his or her vocal behaviors with those of the partner.

Mixed Model: Quantitative and Qualitative Study

An increasingly popular approach to designing a dissertation is to use a combination of quantitative and qualitative methodologies. This approach combines the rigor and precision of experimental, quasi-experimental, or correlational designs and quantitative data with the depth understanding of qualitative methods and data. Thus, the methods can help inform one another or deal with different levels of analysis. There are many ways of mixing models. Tashakkori and Teddlie (1998) enumerated several possible designs, including mixed methodology studies that combine aspects of both paradigms throughout the study. Theirs is a pragmatic approach in which questions of method are secondary to the adoption of an overriding paradigm or worldview guiding the investigation. Thus, it might be possible to mix research hypotheses of a confirmatory nature with general questions of an exploratory nature, structured interviews and scales that are quantitative with open-ended interviews and observations that are qualitative, and methods of analysis that draw on both traditions to expand the meaningfulness of the findings. An example of an innovative mixed methodology was employed by Mary Gergen (1988) to study the way in which women think about menopause. Gergen held a research event by inviting several women to her home to complete questionnaires that addressed attitudes toward menopause, followed by a group discussion on the topic. The research report combined a quantitative analysis of the responses to the questionnaire with a qualitative analysis of themes generated by the discussion. An example from another field would be an analysis of the effect of timber dislocation on a logging community by quantitatively assessing the economic impact and qualitatively assessing the emotional impact on families in the community.

The mixing of methods within the mixed-model dissertation occurs in the data collection phase, the data analysis phase, and the data interpretation phase of the study. A simplified summary might include two main options: One is whether the quantitative and qualitative elements of the study are sequential or concurrent and the other is whether one method is nested within the other or used to confirm the findings obtained by the other. In a sequential strategy, a researcher might begin with one approach and subsequently use the other approach to elaborate on or expand those findings. One variation is to add a qualitative component to a fundamentally quantitative study to help explain or extend the findings. Another option is to begin with a qualitative phase and add quantitative data collection at a later point. This design makes it possible to submit an emergent theory from a qualitative study to quantitative validation (Morgan, 1998). As Creswell (2003) pointed out, it may also be the method of choice when validating an assessment instrument that has previously been developed. In a concurrent design, the researcher would collect or analyze both forms of data at the same time. In the most common variation, the quantitative and qualitative approaches are used to supplement one another in the same study, with each method seeking to confirm or validate the findings from the other and strengthen the outcomes of the study because the advantages of one approach may compensate for the weaknesses of the other. In a nested study (Tashakkori & Teddlie, 1998), there is one predominant method, and the other method is embedded within it to enable the researcher to obtain a richer perspective on the phenomenon being studied. The nested method may be looking at a different question than the dominant method. A common application is when a subsample of a larger group that has been assessed quantitatively is interviewed qualitatively for further information or when quantitative data are also collected in a predominantly qualitative study to learn more about the participants.

Mixed model studies present many logistical challenges, one of which is the sheer burden of collecting data using two very different methodologies. Perhaps the most common application of mixed methodology is to assess a large number of participants using standardized scales and measures in a field study or an experimental study and then conduct open-ended interviews with a subset of the original sample to derive a richer understanding of the phenomenon in question. We find that an increasing number of students are electing this approach to dissertation projects in spite of the increased task demands of such studies. A good example is a study by one of our doctoral students who sought to understand what makes extreme high-risk athletes engage in what laypeople view as self-destructive behavior (Slanger, 1991). The resulting dissertation combined the objectivity of validated measures of sensation-seeking and perceived competence with open-ended interviews conducted with a random subsample of the total group. Slanger discovered that the methods complemented one another: Data from the quantitative scales revealed how the key predictive variables discriminate among extreme risk, high-risk, and recreational athletes, and the qualitative interviews introduced the concepts of spirituality and flow (Csikszentmihalyi, 1991). A recent graduate (Christensen, 2005) adopted a mixed-method design to study conflict at the governance level within Friends schools. Christensen gathered intensive data from interviews with trustees and a focus group with consultants who worked with Friends school boards and supplemented those stories with quantitative data from an electronic survey sent to a larger number of school representatives. The combined data enabled her to identify predictors of growth in organizational dynamics and then design a module-based program for board preparation and education. Similarly, Nelson (2000) took a qualitative interview approach to her dissertation on how relationship themes influence the response to trauma in mothers of medically fragile infants. She supplemented her narrative inquiries with two quantitative measures of growth following trauma as well as detailed medical, developmental, and demographic data from existing records. Finally, David Nobles (2002) took a very different mixed model approach to his dissertation on drug control policy implementation speech acts of President George W. Bush. Nobles analyzed 33 rhetorical artifacts consisting of speeches, exchanges with the media, and other public remarks from the perspective of three different research models: dramatism and metaphorical analysis, both approaches to rhetorical criticism, and communication theory, in the form of the coordinated management of meaning (CMM) and social constructionism. The findings describe the impact of the War on Drugs metaphor on drug use and drug control policies.

Students who decide to take a mixed-model path to their dissertations have a number of decisions to make, including which method, if any, receives priority; how to decide on a data collection sequence; how to explain and integrate findings that may not be congruent; and whether a larger, theoretical perspective should frame the entire research design. Creswell (2003) is helpful in terms of providing criteria for making these strategic choices.

A major reluctance to adopt the mixed model approach comes from scholars with strong epistemological commitments to either quantitative or qualitative research because they view the underlying assumptions of the approaches as fundamentally incompatible. At the risk of oversimplification, quantitative studies generally rest on an objectivist epistemological tradition that seeks to validate knowledge by matching the knowledge claims of the researcher with phenomena in the real world (the correspondence theory of truth). In this tradition, theories are proposed as universal hypotheses to be tested empirically. Qualitative studies, on the other hand, may derive from the constructivist tradition associated with the postmodern movement. Here knowledge is not discovered but invented, situated within a specific context heavily determined by local practices and validated through internal consistency and social consensus (the coherence theory of truth, Neimeyer, 1993). In practice, this means that the researcher maintains an open curiosity about a phenomenon and the theory emerges from the data; there is no one true reality on which to validate theories deductively.

Our own position is that both quantitative and qualitative studies can be approached from a myriad of philosophical perspectives. In the purest sense, statistics is merely shorthand for communicating information about complex phenomena elegantly and precisely. We encourage students to think clearly about a research topic and then apply the methods that make the most sense in answering their questions of interest and that are consistent with their values.

Theoretical Dissertations

Another possible approach to writing a dissertation is to write a *theoretical dissertation* and bypass the need for data collection entirely. This is by no means an easy alternative. Original theoretical contributions are a profound intellectual challenge. One way of describing the difference between a knowledge of the literature required for a standard quantitative or qualitative study and that required for a theoretical study is by referring to the difference between being a native of a foreign country and a tourist in that country. As a tourist in a foreign environment, it might be necessary to learn as much as possible about the country by studying maps, reviewing the customs, and learning the language, but chances are you will never master the country as well as the native speaker. It's the same with research. To make a genuinely original theoretical contribution, you need to know an area of inquiry inside-out and be intimately familiar with the issues and controversies in the field. If you are beginning to review an area of interest to formulate a study, you are probably better off with an empirical design. Of course, most doctoral dissertations need to have theoretical implications, and the data you gather and analyze may even create the opening for a brand new way of thinking in your field. That, however, is quite different from starting with the expectation of creating, let's say, a new theory of consciousness or, a bit more modestly, a revised theory of short-term memory.

If you choose to pursue a theoretical dissertation, you will be expected to argue from the literature that there is a different way of understanding a phenomenon than has heretofore been acknowledged. Some of the more viable theoretical dissertations in the social sciences are those that bring together or integrate two previously distinct areas. For instance, one of our graduate students was of the opinion that there is a significant breach between the theory of psychotherapy and the practice of psychotherapy, which led to an ambitious, high-quality theoretical dissertation on the relevance of personal theory in psychotherapy (Glover, 1994). Another student recently completed a very scholarly, book-length theoretical dissertation titled, *Organic Constructionism and Living Process Theory: A Unified Constructionist Epistemology and Theory of Knowledge* (Krebs, 2005). On a somewhat less abstract level, Rainaldi (2004) developed a new theory of incorporative female sexuality informed by psychoanalytic drive theory and recent advances in the biological sciences. Finally, Demoville (1999) used computer simulation software to create a systems dynamics model of organizational performance. The data that served as the input for the model came from organizational case studies and the social science literature. The model showed the interrelationships among key organizational components under both stable and chaotic environmental conditions. A panel of expert organizational leaders and consultants then helped validate the model by providing feedback on its performance.

Meta-Analysis

Meta-analysis is a form of secondary analysis of preexisting data that aims to summarize and compare results from different studies on the same topic. Meta-analyses have become increasingly common in the social science literature because they pool the individual studies of an entire research community, thus providing the reader with a much richer understanding of the status of a phenomenon than any single study can offer. The term *meta-analysis* has been attributed to Glass (1976) as an "analysis of analyses." A more complete description of the various meta-analytic methods is available in Newton and Rudestam (1999). Meta-analyses differ in terms of the unit of analysis they use (e.g., a complete study or a finding within a study) and the statistical techniques they use to integrate the results from separate studies to draw conclusions about the entire body of research.

The first step in conducting a meta-analysis is screening and selecting existent studies for their methodological rigor. Then statistical techniques are used to convert the findings of all the studies to a common metric. Finally, the summary analysis yields information about the strength of relationships among variables (the effect size) across studies, using the newly expanded sample.

All dissertations, of course, involve a critical review of the literature on the topic in question. In a meta-analysis, it is this review of the literature, including a finely tuned statistical analysis, that constitutes the study. In our opinion, there is no reason why a carefully conducted meta-analysis could not serve as a suitable dissertation.

Action Research

Action research provides another possible approach to completing a doctoral dissertation, although it may be too prodigious a challenge for most graduate students. *Action research* has been defined as "a form of research that generates knowledge claims for the express purpose of taking action to promote social change and social analysis" (Greenwood & Levin, 2006, p. 6). That action research is generally stimulated by the wish to address a particular problematic situation within an identifiable organization or community makes it distinct from theoretical research that is carried out as a purely academic exercise. Another distinguishing feature is that action research is never done "to" someone but is done by or in collaboration with insiders from the organization or community. It is a systematically undertaken reflective process that includes creating theory within a practice context and testing the theory using specific experimental interventions (Herr & Anderson, 2005).

Most action researchers acknowledge the seminal contributions of Kurt Lewin (1948) and his commitment to social change. Action research can be either quantitative or qualitative in nature, drawing on such diverse techniques as surveys, interviews, focus groups, ethnographies, life histories, and statistics. In the early days of action research, the researcher tried to initiate change in a particular direction; more recently, the goals and targets of change are determined by the group members through participatory problem solving. Members of an organization or community that constitutes the focus of the research become coresearchers in the process. Thus, the researcher is a facilitator who needs to possess good group process skills to effectively mobilize a group of participants to study their own behavior, including their defensive reactions to change.

A good action research project proceeds according to a cycle of steps introduced by Lewin (1948) and known as the plan-act-observe-reflect cycle. The planning stage involves the identification of a problem and the formulation of hypotheses and procedures for achieving one or more goals. The action stage consists of implementing the intervention(s). The observe stage consists of recording the actions and their impact on achieving the goal(s). Finally, the reflection stage allows for reviewing the data and the action plan and developing new inferences that lead to a new cycle of research as part of a continuous learning process.

Herr and Anderson (2005) advised that to serve as a dissertation an action research study should contribute generalizable, transferable knowledge as well as knowledge that is useful to those in the setting of the study, a point which we also endorse. Action research may, for instance, generate new theory that is applicable to similar problems in other contexts, as well as new tools or products that are recommended for broader use. Herr and Anderson also noted that students who envision conducting an action research study for their dissertations should be conscious of certain potential complications. One is that action research studies can be "messy" in the sense that the procedures and outcomes are difficult to predict, which means that committee members may need to stay flexible regarding potential outcomes and understand that the methods and procedure may need to be revised as one goes along. Second, students need to realize that they may be walking a tightrope as they serve the multiple roles of student, researcher, and participant in the research, and maybe even employee in the organization. This implies making choices with full awareness of possible consequences and their ethical implications. Finally, it is important to identify the contributions of the author of the dissertation in spite of the fact that several other individuals may have served as coresearchers in conducting the study.

Within our institution, most action research dissertations have taken place in the fields of education and organization development, although fields of social work, nursing, and criminology also attract this approach. The action research cycle was used by one student in her dissertation to explore a community college's use of collaborative organizational learning in its planning and decision-making processes (Witt, 1997). The student worked as a coresearcher with members of the college administration, faculty, and staff. Each member of the team brought specific skills to the project. The dissertation student, of course, provided her expertise in action research. The team analyzed archival data, as well as data from meetings, journals, interviews, and participant observation field notes, to evaluate the effectiveness of the institution's learning processes.

In summary, positivism maintained that there was a single method, that of the natural sciences, that was valid everywhere. Today, postmodern critics are circling like vultures to pick over the spoils of positivism (Smith, 1991). Yet the natural sciences are still very much alive, and their commitment to empirical observation and scientific rigor continues to be dominant in social science research. Whereas some critics maintain that the humanities, with their focus on the interpretation of meaning and values, will ultimately provide a superior ideological alternative, that is far from clear. What is clear is the need to begin the research enterprise by asking an essential question and then asking what you must do to convince yourself and others of the validity of the ideas supporting it (Bevan, 1991). Along the journey, be wary of rigid methodological rules and draw on any method with a clear understanding of its advantages, its limitations, and whether it compromises assumptions about the phenomena you are researching.

Note

1. There are numerous other statistical models that control for extraneous variables; only two of the most common are presented here.

PART II

Working With the Content

The Dissertation Chapters

4

Literature Review and Statement of the Problem

The previous chapters provided an orientation to research in the social sciences and offered suggestions on how to develop an appropriate topic. In this chapter, the research question begins to take shape using the vehicle of the review of the literature.

The Introduction

The Review of the Literature is generally preceded by a brief introductory chapter. The Introduction consists of an overview of the research problem and some indication of why the problem is worth exploring or what contribution the proposed study is apt to make to theory or practice, or both. The Introduction is usually a few pages in length. Although it may begin by offering a broad context for the study, it quickly comes to the point with a narrowly focused definition of the problem. The form of the Introduction is the same for both the research proposal and the dissertation, although there are likely to be some changes made to the understanding of the research problem after the study is completed. Ironically, it is usually impossible to write a final Introduction chapter prior to completing the Review of the Literature and Method chapters because those chapters will inform the problem and its operationalization.

The wording of the research problem should be sufficiently explicit to orient the most inattentive reader. There is nothing wrong with beginning the chapter with a sentence such as "In this study, I attempted to evaluate the impact of environmental protection legislation on atmospheric pollutants in the chemical industry." The chapter would proceed to stipulate the assumptions and hypotheses of the study, identify the key variables, and explain the procedures used to explore the questions. It should include a synopsis of the arguments that explain the rationale for the research question and the study. It is perfectly acceptable to cite one or more studies that are directly relevant to the proposed investigation and may have inspired it or lent it empirical or theoretical justification. But this is not the place to conduct a literature review. Avoid technical details and keep the Introduction short.

Review of the Literature

Often the lengthiest section of the research proposal, the Review of the Literature is placed just after the introductory overview of the study. This chapter of the dissertation provides a context for the proposed study and demonstrates why it is important and timely. Thus, this chapter needs to clarify the relationship between the proposed study and previous work conducted on the topic. The reader will need to be convinced not only that the proposed study is distinctive and different from previous research but also that it is worthwhile. This is also the place where the student's critical abilities as a scholar become evident. Many students erroneously believe that the purpose of the literature review is to convince the reader that the writer is knowledgeable about the work of others. Based on this misunderstanding, the literature review may read like a laundry list of previous studies, with sentences or paragraphs beginning with the words "Smith found . . . ," "Jones concluded . . . ," "Anderson stated . . . ," and so on. This not only is poor writing but also misses the whole point of an effective review of the literature.

A colleague of ours, Jeremy Shapiro, noted that much of the labor that goes into writing is often wasted effort because it is not based on a clear understanding of the purpose of an essay or thesis (Shapiro & Nicholsen, 1986). As a general rule, if you have difficulties in your basic writing skills—that is, in constructing grammatical sentences, using appropriate transitions, and staying focused and concise—a research dissertation will glaringly reveal these weaknesses, and the logic and persuasiveness of your arguments will be diminished. Grammar does not receive nearly as much attention in our educational system as it did in the past. Perhaps the best justification for learning good grammar is some sage advice forwarded by Lynne Truss (2003, p. 7): "Punctuation is a courtesy designed to help readers to understand a story without stumbling." Thus, punctuation marks serve as traffic signals to let the reader know when to pause, pay attention, take a detour, or stop. Consider the following popular example of two sentences with the same words and different punctuation. Notice the different meanings:

A woman, without her man, is nothing.

A woman: without her, man is nothing. (Truss, 2003, p. 9)

One suggestion is to obtain remedial help in strengthening basic writing skills. Furthermore, be aware that the style of writing that is appropriate to research papers is somewhat different from the style of writing associated with literary prose. Scientific writing tends to be more direct and to the point and less flowery and evocative. Effective academic writing is an acquired skill that is taken up as a separate topic in Chapter 10.

A good way to formulate a question that is appropriate to a research study is to determine what bothers you (Shapiro & Nicholsen, 1986). As you consider one or more possible questions and draw on the observations and ideas of others who are interested in the same and related questions, you are in fact formulating the argument. The forum for the argument is the literature review, which is played out in the form of a dialogue between you and the reader. To dialogue effectively, the writer must anticipate the kinds of questions and apprehensions that the reader might have in critically examining your argument. It is common for critical evaluations of academic papers to be peppered with comments such as "What is your point here?", "What makes you think so?", "What is your evidence?", and "So what?" The more you can anticipate a reader's questions, the easier it will be to formulate your arguments in a way that produces mutual understanding. Dissertations go through many drafts, and the revision process consists of asking and responding to these questions from the point of view of a circumspect and knowledgeable reader.

The literature review is not a compilation of facts and feelings but a coherent argument that leads to the description of a proposed study. There should be no mystery about the direction in which you are going. ("Where are you going with this?" is a good question to ask yourself repeatedly in a review of the literature.) You always need to state explicitly, at the outset, the goal of the paper and the structure of the evolving argument. By the end of the literature review, the reader should be able to conclude "Yes, of course, this is the exact study that needs to be done at this time to move knowledge in this field a little further along." The review attempts to convince the reader of the legitimacy of your assertions by providing sufficient logical and empirical support along the way. You will continually need to determine which assertions the reader can accept as common understanding and which assertions require data as support. For instance, if you were to assert that survivors of suicide attempts need professional help, a peer reader probably would want to know the basis of your assertion and request some evidence about the needs of those who attempt suicide and why professionals (i.e., as opposed to nonprofessionals) are necessary. Avoid statements based on "common knowledge" that can easily be verified as false. For example, someone might make the statement that the divorce rate has skyrocketed in recent years. Not only is this statement false, but also the timeframe represented by "recent years" is unclear. On the other hand, the claim that Freud was the father of psychoanalysis is likely to be well established as a fact in the professional psychological community and thus not require further backing.

Becker (1986) noted that there is no need to reinvent the wheel and it is perfectly permissible to draw on the thoughtful arguments of others and incorporate them into your own research project. This is very much in keeping with researchers' understanding of the incremental, cumulative process that characterizes the development of normal science (Kuhn, 1962).[1] On the other hand, a skillful researcher draws on original source material rather than relying on review articles and secondary sources. We advise great caution when reporting summaries of statistical findings from secondary sources because these can often be both incomplete and misleading. For any study whose results are critical to your own central arguments, we recommend careful inspection of the results from the primary source material.

Becker (1986) used the image of a jigsaw puzzle, in which you design some of the pieces and borrow others in their prefabricated form from the contributions of other scholars. In addition, it is worth noting that becoming overly preoccupied with the literature can deform your argument so that you lose your privileged place at the center of the study. Do not let your anxiety about one missing reference delay your forward momentum; you can always insert missing or new material into the review at a later date. In any case, do not neglect to give proper credit to the source of ideas by citing complete references in your writing.

Common Problems

A principal failing of novice researchers at every stage of a project, and especially evident in the Review of the Literature, is giving away their own power and authority. As a researcher, you need to accept that you are in charge of this study and that, in the case of dissertations, it is likely that ultimately you will be the world's leading expert on the narrow topic you have selected to address. One way of giving away authority is to defer to the authority of others in the review, assuming, for instance, that because Émile Durkheim or John Dewey said something, it is necessarily valid. You need to adopt a critical perspective in reading and relating the work of others. The main reason why sentences beginning with "Jones found . . . " are best kept to a minimum is that they shift the focus of the review from your own argument to the work of others. A preferable strategy is to develop a theme and then cite the work of relevant authors to buttress the argument you are making or to provide noteworthy examples of your point or counterexamples that need to be considered. Consider the following examples:

> "Illuminatus (2003) conducted a study on the effects of seasonal light on major depression by comparing the rates of depressive illness among residents of Seattle and San Diego during different times of the year. He hypothesized that there would be more depression in the northern city than the southern city and more depression during winter than during summer. His findings confirmed his hypotheses." This presentation turns the focus of the review toward the opinions of another researcher.

> "There is reason to believe that differences in seasonal light can affect the extent of depressive illness. For instance, residents of Seattle, a northern city, are reported to have higher rates of depression than residents of San Diego, a southern city, and these differences are accentuated during the winter (Illuminatus, 2003), suggesting that relative darkness may exacerbate mood disorders." This presentation keeps the focus on the phenomenon and uses the finding of the cited research as empirical support.

Another way of limiting your own authority is by using quotations in excess. The overuse of quotations tends to deflect the argument away from the control of the author. Restrict the use of quotations to those with particular impact or those that are stated in a unique way that is difficult to recapture. Besides, using your own words to present difficult concepts will help convince you (and others) that you really understand the material.

Once you have read the literature in an area, it may be tempting to report everything you now know. Avoid this temptation! A good literature review needs to be selective, and it is taken for granted that the majority of source material you have read will not make it directly into the literature review. That does not mean that it wasn't necessary to read all those books and articles; they provide the expertise required to make your contribution. But remember, in the dissertation itself your task is to build an argument, not a library. One of our colleagues likens the process to a courtroom trial, where all admissible testimony by the witnesses must be relevant to the case and question at hand. Consistently ask yourself, "Why am I including this study or reference?" Similarly, each sentence in the dissertation needs to be there for a purpose, sometimes to provide relevant content and sometimes to facilitate communication to the reader, but never as filler.

Although the primary task is to build an argument and you are expected to present your own point of view, it is not fair to exclude references that contradict or question your case. You must be objective enough to present both sides of an argument and acknowledge where the weight of the evidence falls. Throughout the review, leave enough signposts along the way to help orient the reader. One way to do this is to inform the reader of what you have done and what conclusions you have drawn on the basis of the available evidence. You also need to convince the reader that your knowledge of the existing literature is extensive and intensive enough to justify your proposed study. That a study on your topic or question does not exist is never sufficient justification. There are many things that are simply not worth studying.

Critiquing a Research Article

The relevant studies need to be critiqued rather than reported. The critique serves to inform the reader about the status of reliable knowledge in the field and to identify errors to avoid in future research. As you read the available research in an area, you need to maintain a critical perspective, evaluating the study on its own merits and in comparison with other studies on the same or a similar problem. A critique does not imply that you must discover and identify a major flaw or weakness in every study you read. Sometimes students offer critiques that read like a list of "weaknesses" of a particular method cited from a research methods text. These are seldom of value.

You are evaluating the content for its application to your research. That means paying particular attention to the following three elements of all empirical studies:

> How was the problem defined? Is this definition similar to or different from the way in which you are conceptualizing and defining the problem and the associated concepts and variables?

What measures were used to operationalize the variables and assess the differences between groups or effects of interventions? Are these measures similar to or different from those you intend to employ?

What population was studied and how was the sample chosen? Is the population similar to or different from the one you intend to address? Was the sample chosen randomly, out of convenience, or in a biased manner?

Answers to these questions will help you evaluate the relevance and limits of generalizability of the study you are reviewing in relation to your proposed study. In addition to these major points, it is always a good idea to ask what the author of the study can properly conclude based on the design. Does the study, for instance, enable you to conclude that there is a cause-and-effect relationship between the study variables or that they merely correlate with one another?

The following outline consists of a rather comprehensive set of recommendations for critiquing a research article. Not all of these items will be included in any given citation within the literature review. The amount of attention a study receives will depend on its direct relevance to the proposed research question and should not detract from the flow of the argument. Nevertheless, this list can act as a reminder for how to read and evaluate critically a research article's contribution to a proposed study:

1. Conceptualization
   a. What is the major problem or issue being investigated?
   b. How clearly are the major concepts defined/explained?

2. Theoretical Framework and Hypotheses
   a. Is there a clearly stated research question?
   b. Are there hypotheses? Are they clearly stated?
   c. Are the relationships between the main variables explicit and reasonable?
   d. Are the hypotheses stated in a way that makes them testable?

3. Research Design
   a. Does the research design adequately control for extraneous variables?
   b. Could the design be improved? How?
   c. Are the variables clearly and reasonably operationalized?
   d. Is the choice of categories or cutting points defensible?
   e. Are the reliability and validity of the measures discussed?
   f. Is the choice of measures appropriate?
   g. Is the population appropriate for the research question being studied?
   h. Is the sample specified and appropriate?
   i. Can the results reasonably be generalized on the basis of this sample, and to what population?

4. Results and Discussion
   a. Are the data appropriate for the study?
   b. Are the statistical techniques appropriate and adequately described?
   c. Are the control variables adequately handled in the data analysis?
   d. Are there other control variables that were not considered but should have been?
   e. Are the conclusions of the study consistent with the results of the statistical analyses?
   f. Are alternative conclusions that are consistent with the data discussed and accounted for?
   g. Are the theoretical and practical implications of the results adequately discussed?
   h. Are the limitations of the study noted?

5. Summary
   a. What is your overall assessment of the adequacy of the study for exploring the research problem?
   b. What is your overall assessment of the contribution of the study to this area of research?

Long Shots and Close-Ups

Our colleague Joseph Handlon drew an analogy between doing a literature review and making a movie. In filmmaking there are "long shots," "medium shots," and "close-ups," which refer to the relative distance between the camera and the subject matter. As a metaphor, a long shot suggests that the material is background for a particular topic. Background material needs to be acknowledged but not treated with the same detail as foreground material; it is not figural. A study on the stressful impact of relocation, for instance, might begin with the following observation:

> There have been three basic ways of approaching the topic of stress empirically. One is by regarding stress as an independent variable and focusing on the nature and strength of the stressor, exemplified in the empirical contributions of Holmes and Rahe (1967). A second approach is to view stress as a dependent variable, focusing on the physiological and psychological impact of stressful events, illustrated by the seminal work of Hans Selye (1956). An alternative approach is to view stress as a transaction between a stimulus and a response, which is moderated by a set of cognitive variables. This approach, elaborated in the work of Lazarus and his colleagues (Lazarus & Folkman, 1984), forms the conceptual foundation for this study.

In this way, considerable literature can be referenced without attending to details or critical evaluations of each study.

The medium shot is somewhere between the long and the short focus and requires a bit more descriptive material. As an example, let us assume that a researcher wishes to explore the effect of social protest and threats of violence on the well-being of workers in abortion clinics. It would be appropriate to obtain a good overview of the impact of potentially violent social protest in other contexts as well as a good understanding of the emotional demands of working in a clinic serving women with unwanted pregnancies. Studies that bear on these relevant issues may not need to be presented in critical detail, but they certainly need to be summarized sufficiently to give the reader a clear indication of the status of the research as it pertains to the orientation of the proposed study.

Finally, the close-up requires a careful examination of the research and is reserved for those studies that have the most direct relevance to the proposed research question. In some cases, this might refer to one or two studies that are being modified or amended in some critical way to form the basis for the current study. More frequently, it refers to a collection of work on a relatively narrow topic that is clearly central to the proposal. These studies are not merely referenced but critically examined so that the reader obtains a clear sense of what is already known about the phenomenon, how reliable and valid the conclusions based on that work are apt to be, and how the proposed study will deal with previous limitations and move the field ahead. The researcher who is interested in exploring the impact of infertility treatments on communication between husbands and wives might present the following close-up statement after having carefully described the samples, measures, and procedures of the two most relevant (fictitious) studies in that literature.

Of the two studies that bear directly on the proposed question, Sterile (2004) found that couples reported improved communication after experiencing prolonged infertility treatment, whereas Ripe and Fertile (2005) concluded that behavioral exchanges between infertile couples more frequently escalated into arguments the longer that medical interventions continued. Of particular concern in Sterile's study is the fact that because men and women were interviewed together the couples may not have been totally honest and responses by one member of a couple may have been prejudiced by those of the other member. Beyond this threat to validity, the conflicting findings of the two studies suggest the need for a more definitive investigation of the impact of infertility treatment on communication patterns within couples.

A good strategy for reviewing the literature can be found by referring to a Venn diagram (see Figure 4.1) of three intersecting circles, which is

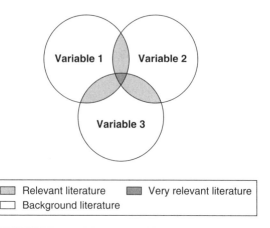

Figure 4.1   Venn diagram guide to the literature review

derived from the previously discussed exercise on formulating research questions. The long shots, or those through wide-angle lenses, are represented by the portions of the three primary variables that are independent of the other two variables. The medium shot is illustrated by the intersections of any two variables. The close-up, or shot through a narrow-angle lens, refers to the joint intersection of all three variables. As a general rule, any studies in the existing literature that incorporate all of the major variables or constructs that are present in the proposed study require very careful scrutiny because they are particularly relevant. Studies that relate some of the variables (e.g., two) also deserve a short description. Studies that deal with only one of the selected variables, perhaps in conjunction with other, less relevant variables, are merely background. They are generally too numerous to examine in detail and include a great deal of content that does not pertain to the current study. Certainly, one need not review all studies dealing with sexual dysfunctions, for instance, to focus on male impotence in midlife. Nor will one need to consider all previous work on men or midlife. Yet gender issues and midlife development issues may provide important background material and a theoretical foundation for the proposed study. Moreover, the researcher will not have to introduce every study on impotence but will probably need to be familiar with a broad range of previous work in the area.

Review of the Literature in Qualitative Dissertations

Each research tradition has its own idiosyncratic approach to writing the dissertation. What you have just read constitutes the prevailing model in the social sciences. However, research studies that are qualitative in nature may have a different approach to the literature review. Because many of these studies are inductive or theory building, as opposed to theory testing, much of the formal literature review may be found in a discussion chapter toward the end of the dissertation, after a theory has emerged and the author is seeking to position it within the existing literature. Ruthellen Josselson (Josselson & Lieblich, 2003), who comes out of the narrative inquiry tradition, sees the need for a review that orients the reader to the existing literature but is concerned about a review that restricts rather than opens the inquiry, fearing that an overly comprehensive or overly focused review preempts the researcher from greeting his or her data with the appropriate level of openness, curiosity, and wonder. The review chapter she favors is more like a research proposal, which demonstrates sufficient sophistication with the literature, including existing theory and relevant empirical studies, but focuses on orienting the reader to the boundaries of the proposed study and launching it. More informally, this background material would say, in effect, "Here's a phenomenon that interests me, here are one or more theories that have been proposed to try to understand this phenomenon, here are some empirical ways in which previous researchers have attempted to understand the phenomenon, this is what they have discovered so far, and this is what I, very tentatively and with great curiosity, think is important here." The researcher is then encouraged to keep reading the literature as the study progresses and tie it in to his or her findings in a very thorough and evolved discussion chapter.

In another context, David Rennie (1998), an admittedly "Big Q" grounded theory researcher who served as external examiner for the dissertation of one of our doctoral students, admonished the student to reduce significantly her 150-page literature review in her proposal as overly inclusive and inappropriate for a discovery-oriented qualitative study and encouraged her to reintroduce those topics in the literature review which were subsequently referred to by her interviewees once the data were collected and examined.

As one might imagine, the same inductive, discovery-oriented mindset finds its way into the Statement of the Problem and Method chapters of the dissertation as well. These distinctions become apparent as we tackle these respective sections of the dissertation in the following chapters. In any case, all students need to give priority to the structural and writing conventions promulgated by their respective disciplines and academic departments.

Statement of the Problem

At the conclusion of the literature review, the reader should have obtained a fairly clear idea of the study. By this time, you will have carefully crafted your argument and moved the reader along as you build your case. You will have convinced your reader of your mastery of the subject matter by having reviewed and critiqued the existent literature that pertains to your study and gives it a suitable context. The next immediate challenge is to form a transition between the literature review and the next section of the dissertation, the Statement of the Problem. One way to build this transition, so that the literature review chapter appears connected to the proposed study, is to write a summary of the review you have conducted. This summary would highlight your main conclusions, including reference to the most relevant literature (which you have previously reviewed), and leave the reader anticipating the next steps.

The Statement of the Problem is sometimes written as a separate chapter and sometimes located at the very end of the Review of the Literature. Although you probably have offered a general statement of the problem early in the introductory chapter of the dissertation, this is the place for a more specific statement. The specificity of the problem statement is very important. A research problem consists of much more (and less) than a misunderstood collection of unidentified relationships. The statement is usually framed in the form of one or more research questions and research hypotheses. Although we recommend the inclusion of formal hypotheses as a general standard, whether or not to include them may depend on the type of study, what is known about the question, and the conventions of your discipline and department. Similarly, the statement of the problem may contain conceptual definitions of major concepts. This is particularly true when competing definitions of the concepts exist within the field of inquiry (e.g., it might be important to point out that the study will focus on trait anxiety as opposed to state anxiety or other conceptualizations of the construct of anxiety).

It is critical that a research question have an explanatory basis. This means that the Statement of the Problem contains a brief summary of the conceptual underpinnings for the proposed research. Dust bowl empiricism is the somewhat derogatory term used to refer to a shotgun approach to research, in which the investigator levels his or her sights to see what is out there without developing a convincing chain of presuppositions and arguments that leads to a prediction. There is no research problem in "wondering" how the variables of gender, voice quality, and persuasion intercorrelate. This will not serve as a suitable problem statement. Hypotheses, on the other hand, have the virtue of being explanatory expressions of research questions because they imply a commitment to a particular understanding of how variables relate.

An example of a research question without a specific hypothesis is "What is the role of male significant others on the criminal activities of female criminals?" This research question implies a study that obtains information from or about women who have been convicted of crimes regarding the influence of boyfriends and male acquaintances in their criminal activities. A study that poses this question without predictive hypotheses (perhaps because of a lack of available information about this topic) might be termed exploratory. Too often, we find, students pose their dissertations as exploratory to avoid the challenging tasks of thinking deeply about underlying concepts and rigorously linking their ideas with previously published work in related areas.

In most instances, it is possible to project hypotheses. Even in those instances where there is a relative lack of research in an area, it is likely that studies and theories exist on related topics that can inform the proposed study. In the previous example, the investigator may have developed some reasonable hunches about the research question from his or her knowledge of women's developmental theory and the role of the peer group in criminal behavior. These hunches would be reflected in one or more hypotheses. An example of a research hypothesis is "There is a negative relationship between positive body image and motivation for augmentation mammoplasty." A second example is "Couples in stable, unhappy marriages use more conflict avoidance methods than couples in stable, happy marriages." The first hypothesis suggests a study in which the variables of body image and motivation for breast augmentation will be statistically correlated, whereas the second hypothesis suggests a study using two groups of couples who will be compared on how they manage conflict. In either case, the variables specified in the hypotheses will need to be *operationalized*, or clarified with regard to how they are to be measured. Such specification usually takes place in the Method chapter. In the first example, the researcher might predict, as did one of our students, a negative relationship between scores on the Jourard-Secord Body Cathexis Scale and a 10-item Likert-type scale of motivation to seek augmentation mammoplasty (Ewing, 1992). It is obviously important to specify each variable. In the second example, the terms *stable/unstable marriage* and *conflict avoidance methods* would need to be conceptually defined and operationalized, and the two groups of couples need to be identified.

It usually takes several rewritings to come up with research questions and hypotheses that are optimally clear, concise, and meaningful. Note that hypotheses typically are written as positive assertions in the present tense. They are not written as null hypotheses. The reader may be aware that inferential statistics work on the assumption of rejecting null hypotheses, that is, hypotheses that assume there are no significant differences between or among groups or no significant relationships among variables. Research hypotheses, on the other hand, should be stated not as null hypotheses but as directional hypotheses (or hypotheses that specify a relationship between variables) that follow from the argument that has been established in the preceding chapter. As research hypotheses, null hypotheses are confusing because they reflect the opposite of the argument you have been proposing. If the logic behind the stated hypotheses is not totally evident, it is always a good idea to follow or precede each hypothesis with a short rationale that reminds the reader how it emerged out of theoretical propositions established in the Review of the Literature.

Recommended criteria for a good hypothesis are that it be free of ambiguity, express the relationship(s) between two or more variables, and imply an empirical test (Locke, Spirduso, & Silverman, 1999). A common pitfall is to have more than one hypothesis embedded in a single, complex statement (e.g., "Women who earn more than their husbands have more self-confidence, have more friends, and receive more help on household tasks than women who earn less than their husbands").

Some dissertations contain both research questions with hypotheses and research questions that stand alone. The hypotheses might cover those relationships that directly challenge previous work or test a theory, whereas research questions without hypotheses are more open-ended opportunities to satisfy one's curiosity. For instance, a student studying self-disclosure patterns among psychotherapists might have specific hypotheses about the relationship between self-disclosure and friendship (e.g., "Therapists who are high in self-disclosure with their patients have fewer personal friends") but no clear expectations about the relationship between self-disclosure and stages of therapy (e.g., "What is the relationship between therapist self-disclosure with patients and the stage of psychotherapy?").

A more popular way of combining research questions and hypotheses is to use research questions as more general investigatory themes, which are then followed by specific hypotheses that make predictions in a testable form. This example is loosely based on a dissertation by one of our students (Davenport, 1991):

Research question: How do dyslexic adolescents cope with the effects of their learning disabilities?

Hypothesis 1: Dyslexic adolescents who accept the diagnosis of having a learning disability use more problem-focused coping strategies than dyslexic individuals who reject or deny the diagnosis.

Hypothesis 2: Dyslexic adolescents who accept the diagnosis of having a learning disability rely more on social support than dyslexic adolescents who reject or deny the diagnosis.

Hypothesis 3: Dyslexic adolescents who reject or deny the diagnosis of having a learning disability use more avoidant coping strategies than dyslexic adolescents who accept the diagnosis.

Hypothesis 4: Dyslexic adolescents who reject or deny the diagnosis of having a learning disability deny negative affect more than dyslexic adolescents who accept the diagnosis.

The preceding hypotheses suggest a research design that focuses on the differences between two groups of adolescents. Another dissertation, by Ellen Goldberg (2003), began with the general research question "What are the parent and child factors that predict diabetes self-care behaviors, particularly around prevention, detection, and treatment of hypoglycemia at home and in the school environment?" The primary hypotheses of the study are framed to suggest a correlational analysis of the results:

Hypothesis 1(a): Parental fear of hypoglycemia is inversely related to parental expectations for child responsibility for diabetes self-care autonomy in school.

Hypothesis 1(b): Parental fear of hypoglycemia is inversely related to parental expectations for child responsibility for diabetes self-care at home.

Hypothesis 2(a): Parental perception of the child's temperamental regularity and task orientation are inversely related to parental expectations for the child's responsibility for diabetes self-care autonomy in school.

Hypothesis 2(b): Parental perception of the child's temperamental regularity and task orientation are inversely related to parental expectations for the child's responsibility for diabetes self-care autonomy at home.

Hypothesis 3: Parental expectations for diabetes self-care autonomy are lower in the home environment as compared to the school environment.

Hypothesis 4: Parental expectations for diabetes self-care autonomy are inversely related to metabolic control.

The variables noted in the hypotheses also need to be operationalized. In this case, Goldberg (2003) tested the hypotheses using measures such as the Fear of Hypoglycemia Survey and the Diabetes Family Responsibility Questionnaire.

Problem Statements in Qualitative Research

The precise form of a good problem statement varies according to the discipline of the study and the research tradition it represents. Qualitative studies are more likely to support more open-ended questions. Within the phenomenological tradition, a dissertation on the exploration of childbirth might have as an overview question "What is the experience of giving birth to a child?" Taking the lead of Moustakas (1994), one chooses a topic rich with personal significance and social meaning, a topic that reflects an experience that the researcher has had and about which there is a passionate interest in understanding its nature. The question should have the following characteristics:

1. Seeks to reveal more fully the essences and meanings of human experience

2. Seeks to uncover the qualitative rather than the quantitative factors in behavior and experience

3. Engages the total self of the research participant and sustains personal and passionate involvement

4. Does not seek to predict or to determine causal relationships

5. Is illuminated through careful, comprehensive descriptions and vivid and accurate renderings of the experience rather than measurements, ratings, or scores (Moustakas, 1994, p. 105)

One of our graduate students, Sara Katz (1995), completed a fundamentally phenomenological study on the experience of coping with chronic, recurrent vulvar pain, a relatively unusual medical condition that can be quite debilitating and extremely resistant to treatment. The primary research questions in her study were as follows:

1. How do women live with chronic vulvar pain?

2. In what ways do women with chronic vulvar pain construct definitions of their illness, self, and situation?

3. How do a woman's somatic perceptions of her vulvar pain develop, change, and give rise to consequences?

4. How do a woman's emotional responses to her vulvar pain develop, change, and give rise to consequences?

5. How is shaping of the self related to the meanings the woman with chronic vulvar pain makes of the somatic sensations of the conditions and her emotional reactions to them?

Note that all of these questions follow up on the themes and contexts that define the experience of the phenomenon of chronic vulvar pain and help to provide a structure for holding the feelings and thoughts about the experience.

Another phenomenological dissertation, by Paul Smith (1998), posed the following question: "How do professional family divorce mediators manage the inner experience of conflicting voices within themselves and their sense of being centered while conducting mediations with polarized parties, developing mediation policies and procedures with other mediators, and advocating for forms of mediation practice within polarized socio-legal contexts?" As can be seen, the overarching research question within the phenomenological tradition usually asks about the meaning of an experience or phenomenon.

The wording of the primary research question in a grounded theory study is likely to be a process question (Morse, 1994), although, as the previous examples suggest, there is often some overlap in practice between these two research traditions. Adopting the previous childbirth theme, a typical research question using the grounded theory approach might be "How do women prepare for childbirth in a managed care health system?" This question is much too broad and open ended for a quantitative study. Recall, however, that the primary purpose of a grounded theory study is to generate a theory that relates to this phenomenon.

The primary question is usually followed by a series of further questions or prompts that have direct implications for data analysis:

- How does the process develop over time?
- What are the noteworthy events in the process?
- What facilitates the process?
- What hinders the process?
- Who are the key participants in the process and what are their roles?
- What are the outcomes?

The dissertation of one of our students, Nancy LaPelle (1997), was conducted to "discover what contextual, personal, and process variables support both motivating and demotivating performance evaluation experiences for intrinsically motivated supervisees in organizations, using a grounded theory design and resulting in a theory that fits the experiential participant data that were systematically obtained and analyzed" (pp. 2–3). LaPelle asked the following primary research question:

What are employees' significant experiences of performance evaluations in organizations and what are the factors that affect motivation and subsequent performance? More specifically, which features of the evaluation and of the surrounding management context will lead performance evaluations to have a positive effect and which will lead to their having a negative effect? (p. 6)

A number of subquestions were subsequently generated:

1. Do organizations intend performance evaluations to have an impact on motivation and performance either positively or negatively? What is their purpose and impact in different organizations or as implemented by different supervisors?

2. What is the process and experience of those who are motivated or demotivated by performance evaluations? Under what conditions is performance appraisal harmful to employees' motivation?

3. Does performance feedback work to improve performance and motivation, and under what conditions? Are providing feedback and evaluating performance the same thing?

4. What hypotheses might experiential data reveal? What existing bodies of theory might be related to the outcomes of this study that could help explain the revealed relationship between performance appraisals and motivation? How might they be integrated to form a unifying theory?

Another student, Lawrence Dong (2005), designed a dissertation to generate/develop a grounded theory of ethnic identity formation for Southeast and East Asian young offenders. His research was based on the following major research questions, which also guided his study:

1. How does ethnic identity develop for Southeast and East Asian young offenders?

2. What patterns or commonalities exist in the process of ethnic identity formation for these adolescents?

3. What factors are influential in their ethnic identity formation?

4. How has their ethnic identity formation influenced their risk for offending?

5. Are there ethnic cultural protective mechanisms that may serve as buffers against offending? (Dong, 2000, p. 68)

In an ethnographic study, the wording of the research question is apt to focus on a description of aspects of a culture (Morse, 1994). Following through with the childbirth example, an overarching question might be "How can the culture of a delivery room in a major urban hospital be described and interpreted?" Such a question would imply describing the context where childbirth occurs, analyzing the main themes, and interpreting the behavior of patients and medical staff. A dissertation example of the ethnographic approach can be found in Julianne Lynch-Ransom's (2003) study of the impact of the Internet on the organizational culture of a Midwestern company. The following research questions foreshadowed her study:

1. In what ways have the ideological inscriptions or domains of values that underlie this organization's unique manufacturing of authenticity as culture emerged?

2. In what ways has the process of construction of meaning through symbols, beliefs, and patterns of action resulted in both unity and division of organizational members' identity claims?

3. In what ways has the process of construction of meaning through symbols, beliefs, and patterns resulted in actions of leadership as culture in the Internet group?

4. In what ways has the process of identity and identification through symbols, beliefs, and patterns manifested in the merging of culture following the acquisition of this organization?

Narrative inquiry assumes that people construct their own meanings of their lives through the stories they tell and retell (McAdams, Josselson, & Lieblich, 2001). Within this tradition a study on childbirth might ask how the experience of having and raising a child has contributed to a woman's sense of self and her relationships with men and other women. A recent dissertation adopting a narrative orientation to a different developmental topic asked the following research questions (Jersild, 2006):

1. When women have grown up with a mother who earned as much money as their father, and received as much recognition for her accomplishments, what role do these processes have in the mother-daughter relationship?

2. What is the impact on the daughters' own experience of agency?

3. How do they perceive the balance of power in their childhood homes, and how do those perceptions shape their understanding of their own possibilities and desires and their ideas of what it means to be female?

4. How have these perceptions informed their own choices in work and relationships and their experience of *having* agency?

5. How do they construct the meaning of work, relationships, financial reward, and personal accomplishments?

6. What (if any) childhood experiences do they point to as preparing them for their adult lives? (Jersild, 2006, p. 65)

Other research traditions have their own chosen formats for presenting the research question. In action research, for example, Stringer (1999) does not specify a research question following the Review of the Literature. Rather, the Statement of the Problem is embedded in the introductory chapter, which describes the following elements:

- The issue or problem to which the study responds
- The location of the study and its stakeholders
- Organizations, policies, programs, and services that affect the problem
- The purposes of the research
- The significance of the study
- An overview of the content of each chapter of the report that follows

The literature review includes both the academic literature and official and unofficial documents (governmental policies, organizational procedural manuals, reports, news articles, etc.) that have interpreted the issue that is being studied. According to Stringer (1999), these materials are deconstructed to expose the underlying assumptions, concepts, and theories that buttress their claims and set the stage for the methodology of the research that is then described. The write-up of these sections, as well as the entire document, may be more narrative in style than, say, an experimental research study. Hameed Williams (2006) recently completed a participative action research dissertation study to gain understanding of the social worlds of gay men of African descent living in the New York City metropolitan area. His primary research question reflects this goal: "What understanding does a group of black men who experience same-sex desire offer about their social world when they are engaged in an embodied, Afrocentric, collaborative inquiry process?"

The statement of the research problem, together with the precise exposition of the research questions or hypotheses, or both, serves as a transition between the Review of the Literature and the description of the methods of the study. The following chapter offers guidelines and suggestions for presenting the methods.

Note

1. Kuhn also identified paradigm shifts as discontinuous, more disruptive changes in the evolution of scientific thinking.

BOX 4.1   Student Suggestions

1. Use the APA style manual (*Publication Manual of the American Psychological Association*, 2004) at the outset. It is much easier to get into the habit of referencing articles and books correctly than to go back and revise the format at a later time. This is especially true for direct quotations, where it is critical to keep page numbers. A software program such as Endnote will make it much easier to use APA format conventions automatically in the text and for references.

2. You'll know when to stop your literature review when the articles you read become redundant and when the authors and articles that are cited become familiar to you.

3. Develop a system for organizing and cataloging what you read. For example, I began to note, in the margins of the books and articles I read, numbers representing the topic being covered. I simply started numbering as I discovered topics, and I ended up with 38 topics that included everything I wanted to be able to retrieve. Later, I organized the references according to the numbers in a computerized filing program.

4. Read the original writings of the theorists you are studying, not just what someone else says about their theories. I have found that other people tend to misinterpret original writings. Piaget, for instance, is terribly misunderstood in America. Plus, the original source is so much richer. Trust yourself before you trust others. Take your time to pinpoint those parts that aren't completely clear to you because those are usually higher level thoughts that you need to struggle to understand.

5. One of the problems that students will likely encounter is tracking a given subject matter through different disciplines, for example, social psychology, sociology, anthropology, communications, and cross-cultural studies. Often research in one discipline is isolated from another not by differences in philosophical orientation but rather by the sociological barriers of a fragmented academia. The subject matter may even have a different name for the same basic phenomenon.

6. Scanning basic textbooks in these different fields can give you clues to follow up in the library directory. Journals are extremely valuable in following academic debates between members of a research tradition or identifying battles between research traditions. Bibliographies can be very useful in tracking down new sources.

7. It is much easier to record complete references for source materials when you initially read them rather than later on. It is very frustrating and time-consuming to retrieve a publication date or page number after an entire paper has been written.

8. Use an ample number of subheadings in your Review of the Literature chapter to maintain organization and flow. Make sure your headings convey enough information to assist readers and orient them to the material that follows.

Tips for Choosing and Reviewing the Literature

1. Know your databases and realize that the articles you find in them depend on the key words you use in your search. Try as many alternative terms as possible.

2. Start with more recent studies and review articles and books and work backward in time.

3. Identify "classic" studies and studies that others in the field regard as especially important.

4. Don't neglect studies that disagree with your point of view or your hypotheses or that have obtained negative outcomes.

5. Check for more recent studies even after you move on to the later stages of your dissertation.

6. Learn the skill of quick reading. There is too much out there for you to read everything in detail. Start by reading the abstract and skimming the beginning and conclusion of each chapter, then move on unless it is a particularly relevant article.

7. Group your articles into themes and categories, look for how studies are related to and differ from one another, and check for gaps in the literature.

8. Don't claim that "there are no studies" on a topic, but rather that nothing was found using your search strategies. Moreover, be prepared to expand your search to other areas that are related to or have implications for your study.

Writing and Grammar Tips

The following advice reflects our experience of some persistent problems with grammar in dissertations:

1. Summarize frequently and provide clear transitions between sections.

2. Learn how to use apostrophes correctly (e.g., it's vs. its).

3. Make sure pronouns agree in number (i.e., singular and plural are used consistently in the same sentence). For instance, the sentence "Whenever a member of the military engages in combat, they are at risk for post-traumatic stress disorder" contains a pronoun that does not agree with its related noun. Alternatively, one could write, "Whenever military personnel engage in combat, they are at risk for post-traumatic stress" or "Members of the military who engage in combat are at risk for post-traumatic stress."

4. Learn to use present tense and past tense correctly. Past tense should be used when an action took place in the past, whereas present tense should be used to refer to enduring findings. Generally speaking, findings from a specific study deal with samples, whereas generalizations from that study refer to populations. For instance, one might write the following statements when referring to a previous study: "The grizzly bears were less aggressive when the campers played music. This enabled the researcher to conclude [or enables us to conclude] that music soothes the savage beast."

5. Learn the correct distinction between commas and semicolons. Semicolons are used to join complete sentences (each contains a subject and a verb) where there is no conjunction, such as *and* or *but*. The semicolon suggests to the reader that the two halves are related or part of the same idea, as in the following sentence: "Jones surveyed men and women; Smith relied exclusively on men."

6. Avoid slang and jargon.

7. Avoid plagiarism at all costs. Ideas and wording that are not your own need citations.

Our colleague Judy Stevens Long offers the following sage (but possibly overstated) advice for students who want to improve their academic writing:

1. Never write a sentence that carries over three typed lines (about 30 words). They tend to be harder to understand.

2. Never put more than three prepositional phrases or infinitive phrases in a sentence. They divert the reader's attention from the main point of the sentence. A prepositional phrase starts with a preposition, such as *in, through,* and *under*. An infinitive phrase starts with the word *to* and is followed by a verb, as in *to discover* and *to prepare*.

3. Put the subject of the sentence first and the verb relatively close to it. This makes it easier for the reader to know your intention. Verbs tend to be the most underrated part of a sentence in academic work, so try to find lively alternatives for linking verbs such as *is* and *was*.

4. The adverb is the enemy of the verb. Adverbs such as *very* and *really* and *uniquely* aren't necessary. Good verbs speak for themselves.

5. The adjective is the enemy of the noun. If you find the right noun, you can reduce your use of adjectives.

The interested reader can find a wealth of additional writing tips online in "Fussy Professor Starbuck's Cookbook of Handy-Dandy Prescriptions for Ambitious Academic Authors or Why I Hate Passive Verbs and Love My Word Processor" (pages.stern.nyu.edu/~wstarbuc/Writing/Fussy.htm).

Citing Studies in Text

APA style dictates how to cite studies correctly, both in your text and in your bibliography. In text, the author of a study can be cited in at least two different ways. Note how parentheses are used differently in the two examples and note where the period is placed:

a. "It has been determined that men are more reluctant than women to ask for directions" (Knowitall, 2004).

b. "A study by Knowitall (2004) determined that men are more reluctant than women to ask for directions."

There is another subtle but important difference in citing multiple authors. Note the difference between the use of the word *and* and the ampersand (&):

a. "There is reason to believe that women enjoy shopping more than men do" (Bargain & Spend, 2005).

b. "Bargain and Spend (2005) found that women enjoy shopping more than men do."

SOURCE: Stefan Kramer. Reprinted with permission of the author.

Learning to Use the Library

A critical piece of nearly all research activities, and most certainly the dissertation process, is efficient and effective exploration of the scholarly (or professional) literature—in your field of study and related ones. Entire books have been devoted to that subject, so we cannot begin to provide a sufficient presentation of the important skills and techniques for this type of research, online and in the library, in this text. Our knowledgeable librarian, Stefan Kramer, offers these pointers on conducting library research:

1. A few hours or days spent honing library search skills and learning effective search techniques may very well save you weeks or months of frustrated, seemingly endless, time-wasting searching.

2. Relying on freely accessible Web search engines and directories alone will not suffice for graduate level research.

3. If you are not already very comfortable with search skills from prior research endeavors, your first stop should be the library's Web site (or a reference librarian of your university), which will likely have tutorials, resource guides, short seminars, or one-to-one consultations based on the resources specifically available at your *library*.

4. Find out what the library can offer you—your tuition already pays for it!—for learning about the following research concerns:

   a. selecting appropriate online databases and other information resources for your subject area

b. effectively searching across multiple online resources
c. going from relevant citations/abstracts you may find to the full text of those items
d. using nested Boolean searching (the *(a OR b) AND (x OR y OR z)* type of query structure)
e. using truncation and wildcards for efficiently searching for variant word forms
f. using proximity operators (includes phrase searching) for controlling distance and sequence of the search terms in your query
g. using controlled vocabularies for targeted subject searching, where available
h. selecting specific fields/indexes of online databases for focusing searches
i. saving and organizing the results of your searches
j. respecting copyright

SOURCE: Stefan Kramer, Fielding Graduate University, personal communication.

Software for Bibliographic Management

Program	Developer-Distributor	Web Site	Comments
Citation	Oberon Development Ltd.	http://www.oberondev.com/9-home.asp	Citation 9 available for 30-day trial download.
EndNote	Thompson ResearchSoft	http://www.endnote.com	EndNote X available for 30-day trial download.
Procite	Thompson ResearchSoft	http://www.procite.com/pchome.html	Trial download available.
RefViz	Thompson ResearchSoft	http://www.procite.com/pubtools/refviz.asp	A text analysis and visualization software application designed to evaluate the literature. Trial download available.
sci PROOF	Thompson ResearchSoft	http://www.procite.com/pubtools/sciproof.asp	A new tool designed to streamline scientific writing. Verifies spelling, style, acronyms, and Greek symbols. New proofreading technology enables authors to integrate and proofread required formats and styles. Trial download available.

5

The Method Chapter

Describing Your Research Plan

T he Method chapter of a dissertation, article, or proposal describes the exact steps that will be undertaken to address your hypotheses or research questions. For this reason, the Method section follows logically from the statement of the problem in much the same way as research questions follow from the Review of the Literature. The goal of this chapter is to provide a clear and complete description of the specific steps to be followed. It is necessary to describe these steps in sufficient detail to help a naïve reader to replicate your study.

In Chapter 3, we suggested that students select a suitable problem before selecting the appropriate method with which to study that problem. In some dissertations, however, the method may in fact be the topic of study. A student may become excited about the possibilities of a particular data collection technique or method prior to generating a suitable problem. In most cases, though, the appropriate method of study is generated by careful consideration of the research questions and the applicable method by which those questions may be studied. The following material is divided into two major sections, one that focuses primarily on the quantitative dissertation and one that focuses on the qualitative dissertation; we strongly recommend that you read both sections. The issues to be considered are not independent of each other, and there is considerable overlap in the content of this chapter, regardless of the method being employed.

The Method Chapter in a Quantitative Dissertation

The Method chapter is the place in which the exact steps you will be following to test your questions are enumerated. The Method chapter typically contains the following three subsections: Subjects or Participants, Instrumentation or Measures, and Procedures. In addition, the Method chapter of a dissertation proposal often contains a Statistical Analysis or Data Analysis section, in which procedures for approaching the data are outlined. Research that uses special equipment frequently contains an Apparatus section, in which the nature and type of equipment are described.

A frequent mistake contained in first drafts of Method chapters involves overuse of the opportunity to rehash the material contained in the Review of the Literature or Statement of the Problem, which were presented in another chapter. The Method chapter should be viewed primarily as a set of directions for conducting a specific piece of research. We follow this perspective in describing each of the subsections of a Method chapter.

How to Begin a Method Chapter

A reasonable way to begin a Method chapter is to develop an introductory paragraph that describes both the design of the study and the organization of the chapter. This prepares the reader for what is to follow and provides a framework within which to incorporate the materials. This paragraph says to the reader, "This is the Method chapter, this is how it is organized, and this is the type of design I used." The most difficult component of the introductory paragraph may appear to be the design statement. There are dozens of books that take research design as their sole topic. Our purpose here is not to review this extensive material. In this context, we are suggesting only a short sentence or two that informs the reader of the general type of design and any suitable label that may be applied to it.

For example, imagine a study in which you plan to mail 700 surveys to retired male executives in an attempt to assess their adjustment to retirement. It is probably sufficient simply to state something like the following: "This study used a cross-sectional survey design to assess adjustment to retirement of a sample of retired male executives." Similarly, imagine an experimental design in which two dichotomous variables will be used as independent variables. It may be sufficient to describe the design as "an experimental study using a 2 × 2 factorial design." An example of such a design is described in a dissertation by Sangster (1991):

> An experimental, 2 × 2 factorial, pretest-posttest design was used to test the hypothesis. The independent variables were (a) training type and (b) management experience. Respective levels of independent variables were descriptive and prescriptive training, and high and low management experience. (p. 102)

Determining exactly which type of design description best fits your study can be accomplished by referencing one of the many texts that describe designs (e.g., Campbell & Stanley, 2005; Kerlinger & Lee, 1999), but a specific label may not be as important as a clear explanation of the structure of your study. For example, a dissertation by Macdonald (1990) examined the relationships among empathy, personal maturity, and emotional articulation. Macdonald described her design as follows:

> The research design was a correlational design utilizing cross-sectional survey methodology and includes a number of survey instruments. The purpose of the design was to correlate the scores of the personality tests listed below with the scores on responses to the short stories, as well as measure the interrelationship of the responses to the short stories. (p. 115)

Describing Your Sample

The Subjects (or Participants) section of the Method chapter describes the source and number of subjects you will be using (in a proposal) or the source and number of subjects actually obtained (in a completed project). Note that we use the term *subjects* in a very broad context. The subjects may be informants or participants in the research, organizations or events, documents or segments of commercials edited from television programs, or even an entire society, as in the case of anthropological research. In studies of human beings, the term *participants* is generally preferable to the term *subjects*. One goal of this section of the Method chapter is to describe why and how the particular unit of analysis was selected.

A frequent problem we have observed is that students often confound a description of the sampling of subjects with the procedures used to collect data from these subjects. The former belongs in the Subjects section, whereas the latter belongs in the Procedures section. Of particular importance in the Subjects section are the specific sampling procedures used, the rationale for selecting a given number of subjects, and the source of the subjects. Which type of sample will you draw: random, stratified, purposive? Where will your subjects be located? How many subjects are necessary for your particular design? Each of these questions is important and should be dealt with in the Subjects section. We discuss each in turn in this section.

The Sampling Design. As is the case with research design in general, the issue of sampling is a complex one. Our purpose, however, and your purpose as researcher, is not to discuss the knotty problems of sampling. Your job is to describe how you will accomplish this task in your study, taking all the theoretical and practical issues into account. Knowledge of the various types of sampling design is a prerequisite to developing an appropriate description of your particular sampling problem.

Two examples may be of assistance in developing your approach. In a dissertation examining gender differences in professional identity among practicing psychotherapists, New (1989) obtained a mailing list of all licensed psychologists in the state of California. Beginning at a randomly selected start point, she then sampled every nth name until she had exhausted the list. Her dissertation described this process as follows:

> A systematic random sample was drawn from a list of all psychologists who have been licensed in the state of California for five or more years. The sample was obtained from a research center specializing in the distribution of selected sampling lists. A table of random numbers was used to locate the initial sampling point. Every 20th person was selected such that an initial group of 400 was obtained. These persons were mailed the study materials.

In a second instance, illustrating a nonrandom procedure, Caddell (1989) selected students from classes at three universities to examine moral education in the college environment. He described his sampling procedure as follows:

> The questionnaire was administered to selected undergraduate and graduate level classes at California State University–Fullerton, California Baptist College and Pacific Christian College. The sample was divided into a subset from the morally nondirective institution (Cal State–Fullerton, $N = 178$) and a subset from morally directive institutions (Cal Baptist College, $N = 104$ and Pacific Christian College, $N = 71$).

Locating Participants. Of the two examples presented in the previous section, only one describes both where and how the participants were obtained as well as the sampling design used. In the study using university students, Caddell (1989) failed to describe how the "selected undergraduate and graduate level classes" were obtained. In fact, the procedure was one of asking professors at each institution for permission. This decidedly nonrandom procedure could probably best be described as a convenience sample.

In many studies, it may not be practical to obtain a truly random sample. Even college sophomores, who constitute the classic population of many university-based studies, are a select group with their own idiosyncracies that exert limitations on the ability to generalize findings to people in general. Students who choose to study relatively unusual phenomena, such as men who continue to live with their parents into and beyond midlife or adults who grew up in foster homes, may end up relying on a snowball technique to obtain a sufficient number of participants. This technique consists of other individuals, including previously identified participants, knowing of and recommending additional potential participants. This approach to sampling may or may not be suitable, depending on the tolerance of the study to absorb the potential bias inherent in the method. One relevant example is Carol Crane's (2005) dissertation, which required her to locate an adequate number of participants with developmental synesthesia, a rare neuropsychological condition. A snowball technique for identifying participants is more common in qualitative studies. Take, for example, Diane Armstrong's (1994) fascinating dissertation on the nature of dreams of 18 congenitally and adventitiously blind men and women or Devon Jersild's (2006) exploration of women who grew up with particularly successful and accomplished mothers.

An increasingly popular way of identifying participants and collecting data is through the Internet. Our students have used two different approaches. One is to design or hire an individual or company that designs Web sites for research data collection. All of the questionnaires and measures for the study are available on the Web site and presented in a clear, systematic way that enables eligible participants to complete them on their home computers at a time of their choosing. Each participant's responses are downloaded into a database so that the results can easily be manipulated and analyzed statistically. Sometimes the participants are recruited on the same Web site or via Internet discussion lists that appeal to individuals who have the required characteristics to qualify for the study. Tracy Zemansky (2005) helped design her own Web site to complete a recent dissertation on the recovery process of long-term members of Alcoholics Anonymous. She obtained 164 qualified participants in a short period of time. A slightly different approach is to use an existing service that allows researchers to post their measures on a secure domain within a public Web site that is available exclusively for such survey and data-gathering activities. Potential participants are recruited by the researcher through e-mails, electronic discussion lists, letters, or personal contact and directed to the Web site, invited to create a secure online identification code and password, and asked to type in the appropriate survey number to access the study. The site also provides the necessary informed consent forms. Corinne Goodwin (2006) recently used this kind of online research service (www.psychdata.com) to complete her dissertation on the quality of the supervisory relationship in the training of clinical psychologists. She too was gratified to obtain more participants than she anticipated within a very short period of time using this strategy.

What are the advantages and disadvantages of selecting participants based on their willingness to access an Internet Web site and complete surveys electronically? We do not yet know enough about the comparability of these samples, but what we do know is encouraging (Wright, 2005). Though there may be bias in terms of computer access and computer savvy, there is also the possibility of obtaining geographically heterogeneous samples that may not be available when using traditional data collection strategies. Also, many participants seem to trust and appreciate the anonymity they have by addressing a machine rather than the researcher directly. Of course, the accompanying risk is that when might be more likely for participants to fudge their responses using this more impersonal format. It does seem clear that researchers can obtain a large number of responses very efficiently over the Internet and collect data in a form that allows for relatively painless analysis. The previous discussion does not exhaust the varieties of Internet-based data collection. This is so critical for the dissertation process that we have devoted all of Chapter 11 to a thorough discussion of the many sources of data and strategies for data collection through the Internet.

The Appropriate Number of Participants. Determining the appropriate number of participants for a given design is one of the most difficult sampling problems. Generally, given considerations of cost and time, students wish to obtain as few as their committee will allow; however, this decision is not arbitrary. Most students tend to underestimate the number of participants necessary to draw meaningful conclusions from the data. For example, imagine a study from the field of education in which the researcher wishes to compare the level of creativity of students who are sent to public schools to those who receive home schooling. If in fact there is a difference, the student-researcher must collect enough data for this difference to appear in the results. The smaller the difference, the more data the student-researcher must collect.

The best method to approximate the number of participants is to conduct a power analysis. A power analysis advises the researcher regarding how many subjects are necessary to detect any effects that result from the independent variables, given (a) the size of the effect of these variables in the population, (b) the type of statistical tests to be used, and (c) the level of significance (or alpha level) of the study. The level of power, expressed as a probability, lets the researcher know how likely he or she is to avoid a Type II error. A Type II error occurs when one fails to reject the null hypothesis, even though it is false. Failing to reject a false null hypothesis means that an effect existed but was not detected by the study. As the probability of a Type II error increases, the power of the study decreases. In fact, power is equal to 1 minus the probability of a Type II error. Thus, if a probability of a Type II error is .15, power is .85 (1 − .15 = .85). Said less technically, an underpowered study is likely to obtain nonsignificant findings.

Historically, power calculations have been difficult to conduct, and students and their committees frequently relied on general rules of thumb to determine the appropriate number of subjects. Computer programs now simplify these calculations, and we strongly recommend that they be used in dissertation planning. Most power analysis software exists as programs that are either individually purchased or purchased as add-ons to existing software. An example of an individually purchased program is nQuery Advisor 6.0 (http://www.statsolusa.com). nQuery Advisor is an easy-to-use program that helps researchers determine the effect sizes and sample sizes necessary to conduct a sufficiently powered study for a wide variety of statistical procedures and designs. An example of a program that is an add-on to an existing program is the SPSS module, Sample Power (www.spss.com). One problem with these programs is that they may be quite expensive; however, cooperative arrangements with the academic community often permit deep discounts for students. Check with your college or university software vendor to determine the exact pricing of this software. An alternative is to calculate power by hand. Though the calculations can be confusing for the novice, with a little help a student can often successfully estimate the appropriate sample size using formulas and tables. Three sources that we recommend are Cohen's (1988) *Statistical Power Analysis for the Behavioral Sciences;* Kraemer's (1987) *How Many Subjects? Statistical Power Analysis in Research;* and Wilcox's (2001) *Modern Statistical Methods: Substantially Improving Power and Accuracy.*

Finally, for more detail on the concepts of power and effect size, we recommend Chapter 4 of our own text *Your Statistical Consultant: Answers to Your Data Analysis Questions* (Newton & Rudestam, 1999). This chapter contains an extended discussion of the issues raised here and alternative formulations of the logic of statistical hypothesis testing.

In our earlier example of the student interested in comparing home-schooled with traditionally schooled youngsters, a *t* test might be used to compare levels of creativity between these two groups. Table 5.1 gives an example of a power analysis designed to answer the question "How many participants will I need to test the difference between the means of two groups, if I use a level of significance of .05 and desire a power of .80?" The table shows the number of subjects necessary to obtain the specified power level of .80 (a standard level, generally considered acceptable) using an alpha level of .05 (also a generally acceptable criterion) if the size of the effects (i.e., the mean differences relative to the standard deviation) are small, medium, or large.

Table 5.1 shows that if medium effects were predicted, it would require 64 participants per group to achieve a power of .80 when using an alpha level of .05. Even if the effects are large, the researcher would need at least 26 participants per group to achieve the same power level (.80). Another way to say this is that even if the research hypothesis is true, the researcher may fail to support this hypothesis because of insufficient sample size. As the sample size increases, it becomes more likely that the statistical tests will detect any effects that exist in the data.

Finally, it is important to make three critical points about the use of power analysis. First, in many dissertations the use of power analysis may be unrealistic. Enough subjects to meet the requirements of a purely mathematical procedure may not exist in some cases, and qualitative dissertations, case studies, oral histories, and intensive interviews may rely

Table 5.1   Power Analysis for a *t* Test

Effect Size	N Per Group	Total N
Small	393	786
Medium	64	128
Large	26	52

NOTE: To achieve a power level of .80, while setting the level of significance (alpha) at .05.

more on what the student and committee deem reasonable to develop a convincing argument, independent of statistical testing. Second, in cases where quantitative analysis is essential, students often use a multivariate framework with many variables. The number of subjects necessary in these contexts is likely to be much higher than that suggested earlier for a simple two-group t test. Third, even in highly quantitative studies, the use of statistical inference may not be appropriate, and thus power analysis would also be meaningless. In these cases, it is unreasonable to critique the study for failure to use significance testing or for lack of power. Not all quantitative studies rest solely on finding significance.

Instrumentation: Describing Your Research Tools

The Instrumentation (or Measures) section of a Method chapter describes the particular measures you will employ and how they will measure the variables specified in your research questions and hypotheses. This section makes your case for the use of particular measures as the best and most appropriate to your specific research environment.

If you are using instruments that have been used previously, especially standardized and widely recognized scales, then you should consider the following information as particularly relevant to your description: information about the appropriateness of the use of the instrument with the population and setting described in the proposal, information about the measurement characteristics of the instrument, and information about the administration and scoring of the scales. Each of these three areas is discussed separately.

Is the Measure Appropriate? A number of scales may exist that measure the same phenomenon. How is the researcher to select the "best"? (Or how does one guard against the claim that he or she should have used something else?)

The first step is to support the use of a given instrument with the population selected for your study. Measures that work well with adults may not be particularly effective with adolescents or children. Measures designed for use in one culture may work poorly in another. The writer's goal is to locate empirical studies that demonstrate the use of an instrument with a population as closely representative as possible of the population to be used in his or her study.

The second step is to demonstrate that the authors of the measure you select conceive of the phenomenon in terms similar to the manner in which you have conceptualized the same phenomenon. For example, all measures that assess depression are not the same because those who originally designed the measures viewed depression from different theoretical positions. The contents of the measures reflect these different positions. Thus, it may be important to indicate that you have chosen a particular instrument because it reflects the conceptualization of the phenomenon in a manner that is consistent with your perspective.

What Are the Measurement Characteristics of the Instrument? By *measurement characteristics,* we mean the reliability, validity, and structure of the measure. Reliability refers to the ability of a measure to produce consistent results. Validity indicates that a measure in fact measures what it purports to measure. Structure refers to the number and meaning of subscales contained in a given instrument.

It is important to realize that in a proposal the only information likely to be available regarding an instrument's reliability and validity is that contained in the existing literature. After the student collects his or her data, it is important to add to this body of literature by reporting the reliability and validity of the instrument as evidenced in the new sample. The reliability of an instrument is a characteristic of the population in which that instrument is used. Thus, an instrument that achieves high reliability in one sample will not necessarily receive that same level of reliability in another sample representing a different population.

How Does One Administer and Score the Measures? It is important for the reader to understand how an instrument is administered and scored. Some measures are self-administered and may simply be mailed or passed out with instructions to, for example, "check the box that most represents your feelings at the present time." Others, such as the Rorschach, require extensive training to administer and score. For others, the scoring methods are a well-guarded secret, and completed protocols must be sent to a central location for computerized scoring (for a fee, of course). In any case, we recommend that you pilot test any instruments you use, whether you make them up yourself or whether they are standard research tools. It may help to ask your pilot participants which instructions and items they found difficult or confusing.

If possible, include a copy of each instrument, with its instructions to the respondent, in an appendix to the dissertation. However, this usually is not appropriate with copyrighted instruments.

The following example, drawn from a doctoral dissertation (Hardwick, 1990), provides what we consider to be a clearly written description of a rather complex instrument. The section we quote contains information about the structure, scoring, and administration of the instrument. Information about the reliability and validity of the instrument is contained in materials we have not chosen to quote here.

> The Bell Object Relations Reality Testing Inventory (BORRTI) is a 90-item "true-false" self-report inventory which was used to operationalize the dependent variables, object relations and reality testing. It yields four object relations (OR) subscales and three reality testing (RT) subscales. Each dimension, OR and RT, is measured by 45 items which are worded to reflect various levels of object relations and reality testing. The four OR subscales are: Alienation, Insecure Attachment, Egocentricity, and Social Incompetence. The three RT subscales are Reality Distortion, Uncertainty of Perception, and Hallucinations and Delusions. The test also yields a quasi-summary score for each overall OR and RT construct. This score is the sum of all items to which the participant responded in a pathological direction. Thus, a participant could conceivably have normal subscale scores while still responding to any number of pathological OR and/or RT items.

The author goes on to describe examples of test items and the meaning of each subscale, including the interpretation of high and low scores as well as the measurement characteristics of each subscale. As noted earlier, it is important to include a brief assessment of the reliability and validity of each measure, especially as they pertain to previous research conducted on populations as similar as possible to those in the proposed study. A dissertation by Gilbert (2007) provides the following description of the Levels of Emotional Awareness Scale (LEAS):

> The LEAS is a self-report instrument in which the respondent is asked to imagine 20 scenes described in the form of brief vignettes. A sample item is: "A neighbor asks you to repair a piece of furniture. As the neighbor looks on, you begin hammering the nail but then miss the nail and hit your finger. How would you feel? How would the neighbor feel?" Responses are scored separately for each scene according to a Glossary and Scoring Manual and summed to determine the total score. (p. 101, cited in Gilbert, 2007)

> The LEAS has demonstrated high interrater reliability ($r(20) = .84$). Internal consistency is also high (Cronbach's alpha = .81). Construct validity has been established by comparing the LEAS with scores on measures of emotion perception and of the ability to reason in terms of hypothetical emotions. The LEAS has been found to correlate with measures of ego development and the cognitive complexity of descriptions of parents. (Lane et al., 1990, p. 101, cited in Gilbert, 2007)

Copyrighted scales typically are not reproduced in a dissertation or research publication. To use copyrighted scales in a study, permission should be obtained in writing from the holder of the copyright.

What If I Design My Own Instruments?

In rare instances, a student may not be able to locate any existing measures that tap the construct the student wants to measure. Our first recommendation is to send the student back to the library with the instruction "keep looking." This advice reflects our strong belief that developing your own instrument is generally not a good idea. Research based on hastily thrown together instruments, which lack sufficient pretesting and are questionable in terms of reliability and validity, is of little scientific value. If the student is unable to locate a satisfactory instrument, he or she may wish to consider changing the focus of the research from one that attempts to relate the construct in question to other constructs, to one that attempts to design and assess a new instrument, a valid dissertation topic in and of itself. In this case, building the instrument becomes the central topic, and examining its relationships to other variables becomes part of the process of establishing the validity of the new instrument. Woodard (2001) set out to examine the relationship between the personality construct of hardiness and stress, coping, and physiological functioning in his dissertation. He ended up constructing and validating a measure of courage, which he proposed to be an integral component of the existential concept of authenticity, which is postulated to include the three components of hardiness: control, commitment, and challenge.

Research that concentrates on instrument development is a valuable enterprise and often makes greater contributions than research that attempts to relate existing measures to each other in some new and as yet untried fashion. Nevertheless, such research requires large numbers of subjects, frequent retesting, and sophisticated statistical models. Both the student and his or her committee must carefully weigh the pros and cons of undertaking such an enterprise. We provide six steps that are commonly involved in the process of instrument design:

1. Identify suitable content for an initial pool of items. This helps shape the content validity and face validity of the instrument and is facilitated by reading the theoretical and empirical literature and surveying the opinion of experts.

2. Create an initial pool of items, including items that may be parts of other instruments. This involves deciding on an item and response format

(e.g., 7-point Likert scale) and writing a large pool of logical, unambiguous, understandable items that reflect some dimension of the underlying construct being measured.

3. Obtain a group of expert judges to rate the pool of items for appropriateness (content validity) and clarity (wording). Eliminate poorly rated items based on systematic criteria.

4. Survey an initial pool of respondents with all of the remaining items. Perhaps include other measures to correlate with the items, such as a social desirability scale to control for the tendency to make a positive impression. The respondents should represent the population for which the instrument is being designed.

5. Determine the structure and reliability of the instrument and its subscales. This includes assessing the internal consistency of the scale(s) (i.e., how the items correlate with one another, using a reliability measure such as a coefficient alpha, and how each item correlates with the total score of the instrument or the individual subscales, or both) and may involve the use of exploratory and confirmatory factor analytic procedures. Reduce the item pool by discarding items that do not correlate sufficiently (either positively or negatively) with the total score as well as items that do not discriminate well (e.g., items that almost everyone endorses or rejects).

6. Survey a new pool of suitable respondents to validate the new measure. This includes correlating the responses to the scale with responses to other measures with which it is hypothesized to correlate positively (convergent validity) and negatively (discriminant validity). It might also include some form of predictive validity measure by testing to see if the scale effectively predicts a relevant criterion (e.g., a test of academic potential predicting subsequent school grades). Confirmatory factor analytic procedures are also likely to be used in this step.

What If I Modify an Established Instrument?

It is not uncommon for a student to modify questions or add questions to a validated instrument to facilitate its use. For example, when using some instruments with younger populations, it may be necessary to reword or eliminate questions regarding relations with the opposite sex. Phrases such as "My sex life is satisfactory" may not be appropriate for 7-year-old children.

Our position is that the modification of an existing instrument is perfectly acceptable but that such changes may make the norms invalid and may affect both the reliability and validity of the instrument. A close examination of many instruments currently in use reveals that there has been considerable borrowing among various authors over a lengthy time period. When borrowing or modification occurs, it becomes the responsibility of the student to justify such changes and make his or her case for the reliability and validity of the instrument in its revised form. It is often advisable to use an existing instrument in conjunction with a new instrument of the student's design. Even if the student feels that his or her instrument is better, the use of multiple measures of a single concept can be very useful when establishing the reliability and validity of a new instrument. Of course, when a new instrument fails, as it often does, the old standard can be used in its place. When Slanger (Slanger & Rudestam, 1997) designed her dissertation on participants in extreme risk sports, she knew that the application of the self-efficacy measurement to new domains was limited by the situational specificity of the measure. Thus, she supplemented a generalized self-efficacy scale with a new scale of her own design that focused on significant physical risk taking. To her surprise and delight, her previously invalidated scale was a better predictor of her dependent variable than previously existing measures.

Most dissertations contain some form of demographic data sheet. These sheets contain questions that assess gender, ethnicity, years of employment, marital status, education, and the like. Although such questions need to be thought through carefully, we do not consider adding such questions to a battery of existing instruments in the same context as scale development. We suggest examining surveys from the National Opinion Research Center General Social Survey (GSS) for examples of how to solicit demographic information. For GSS survey information, including the exact wording of hundreds of demographic questions, visit http://webapp.icpsr.umich.edu/GSS/.

What If I Want to Use Archival Data?

Questionnaires are not the only type of data collection instrument. Behavioral observations, extended interviews, and archival data all constitute valid sources of data for dissertation research. Students need to be cautioned about the potential problems of relying on archival data (i.e., data previously gathered and available from other sources prior to the design of the current study) for their dissertations. Here are three issues that must be considered by the student and his or her dissertation committee when considering this option:

1. In our experience, it is not uncommon for students to stumble on or be given a large data set prior to formulating a research question—or even to having a specific research interest. When this happens, students are

tempted to generate a suitable research question and set of hypotheses to conform to the available data. This is putting the cart before the horse: Whenever possible, the method follows from the question rather than precedes it. Research questions need to be justified on their own merits.

2. Archival data sets often suffer from missing, incomplete, or compromised data. This can take the form of an insufficient sample size, the absence of information on important variables that were not included in the original data collection, or the reliance on flawed or out of date measures. The dissertation student is responsible for the adequacy of the data set, and blame for any deficiencies in design or data should not be passed off on other agents.

3. Archival data are usually owned or controlled by others. Students who use them for their dissertation research must ascertain that they will have total access to the data and authorship and control over the resultant dissertation and, in most cases, associated publications.

In one telling example, a student we know who relied on someone else's data discovered, in the middle of data analysis, that the owner of the data had moved out of the country and taken the data with him. Although we have our misgivings about students relying on archived data, we are certainly aware of many excellent studies emanating from them. For example, Newton's (1991) dissertation examined the incidence of depression, substance abuse, and eating disorders in the families of anorexics. Data were obtained from existing medical records. Newton supported his data collection procedures as follows:

> A number of authors have studied the validity of data found in medical records (Harlow & Linet, 1989; Horwitz, 1986; Paganini-Hill & Ross, 1982; and Hewson & Bennett, 1987). Horwitz (1986) compared epidemiological data collected from medical records and by interview for 462 subjects who were part of a case-control study of chronic disease. Results showed that agreements between medical record and interview data are variable, and depend on the type of data examined and the strategy for handling incomplete or ambiguous responses. Horwitz did find a 93% agreement between medical records and interviews for family history of breast cancer. (p. 45)

In this quotation, the author let the readers know that he is aware of potential problems with his method, he has read the literature, and the literature supports the validity of this technique in some instances.

Many large archives provide rich opportunities for further study, and there is probably no persuasive reason for re-collecting data that already exist. One situation that merits using archived or secondary data is when important and relevant data exist that cannot effectively be duplicated by another researcher. The previously mentioned National Opinion Research Center General Social Survey is a good example. Another example is when archived data are critical to a new study, such as the student who wishes to discover how romantic relations have been expressed through the decades by analyzing popular song lyrics over the past 50 years.

Another situation calling for the use of secondary data occurs in academic departments or research centers when several (student) investigators collect or use the same large data set to ask and answer different research questions on the same general topic.

Procedures: Describing How You Did (or Will Do) It

The Procedures section provides a detailed description of the exact steps taken to contact your research participants, obtain their cooperation, and administer your instruments. After reading this section, one should know when, where, and how the data were collected. For example, in a mailed survey, one might describe the following steps: (1) mail precontact letter; (2) 1 week later, mail survey packet; (3) 2 weeks later, mail follow-up survey for nonrespondents. Exact copies of the precontact letter and cover letters accompanying the survey measures should be provided in appendices. Note that the sampling procedures have been described in the Subjects section and the measures described in the Instrumentation section. There is no need to repeat this information in the Procedures section. When procedures are complex and require the administration of multiple instruments over multiple time periods, a flowchart or table presenting the procedures visually becomes very helpful.

It is important that any information that might potentially affect the number of participants or their characteristics be included in this section. For example, much social research is conducted with college students. Were the students asked to volunteer? Were they given extra credit? Was participation mandatory as part of a course requirement? Similarly, when administering mailed surveys such simple information as whether the addresses were handwritten or mailing labels were used can affect response rates. Such information is critical to replicating the experiment and understanding the exact nature of the population sampled. It is also important to describe the procedures undertaken to gain access to the population. For example, if working with high school students, was it necessary to obtain permission of the school board or the principal, or did one simply sample all sixth-period classes? Finally, the procedures for obtaining informed consent should be described in detail and a copy of the informed consent statement, if any, provided in an appendix. This is particularly important when working with minors, who are legally not permitted to provide their own consent to participate in research. (Chapter 12 contains a more detailed discussion of informed consent and other ethical issues.)

Typically, instructions to participants, as well as ethical release forms, are included in the appendices. The ethical release forms are crucial because they inform participants about the potential hazards of partici-pating in the study (e.g., emotional upset), limits to confidentiality, and use of the data, and they make it clear that participation is voluntary. (In some rare instances, participation may not be voluntary.) The purpose of the release forms is to protect both you and those who participate in your research. Release forms also force you to think about the implications of your study on the physical and emotional well-being of humans or ani-mals employed as subjects. Most universities have stringent procedures for conducting ethical research, which generally include passing propos-als through an institutional review board or human subjects committee. A sample copy of a typical human subjects release form can be found in Chapter 12. These forms should include a description of the study, the right of refusal, an explanation of risks and potential discomfort, an opportunity to withdraw without penalty, and the potential for feedback.

Data Analysis: How to Justify and Describe an Analysis

A research proposal often includes a statement that describes the statisti-cal tests that will be used to address the hypotheses and research ques-tions. This section is usually the one that scares students the most (because students learn statistics in the abstract, not as applied to specific research questions). The great benefit of including this statement is that it forces you to think through how you will treat the data from your disser-tation at the time the proposal is generated, rather than after the data are collected. Time spent thinking about these issues at the proposal stage saves considerable time and pain later. In this way, one can avoid spend-ing countless hours collecting data that ultimately are not analyzable because they are not in the correct format in the first place. In the next chapter, we describe in detail how to present the results of a study once the data have been analyzed. In this section, we discuss how to propose a particular sort of analysis prior to having actually undertaken it.

This section is particularly difficult for a number of reasons, beyond the fact that students may not be prepared to apply statistics to their own research. First, statistical analysis is virtually never a one-shot affair. Data may be analyzed and reanalyzed many times before the researchers are satisfied that the data have been given the correct treatment. A technique that initially seemed perfectly reasonable will later seem inappropriate because of the number of cases or distributions presented by the completed sample. Second, interesting questions often arise after initial analyses are completed. If a hypothesis is not supported, one may search for alternative variables that might help explain the lack of support. For example, a hypothesis may be supported only among the highly educated. Research with a large number of noncollege graduates in the sample may obscure the relationship until the college graduates are analyzed separately from the noncollege graduates (i.e., education becomes a moderator variable).

What, then, is the student to do? First, we strongly recommend that, in consultation with your advisors, and experts if necessary, you describe which technique seems most appropriate given the nature of your hypothesis, the number of independent and dependent variables, and the level of measurement of each of the variables. The following chapter contains recommendations regarding the use of statistical techniques. Computer programs also can assist with the selection of statistical techniques, and many statistics texts present flowcharts directing students to appropriate statistical methods. Do not turn your data analysis section into a treatise on a particular technique paraphrased from a statistics text; instead, present a short, reasoned statement that a particular technique seems most appropriate. An example of a straightforward data analysis proposal is provided by Connell's (1992) study of stress in psychotherapists:

> The primary hypothesis, that there will be a significant difference between Group 1 and Group 2 on level of stress, will be tested using a one-tailed t test. . . . The expectation that Group 2 will score differently than Group 1 in 12 of the subscales of the Essi System StressMap will be tested using a multivariate analysis of variance (MANOVA).

When analyses are complex and based on a multivariate theoretical model, a broader statement of analytical strategy may be required. For example, a dissertation proposal by one of our students, Lisa Stewart (2006), examined the relationships among perceived stress, self-efficacy and depression, hopelessness, and suicidal ideation. She described the analysis of her theoretical model as follows:

Path analysis techniques will be used to examine the direct and indirect effects between the variables of initial stress, self-efficacy, depression, hopelessness, and suicidal ideation. Path coefficients will be computed via a series of bivariate and multiple regression analyses based on the hypothesized model.

Five direct, nonmediated relationships will be tested using multiple regression. These include self-efficacy and initial stress, self-efficacy and depression, self-efficacy and hopelessness, depression and hopelessness, and depression/hopelessness and suicidal ideation.

Three mediated relationships will be tested using multiple regression analyses: the effect of self-efficacy on suicidal ideation, the effect of self-efficacy on depression/hopelessness, and the effect of initial stress on suicidal ideation. (p. 65)

Should You Discuss the Limitations of Your Research?

A final section of the Method chapter that we encourage students to include in a dissertation proposal is a statement on limitations and delimitations of the study. Delimitations imply limitations on the research design that you have imposed deliberately. These delimitations usually restrict the populations to which the results of the study can be generalized. For example, you may decide to study only males, either because the theory on which your hypotheses are based has not been studied in females or because you have a readily accessible population of males but not females. Limitations, on the other hand, refer to restrictions in the study over which you have no control. For example, you may be limited to only a narrow segment of the total population you wish to study, or you may be limited by the method you elect to use.

The Method Chapter in a Qualitative Dissertation

Too often students view the relatively unstructured nature of qualitative research designs as license to omit clarity and specificity in the Method chapter of their dissertations. Qualitative studies should not be considered as opportunities to ignore the planning process in research. Issues of identifying and soliciting participants, selecting and preparing research materials and data collection tools, and formulating procedures pertain here as in all studies. The reader needs to understand what you did and how you thought about it in order to appreciate the links among the research problem, the method, and the results.

The organization of the Method chapter, as well as the content that goes into it, may depend on your research model as well as the conventions of your discipline and preferences of your committee members. Josselson and Lieblich (2003) prefer the term *Plan of Inquiry* to *Method* because the word *method* seems to focus on the procedure rather than on how one thinks about the question. We find that students who conduct qualitative studies are prone to spend an inordinate amount of space explaining the philosophy of science supporting the design. Such long-winded explanations seem unnecessarily apologetic; after all, a quantitative dissertation doesn't require a treatise on logical positivism. Basically, the reader needs to know about your research strategy and how your data will be generated with as much specificity as you are able to offer at this stage of the project.

Qualitative research adopts views of sampling, instrumentation, and data analysis that are often directly contrary to views held by those conducting more traditional "rationalistic" inquiry. Lincoln and Guba (1985) called this "the paradox of designing a naturalistic inquiry" and argued that "the design specifications of the conventional paradigm form a procrustean bed of such a nature as to make it impossible for the naturalist to lie in it—not only uncomfortably, but at all" (p. 225). Nonetheless, there are some practical distinctions between these issues in quantitative and qualitative studies that are worthy of consideration.

Sampling and Sample Size in Qualitative Studies

Determining where and from whom data will be collected is directly analogous to our consideration of sampling. Quantitative studies generally rely on random or representative sampling to generalize findings from the sample to the population. The qualitative researcher is more apt to elect purposive or theoretical sampling to increase the scope or range of data exposed (random or representative sampling is likely to suppress more deviant cases) as well as to uncover the full array of multiple perspectives (Lincoln & Guba, 1985, p. 40).

A phenomenological study usually involves identifying and locating participants who have experienced or are experiencing the phenomenon that is being explored:

> Phenomenological research uses sampling which is idiographic, focusing on the individual or case study in order to understand the full complexity of the individual's experience. From this perspective, there is no attempt to claim an ability to generalize to a specific population, but instead, the findings are relevant from the perspective of the user of the findings. (Bailey, 1992, p. 30)

The participants, if you will, are the experiential experts on the phenomenon being studied. This means that the sample probably would not be randomly drawn from a group of college sophomores. Rather, the researcher uses criterion sampling, selecting participants who closely match the criteria of the study. Katz's (1995) participants, for instance, had to meet both inclusionary and exclusionary criteria: a deliberately diverse and representational sample of women who had experienced "ongoing, intractable symptoms of discomfort in the skin of the vulva and/or the vaginal vestibule, which may be diffuse or in specific loci, and either persistent or episodic" (p. 91) for a period of 1 year or more. Referral of participants came directly from medical providers. Moreover, most phenomenological studies engage a relatively small number of participants (10 or fewer might be appropriate) for a relatively long period of time (at least 2 hours). These factors should be carefully noted in the Method chapter.

Because the grounded theory study is inductive and theory evolves as the data are collected and explored, it may be neither possible nor advisable to establish the precise sample size beforehand. Strauss and Corbin (1998) stressed that several forms of sampling are appropriate at various stages of the study. The trick is to choose participants who can contribute to an evolving theory, participants whose main credential is experiential relevance. Thus, at the outset, open sampling might be most appropriate. This means selecting participants or observations without prejudice because no concepts have yet proven to be theoretically meaningful. In practice that might mean systematically choosing every nth name on a list, staying maximally flexible and open to discovery. Researchers who support this approach might regard 20 to 30 participants as a reasonable sample (e.g., Creswell, 1998). Other representatives of the grounded theory approach are leery of processing the amount of data accumulated from that many respondents. They recommend beginning with perhaps 5 or 6 participants who have been selected because they seem to have the phenomenon of interest in common, a process called homogeneous sampling (Glaser & Strauss, 1967). Participants who are different from the initial sample are added only if they represent some quality that emerges as significant for understanding (and perhaps generalizing) the phenomenon under study.

As the study proceeds, the chief criterion for sampling moves toward theoretical relevance. At this point, the researcher has begun to assimilate some early theoretical hunches and wishes to identify examples that demonstrate the range or variation of a concept in different situations and in relation to other concepts. The sampling is done to saturate a concept, to comprehensively explore it and its relationship to other concepts so that it becomes theoretically meaningful. Because the theory emerges from the data, there is no viable way of determining these sampling dimensions beforehand. The researcher becomes increasingly selective in collecting a sample by adding to it based on the core variables that emerge as important to the theoretical understanding of the phenomenon under study. This process is sometimes known as discriminate sampling—choosing persons, sites, and documents that enhance the possibility of comparative analysis to saturate categories and complete the study. This might mean returning to previous interviews or sources of data as well as drawing on new ones. The study proceeds until there is theoretical saturation—gathering data until no new relevant data are discovered regarding a category and until the categories are well developed and validated. For the interested reader, Strauss and Corbin (1998) go into significant detail in describing the varieties of sampling relevant to grounded theory research.

Josselson and Lieblich (2003) agree that saturation—that is, stopping data collection when the results start to become redundant—is the key determinant of sample size. They caution, however, that real saturation never occurs because each new respondent has something unique to contribute to the study. They noted that it is usually the researcher who becomes saturated and that it is important to collect sufficient data to represent the breadth and depth of the phenomenon without becoming overwhelmed. Generally speaking, the longer, more detailed, and intensive the transcripts, the fewer the number of participants. In practice, this may mean specifying a range between 5 and 30 participants.

The ethnographer has different challenges to anticipate. The researcher's relationship with the group to be studied must be fully acknowledged and described. In some ethnographic studies, the researcher may already have membership status. More frequently, there is a gatekeeper or conduit for accessing the group. Once contact has been established, will everyone be approached to participate? Will sampling take place according to some thoughtful criteria? Will participants be selected opportunistically, according to convenience or eagerness to participate? The same rules apply in describing the use of artifacts and other sources of data that the ethnographer observes and records.

Elizabeth Moore's (1995) ethnographic study of organizational culture includes her list of 11 criteria for choosing an appropriate company to study, including issues of size, age, and tenure of employees; opportunities for observation; and access to company documents and employees. She received entry into a chemical company that met her criteria and gave her unlimited access to the organization. She offered all 29 employees the opportunity to participate in confidential interviews and ended up inter-viewing a majority of the employees as well as the founders and their wives. The interviews were of four types:

1. Critical event interviews, which focused on critical periods in the evolution of the organization

2. Ethnographic interviews, which dealt with the artifacts and values within the organization

3. Spouse interviews

4. A customer interview

She also relied on a month of participant observation activities and analysis of organizational documents. The sampling procedures, interviews, observation activities, and documents were described in the Method chapter, and the interview protocols were placed in appendices to the dissertation.

Instrumentation (or Measures) in Qualitative Studies

The instrument of choice for the qualitative researcher is the human observer. Thus, qualitative researchers place particular emphasis on improving human observation and make no claims for the reliability and validity of the instrument in the rationalistic sense. (A discussion of relia-bility and validity in qualitative studies follows later in this chapter.) The task for the student proposing an observational study would be to place considerable emphasis on the training and practice of the observer(s).

Qualitative researchers also recognize the use of other, more traditional sorts of instrumentation, provided they are grounded in the central focus of the research and axioms underlying the method. Typically, our students have used interviews to generate discussion surrounding the major research questions. In these instances, the task of the instrumentation section is to describe the interview and demonstrate how the interview serves as a suffi-cient device to focus discussion on the research questions of the study.

Although the interview itself may be quite loosely structured and flexible, phenomenological researchers generally prepare some questions in advance, preferring to alter them if it seems appropriate as the inter-view progresses. Although the precise wording of questions may vary from time to time, certain types of questions are pro forma. Think of the questions as tools to draw out the participant to reflect on the experi-ence and its implications in his or her life. Thus, one might request that a participant relax and focus on the incident or the phenomenon and "describe the experience, how you felt, what you did, what you said, what thoughts you have about it." Further questions serve as probes to encourage the interviewee to dig deeper and reflect on the meaning of the experience:

What aspects of the experience stand out for you?

How has the experience affected you?

What changes have you made in your life since the experience?

Grounded theory studies generally make primary use of interview techniques as well, although journals and other written records, as well as participant observation methods, may also be employed. Interviews may be either individual or group based, including what are popularly known as focus groups. LaPelle's (1997) dissertation provides a good example of a prepared opening statement to the interviewees:

I would like you to think about performance review experiences that significantly affected your interest, motivation, or performance in your job or subsequent career decision. Please describe, in as much detail as you can remember, the circumstances surrounding these experiences. (p. 37)

Subsequent probes included possible circumstances, such as work responsibilities, interaction with supervisor, inclusion of rewards or recognition of work, skill development as a function of the review, and personal meaning of the review, among others. More objective questions were included to obtain clarification of work history and work environment after the narrative portion of the interview was completed. Note that the initial question is a question of discovery, to identify what is common among the experiences of an aggregate of individuals. In this light, David Rennie (1998), a well-known grounded theory researcher, cautioned researchers not to begin with a set of questions that are really categories for coding so that the categories don't emerge from the data and the data analysis becomes content analysis.

Whereas survey researchers typically insist on preparing a specific set of questions that need to be asked precisely and in a particular order, most qualitative interviewers start with a general plan of inquiry but not a formal set of questions. The Method chapter would include at least one opening question and then some detailed follow-up questions that the researcher may or may not use depending on the subsequent flow of the interview. A student who intends to take this route needs to obtain ample training in conducting qualitative interviews prior to embarking on a dissertation. People construct meaning out of life events, and good interviewers learn to appreciate how they must listen patiently and sensitively and invite these stories by the way they frame their opening questions and follow-up interventions. In this spirit, some of our colleagues insist that students conduct a demonstration interview and include the analysis of it in a qualitative dissertation proposal (Josselson & Lieblich, 2003).

Several excellent texts are available for guidance in preparing and conducting qualitative research interviews. Among the more popular ones are Mishler (1991), Kvale (1996), Weiss (1994), and Rubin and Rubin (2004). Because these authors take somewhat different perspectives, it is a good idea to become familiar with more than one approach, then determine what best suits your own style and orientation.

Data Collection in Qualitative Studies

Issues of determining the successive phases of a study and planning data collection and logistics are subsumed under what we have described as Procedures. Regardless of the sort of study one is conducting, attention always must be paid to how the data are to be collected, independent of the form the data might take. Data recording may be described along two dimensions: fidelity and structure. An open-ended interview, when properly recorded, has high fidelity and little structure, whereas a standardized paper-and-pencil test has both high fidelity and high structure. We recommend the use of tape recorders to record interviews and place little reliance on the use of field notes (i.e., low fidelity and low structure). A diary or journal to record impressions, reactions, and other significant events that may occur during the data collection phase of research, however, is recommended as a useful source of supplementary information.

Data Analysis in Qualitative Dissertations

The issue of describing the data analysis in the Method chapter of the dissertation may be more problematic for those considering qualitative research than it is for those undertaking conventional quantitative research. One perspective comes from Lincoln and Guba (1985), who stated, "Not very much can be said about data analysis in advance of the study" (p. 241). This leaves the student in a difficult position, particularly if a committee is clamoring for a data analysis section in the proposal. Quite a bit has been said about data analysis within the context of qualitative studies, starting with an entire chapter of Lincoln and Guba's *Naturalistic Inquiry* (1985), which considers the issue of processing naturalistically obtained data in considerable detail. Miles and Huberman (1994) devoted an entire book to the issue of qualitative data analysis, and many recent texts on qualitative research, such as Marshall and Rossman (2006) and Silverman (2006), discuss the topic extensively. We consider some of these works in more detail in the following chapter. The main point is that even though a student may not be able to refer to specific statistical procedures, we believe that the general framework of an analysis can be specified in advance. Students should expect that both qualitative and quantitative dissertations are likely to involve multiple phases of data analysis.

Validity and Reliability in Qualitative Dissertations

In traditional empirical research we are mindful of the importance of reliability, internal validity, and external validity of measures and procedures. Many qualitative researchers, on the other hand, forgo the use of the terms *validity* and *reliability* because of the historical link of these concepts to objectivist research and the argument that they are inappropriate to naturalistic inquiry. Nonetheless, all research carries the responsibility of convincing oneself and one's audience that the findings are based on critical investigation. The possibility that the results of a qualitative study rest on a few well-chosen examples has been pejoratively described as anecdotalism (Silverman, 2005). In contrast, the trustworthiness of a design becomes the standard on which it is likely to be judged, and the Method chapter is the place where evidence for methodological rigor is introduced.

Validating an argument or research process basically means showing that it is well founded and sound, whether or not the results generalize to a larger group. On the other hand, when a procedure or result is reliable, it means that we can depend on it (i.e., rely on it). As Richards (2005) pointed out, reliability is not the same as total consistency, anymore than the basic regularity of train schedules implies perfect predictability. She went on to note that the goal of employing standardized measures in a controlled setting is likely to be incompatible with naturalistic research.

It may not be necessary to use the traditional terms *reliability, internal validity*, and *external validity* in writing a qualitative dissertation. Guba and Lincoln (1985), for example, recommended the alternative constructs of credibility, transferability, dependability, and confirmability, and the interested reader is referred to their text for a more complete understanding of these terms. However, the Method chapter needs to attend to these issues in some convincing way. What follows is an overview of recommended approaches.

Reliability concerns the replication of the study under similar cir-cumstances. It pertains to issues such as training interviewers and systematically recording and transcribing data. The naturalistic investigator derives consistency through coding the raw data in ways so that another person can understand the themes and arrive at similar conclusions. The researcher's coding scheme needs to be introduced in the Method chapter, with the understanding that the analysis is likely to be modified both during and after data collection.

Internal validity refers to the validity of a causal inference. From a social constructivist perspective, validation is the process of evaluating "the 'trustworthiness' of reported observations, interpretations, and generalizations" (Mishler, 1990, p. 419). In qualitative research, we ask about the extent to which the investigator's constructions are empirically grounded in those of the participants who are the focus of study (Flick, 2002). The credibility or truth value of findings might be ascertained by spending sufficient time with participants to check for distortions, exploring the participant's experience in sufficient detail, videotaping interviews for comparison with the recorded data, clarifying tentative findings with the participants, revising working hypotheses as more data become available, and checking multiple sources of data such as other investigators, written records, diaries, field notes, and so on. These procedures for adding to the credibility of the study need to be noted in the Method chapter, with the understanding that they might be amended as the study evolves.

External validity refers to the generalizability of the findings of the study. The qualitative study emphasizes the "thick description" of a relatively small number of participants within the context of a specific setting. The descriptions of the participants or setting under study are sufficiently detailed to allow for transferability to other settings. Samples can change as the study proceeds, but generalizations to other participants and situations are always modest and mindful of the context of individual lives. Moreover, generalization is the task of the reader rather than the author of qualitative studies.

Part of the challenge of completing a dissertation proposal using qualitative methods is to master the language of the qualitative paradigm of inquiry. The following procedures can be employed to enhance the trustworthiness of a qualitative research project. No study needs to include all of them, but whatever procedures are adopted should be described in the procedure section of the Method chapter.

Criteria of Adequacy and Appropriateness of Data (Morse, 1998). *Adequacy* pertains to the amount of data collected in a qualitative study, analogous to ensuring sufficient power by insisting on an adequate number of participants in a quantitative study. Adequacy is achieved when you have obtained enough data so that the previously collected data are confirmed (saturation) and understood. *Appropriateness* means that information has been sampled and chosen purposefully rather than randomly to meet the theoretical needs of the study. Multiple sources of data are obtained to provide saturation and confirmation of the emerging model.

Deviant Case Analysis. The constant comparative method implies that the researcher continues to build and test the completeness of a theory by reaching across participants to determine how the findings apply to cases that appear to be exceptions to the rule. By deliberately searching for these "deviant" cases, it becomes possible to test a provisional hypothesis and amend it to incorporate new and different data.

The Audit Trail. An audit trail refers to keeping a meticulous record of the process of the study so that others can recapture steps and reach the same conclusions. An audit trail includes not only the raw data but also evidence of how the data were reduced, analyzed, and synthesized, as well as process notes that reflect the ongoing inner thoughts, hunches, and reactions of the researcher. This critical self-reflection component (previously described as reflexivity) illuminates the researcher's potential biases and assumptions and how they might affect the research process. A further possible step, called an external audit, involves asking an external consultant who has no relationship to the study to review the materials and assess the findings and interpretations for consistency.

Member Checks. It is common in the qualitative literature for researchers to return to informants and present the entire written narrative, as well as the interpretations derived from the information, with the intention of confirming the accuracy and credibility of the findings. For some researchers, this is consistent with elevating the informant from the role of a participant in the study to the role of co-researcher. Others, such as Silverman (2005), advise caution when putting respondents in a "privileged" position by asking them to verify or validate the research findings.

Triangulation. Soliciting data from multiple and different sources as a means of cross-checking and corroborating evidence and illuminating a theme or a theory is known as triangulation. The different sources may

include additional participants, other methodologies, or previously conducted studies. Of course, it is equally likely with qualitative studies that
different kinds of data will yield different interpretations.

Peer Review or Debriefing. Many qualitative researchers make use of peers or
colleagues to play the role of devil's advocate, asking tough questions
about data collection, data analysis, and data interpretation to keep the
researcher honest. The other role of the peer reviewer is to provide professional and emotional support by being an empathic listener to the
researcher along the way. Both the researcher and the debriefer typically
keep written accounts of their sessions together.

This concludes the presentation of the basic elements of a Method chapter
for a thesis or dissertation. When the study is completed and the Results and
Discussion chapters have been added to the document, it is necessary to go
back to the Method chapter and change the verb tense from future to past.
We also recommend removing any detailed sections on data analysis from
the Method chapter and incorporating that material into the Results chapter.

BOX 5.1   Student Suggestions

1. Pilot test any instruments you use, whether you make them up yourself or
    they are standard research tools. Every person can misread or misunderstand
    something. It also helps to ask your pilot participants specific questions, such
    as inquiring if a section was interesting or difficult.

2. I was amazed by the vague and ambiguous items often present in well-known
    instruments. You can't trust that other researchers have constructed scales that
    will be appropriate for your use. If you want to compare your results to scores
    reported in the literature, however, you can't tamper with the instrument.

3. If you decide to construct your own instrument, never start with demographic
    items. Most researchers put them at the end. They are boring. Be sure your
    questionnaire looks nice and aesthetic. It must be clear and easy to under-
    stand. Put your response alternatives in columns rather than rows. It is easier
    for the eye to follow.

4. It helps to give an incentive to participants. Include a stamped, self-addressed
    envelope. Most important is personal contact with participants. My commit-
    tee thought I would get a 10% return rate from a mailing to American
    Psychological Association members, so I made sure to contact people who had
    access to subjects directly.

5. One relatively inexpensive way to encourage people to participate is to offer a
    lottery or drawing for money, a gift certificate, or some item of value. That way
    it will not cost an arm and a leg to pay every participant but will provide a
    worthwhile reward for one or a few participants.

6

Presenting the Results
of Quantitative Studies

The purpose of a Results section is to present the findings as clearly as possible. To do this it is necessary to plan the presentation before writing it. One major difficulty students have is that they do not begin with a plan for ordering the results. A second problem is students' inexperience. The insecurity generated by this inexperience tends to result in the inclusion of too much information in the Results chapter. In most dissertations, the Results chapter contains simply the facts: tables, figures, transcript summaries, and the author's description of what is important and noteworthy about these items. Extended discussion of the implications of the results, though very important, belongs in the Discussion chapter. Additional literature summaries and a rehash of the conceptual framework or methods are unnecessary and detract from the purpose of the Results chapter.

Of course, there are counterexamples to these general organizing principles, particularly in the case of qualitative dissertations that may combine Results and Discussion chapters, and some departments may encourage students to present the results and discussion as a single interconnected chapter. We are aware of these alternative formats and agree that in some cases these may improve the readability and flow of the dissertation. Nevertheless, we base the organization of this chapter on the assumption that the student's dissertation will contain separate Results and Discussion chapters.

How should the results be organized? There is no single standard answer that applies to every case, and it may not matter, particularly if there is an organizational logic that can be described to the readers and if one does a good job of leading the reader through the results. A few suggestions might be of benefit:

1. Begin with a simple statement that describes the structure of the results chapter. Usually, this is a short paragraph that essentially states, "This is the Results chapter and this is how it is organized." When this is clearly done, the reader begins with an understanding of the logic behind the organization of the Results chapter and a sense of what the chapter contains.

2. Second, the results should be organized in such a way that the reader is not confronted with a large mass of data. Although it is true that computer printouts provide extensive information, not all of this should appear in your dissertation.

3. Third, forgo engaging in an extended discussion of the meaning of the findings; these discussions belong in the Discussion chapter. Also, avoid rehashing all of the information in the tables. Your task is to give a simple, clear, and complete account of the results. Take the reader carefully through the findings, making sure that the reader knows what you consider to be the important observations.

Where to Begin?

Most Results chapters can be divided into three basic sections: a description of the sample, the examination of research questions or testing of hypotheses (or both), and the examination of additional questions generated by earlier analyses or further exploratory investigation.

The Results chapter typically begins with a description of the sample. Descriptive data, including descriptive statistics, are primary evidence. Simple demographics (sex, marital status, age, etc.) can be presented in written or tabular form. If the unit of analysis is not a person, then variables that describe the characteristics of the unit being studied should be presented. For example, if the unit of analysis were the city, then it might be appropriate to describe population density, ethnic composition, median house price, and so on. This gives the reader a picture of the basic unit or units in the study. Such information may be presented in a table or a figure or simply discussed in the text—whichever provides the reader with the best overall picture of the results. It is not necessary to supply the raw data, but one must make sense of the data for the reader. (If you are not sure which way to present the data, try presenting it in different ways and ask a friend to read the different presentations, and always consult with your committee.)

The beginning of the Results chapter may also include descriptive statistics on the variables involved in the hypotheses, such as scale scores from the major instruments and information describing the nature of their distributions. Alternatively, this information is sometimes presented in the Instrumentation section of the Methods chapter. This information may be critical for validating the assumptions of statistical tests that are used later. Statistics texts refer to this process as exploratory data analysis (EDA) or preanalysis data screening. There are generally four main purposes for the process, which can be extremely complex: (1) assessing the accuracy of the data, (2) dealing with missing data, (3) assessing the effects of outliers, and (4) assessing the adequacy of the fit between data characteristics and the assumptions of a statistical procedure. It is unlikely that you will need to describe every data screening technique in great detail. For example, you may simply state that the data were checked for accuracy and all responses were within range. On the other hand, if missing data are dealt with using a complex imputation technique, the technique might be described in detail. We recommend our own text (Newton & Rudestam, 1999, Chapters 5, 7, 8) for a more detailed discussion of this topic.

Addressing Research Questions and Hypotheses

After describing the sample, the next step is to address research questions or hypotheses, or both. Sometimes it may be appropriate to address one at a time under separate subheadings, but subheadings such as "Hypothesis 1" tend not to work because more than one hypothesis is often addressed by a single analysis, and use of a hypothesis number as a section heading provides insufficient information. It is much more effective to create subheadings that describe the content of the hypothesis being addressed. For example, "The Relationship Between Anxiety and Employee Performance" makes a better heading than "Hypothesis 2." It also may be awkward to use subheadings that isolate a single statistical procedure, such as "Results of Analysis of Variance." This is because a number of different statistical procedures may be needed to address a single question, such as the relationship between performance and anxiety suggested earlier. One method that appears to work is to address one research question at a time. This may involve discussing the results of several different statistical analyses and the testing of several different hypotheses. Every situation is different, so remember the main goal: a clear and simple presentation.

For example, suppose you are interested in susceptibility to group influence. One research question (there probably would be more than one) might ask about the specific relationship between gender and conformity. (Conformity is one indicator of group influence.) One research hypothesis (there may be more than one) might be that females are more conforming than males. The specific statistical hypotheses might be that (1) the mean conformity rate for females will be equal to or less than the mean conformity rate for males (the one-tailed null hypothesis) and (2) the mean conformity rate for females will be higher than that of males (the one-tailed alternative hypothesis, suggesting a specific direction of influence to be examined by a one-tailed statistical test). In this design, a one-tailed t test probably would be used, if the conformity rate were a continuously distributed dependent variable. If the null hypothesis were rejected, the alternative hypothesis would be supported, thus providing support for the research hypothesis. Note that though we have described the null and alternative hypothesis earlier, we want to discourage the expression of your hypotheses in this form. It is the research hypothesis that describes the relationship to be tested; a statement of the statistical null and alternative hypothesis is implicit in the research hypothesis.

It is typically best to organize the results as to answer the research question(s). For example, the earlier question concerning the relationship between gender and conformity would compose one section of the Results chapter. Remember that there may be a number of statistical analyses that bear on a specific research question or hypothesis. For example, given the question of gender differences in conformity behavior, there may be two indicators of conformity. Thus, one would examine gender differences for each measure, resulting in two statistical tests. One or more paragraphs in this section would present these analyses. Each analysis would specifically address one (or in some cases more than one) null and alternative hypothesis (i.e., the statistical hypotheses). When all analyses relating to this research question have been presented and explained, the analyses relating to the next research question would begin, typically starting a new section.

One should try to avoid presenting tremendous amounts of data, but this is not always possible. Complex studies, with many measures, may leave the author no choice but to present a large amount of information. The more data that must be presented, the greater the burden on both the author and the reader. Later in this chapter, we present some hints for reducing large amounts of data. Sometimes it is appropriate to note that certain findings were not significant, without actually presenting the findings, but this is usually not appropriate if the findings confront major hypotheses. Lead the reader carefully through the findings, making the reader aware of what you consider important. Accept that, as an author, you are in a better position to judge the importance of specific findings than anyone else, and organize the results to emphasize these important findings. It is reasonable to ignore or give passing reference to what is unimportant, but remember that there is a difference between what is unimportant and what fails to support your hypotheses.

The material that follows is directed primarily to quantitative analysis. We address the issue of qualitative analysis in the following chapter. We suggest that the reader read both chapters.

The Nuts and Bolts of Describing Quantitative Results

The Results section usually presents the outcome of multiple analyses of data. Each analysis can be broken down into a series of different statements. These statements present the major findings, some of which may also be presented in tabular or graphic form (i.e., tables and figures). The major focus, however, remains the text and the presentation of important findings, together with test statistics, within the text. Here we provide explanations of four different types of statements:[1]

Statement Type I. Refers the reader to a table or a figure and describes what is being measured or presented. These typically become a topic sentence in a paragraph describing results.

Example 1—Description of a table of correlations.

The correlations between student ratings and final examination marks are given in Table 1.

Example 2—Description of a table of percentages.

Table 1 presents the percentage of responses for each of the five possible categories.

Example 3—Description of a table of means.

Table 1 presents the means and standard deviations by drug category.

Statement Type II. Describes the major findings shown in a table or figure. Comparisons of means, standard deviations, frequencies, and correlations between the various measures or conditions represent examples. Frequently these sentences are combined with the third type of statement discussed later.

Example 1—Description of correlational table or figure.

Of the 10 correlations, it can be seen that 9 are positive and 8 are above $r = .32$.

Example 2—Description of an experiment.

Males rated applicants who wore cologne as lower in intelligence and friendliness. In contrast, females rated the applicants who wore cologne higher in intelligence and friendliness.

Example 3—Description of a figure.

As shown in Figure 2, the rate of typing increased from a baseline of about 0.7 words per minute to about 1.5 words per minute during the treatment period.

Statement Type III. Presents the results of a statistical (inferential) test, such as F or t. These statements typically are combined with statement type II. We recommend that you make a habit of citing the exact probability levels observed in your analyses, except when summarizing a number of analyses simultaneously. When findings are not statistically significant, we recommend that you also report the probability level. For example, you would report $p = .024$ rather than $p < .05$ for a statistically significant finding, and you would report $p = .324$ rather than *ns* for a nonstatistically significant finding. This is consistent with the *Publication Manual of the American Psychological Association* (2004), which states, "Because most statistical packages now report the p value. . . . in general it is the exact probability (p value) that should be reported" (p. 25). There are numerous reasons for following these suggestions, which are by no means unique. First, reporting the exact probability level provides more information than simply reporting that a value is or is not statistically significant at some predetermined level. For example, a probability level of .051 and .859 could both be reported as *ns*, but clearly these values are quite different. This helps avoid unsatisfactory language, such as *marginally significant* or *almost significant*, which is discouraged by all authors discussing good practice in this area. Second, the information contained in probability (p) values is valuable to those who wish to conduct a meta-analysis of your dissertation findings. The difference between a p value of .051 and one of .859 would be extremely valuable for such an analysis, but with a report of ns it would be difficult, if not impossible, to reconstruct these values, particularly in the absence of an effect size indicator. The practice of reporting p values as not significant or as less than some predetermined level (e.g., $p < .05$) is based on conventions developed prior to the ready availability of exact probability levels from computer printouts. Using these earlier conventions, one would hand calculate a test statistic and look up a critical value in a table. These two values (the calculated and the critical) would be compared, and the comparison would provide the basis for the decision to reject or fail to reject the null hypothesis. Our argument is simply that these procedures are no longer necessary and exclude valuable information from your presentation of findings.

Example 1—Description of correlations (summary statement).

Six of the correlations between amount of homework and GPA were found to be positive and significant at $p < .05$.

Example 2—Description of an experiment.

The retention of communication content was found to vary significantly as a function of the time and method of measurement, $F(2, 80) = 34.45, p = .003$. The image instructed groups were significantly faster, $F(1, 60) = 7.34, p = .007$, and made fewer errors, $F(1, 60) = 9.94, p = .004$, than the no image groups.

Some cases require you to combine statement types II and III.

Example 1—Description of correlations.

The correlation between mean parent IQ and child IQ was statistically significant, $r(190) = .87, p = .041$.

Example 2—Description of an experiment.

The mean score for females (75.5) was significantly greater than the mean score for males (70.7), $F(1, 28) = 23.1, p = .022$.

Statement Type IV. Provides summary statements of the major findings or conclusions. These statements typically end a paragraph.

Example 1—The results suggest that students who reported very heavy drug use had significantly higher maladjustment scores than did other students.

Example 2—In sum, these analyses suggest that educational achievement among those raised in single-parent families is consistently lower than among those raised in two-parent families, even when controlling for parents' education and income.

These statements provide examples of the variety of comments that might be used to describe the results of an empirical study. When describing results, try to avoid editorializing with such statements as "Unfortunately, the findings were not significant" or "This result was quite surprising." Such statements do little to enhance the reader's understanding of the results and may make your writing appear sophomoric.

Speaking of Significance

Students often have difficulty summarizing the results of statistical tests, or tests of statistical significance. In this section, we present a few examples of poorly written statements that describe the results of statistical tests and explain why the writing is poor. These examples are all taken from an exercise in which students were asked to write a Results section explaining an analysis of variance of the differences in recorded number of behavior problems for foster children. The three independent variables were ethnicity (Black, Hispanic, or White), gender (male or female), and placement type (placement with a relative or nonrelative). We try to cite examples of typical errors in an attempt to help you avoid such pitfalls in writing about quantitative results.

Statement I

The Black males show a slightly higher number of problems when placed in foster care but not of enough significance.

Comment: The author is trying to indicate that the results were not statistically significant, but as written the statement makes little sense and the comparison group is unclear.

Better: When placed in foster care, the Black males showed a slightly higher number of problems than did Hispanic or White males, but these differences were not statistically significant.

Statement 2

The main effects are only statistically significant for type of placement, which has a higher effect than any other factor with $p < .01$.

Comment: The author misinterprets significance level as size of effect by assuming that because the p value for type of placement was smaller than the p value for the other factors in an analysis of variance, the effect of placement was larger or stronger. This is not generally true.

Better: Of the main effects for type of placement, race/ethnicity, and gender, only the main effect of type of placement was statistically significant, $F(1, 60)$ = 7.34, p = .003.

Statement 3

Hispanic females and Black males also show a slight effect of the type of placement, the mean scores of behavioral problems being significantly lower for the relative placement.

Comment: When there are multiple independent variables, it is important to make clear which categories of which variables are being compared. In this statement, it is not clear if the comparison is being made across gender, ethnicity, or placement type. It is also not clear what a "slight effect" is.

Better: Within the relative placement group, the mean number of behavioral problems for Hispanic males is slightly larger than that for Hispanic females (Hispanic males, 36.3; Hispanic females, 33.5).

Statement 4

The effect of ethnicity by itself is slightly significant, as shown in Table 1.

Comment: Avoid statements such as "slightly significant," "highly significant," and "marginally significant." These are statistically incorrect. An effect is either significant at some preset level of significance or it is not.

Better: The main effect of ethnicity was statistically significant, $F(2, 80)$ = 3.45, p = .026.

Statement 5

Apparently, the analysis of variance sheet listed the significance of F ratio to be .003. Therefore, one can say that the probability of random error that may have produced this effect will be at the $p < .003$ significance level.

Comment: Often writers think that they need to explain the meaning of a statistical test; however, it is generally acceptable to assume that this is within the realm of common knowledge. Thus, unless your statistical analysis is novel or unique, avoid language like that in the example. If you sound like your statistics text, you probably are on the wrong track. Note also that the specific effect being evaluated is not stated.

Better: The analysis of variance in Table 1 shows the main effect of type of placement to be statistically significant, $F(1, 66)$ = 34.45, p = .003.

Following the guidelines presented earlier, one would most likely address the issue of mean differences in behavior problems using a combination of statement types I, II, and III, as follows:

> Table 1 presents the mean differences in behavior problems by gender, ethnicity, and type of placement. As can be seen in Table 1, for every gender by race/ethnicity comparison, children placed in relative foster care evidence fewer behavior problems than children placed in nonrelative foster care. An analysis of variance of these results is presented in Table 2. The results reveal that of the three main effects, only placement setting (the home of a relative vs. the home of a nonrelative) had a significant effect on children's behavior problems, $F(1, 609) = 9.089, p = .007$.

Four Steps in Reporting Results of Research Hypotheses Tested With Statistical Analyses

The process of reporting the results of statistical tests can be summarized in four main steps: (1) clearly state the hypothesis, (2) identify the statistical test used to evaluate the hypothesis, (3) provide the results of the statistical test, and (4) clearly state the results of the test.

Here is an example from a dissertation by Deborah Bower (2006):

> Hypothesis 1 predicted that overt narcissism, self-concept clarity, and the interaction of narcissism and self-concept clarity would be significant predictors of overt aggression. The overall regression was significant ($F[3, 99] = 3.99, p < .01$), yielding a small effect size ($R = .33$, R squared = .11, adjusted R squared = .08). The hypothesis was partially supported. Only self-concept clarity is a significant predictor of overt aggression (beta = .31, $t = 3.25, p < .01$).

Presenting Tables and Graphs

Nearly all dissertations contain one or more tables or figures (i.e., graphs) designed to organize the results of statistical analyses. This section and the sections that follow present the basic principles and logic of describing statistical analyses. The first question an author should ask is "Should these results be presented in a table, in a figure, or simply as part of the text?" Generally, a table containing only a few numbers is unnecessary. For example, a table showing the sex distribution in a sample is unnecessary because this information could be covered adequately in the text by simply stating the percentage of males or females in the sample. In a study with many groups, however, where the sex distribution within each group is important, it probably would be more efficient to present this information in tabular form.

Many dissertations contain graphic presentations of data, or figures. A figure may be a chart, graph, photograph, line drawing, or just about anything else that is not a table. The decision to use a figure is an important one and should be thought through carefully. Figures take considerable space and may clutter a dissertation rather than make it easier to follow. For example, there is little value in using bar charts to present information that can be displayed easily and economically in a table, unless the presentation dramatically illustrates a comparison that is not readily apparent from a table. Students may become enthusiastic about their ability to produce bar and pie charts with existing computer programs; however, the tendency to fill a dissertation with such charts should be avoided.

Considerable planning should precede the construction of tables and figures. You need to think carefully about the optimal number of tables and their content, as well as how to design the specific organization of each table to most effectively illustrate the important aspects of the analyses you wish to emphasize. In addition, you may be required to meet the formatting demands of your university or style requirements of an organization such as the American Psychological Association (APA). In this chapter, we follow many of the guidelines and recommendations of the APA for constructing tables and figures. You should check both your department's and your library's requirements before assuming that the exact format presented in this chapter, or by the APA, is appropriate for your needs.

The following guidelines can greatly improve the look and readability of tables, regardless of the specific requirements of your university:

1. Even though computer analyses produce values with many decimal places, a rounded value often conveys information more clearly than a value with many decimal places. Is there really any logic to reporting that 36.92273% of the sample was single, when you can simply report that 37% was single? (It is generally important to report correlations or covariances to three decimal places to facilitate the reproduction of analyses based on these values. Otherwise, keep it simple and round to a reasonable number of decimal places.)

2. Values can be compared both down columns and across rows. There is some debate over which is best and easiest to visualize for the purpose of comparisons. The following two sections suggest that percentages in univariate (one-variable) and bivariate (two-variable) tables be calculated within columns to facilitate comparisons across rows; however, it may be necessary to do the opposite when attempting to include many comparisons within one table. Try to be consistent in this regard.

3. Column and row averages and totals can provide much additional information, without cluttering the table. When excluding these values, make certain that the base number and direction for calculating percentages (i.e., within rows or columns) are clear.

4. It is unnecessary, and undesirable, to cram every number on a computer printout into a table. Select the information to be included carefully, organize it to make the information visually appealing, and use plenty of white space to improve visual organization.

5. The tables and figures in a Results section should relate to one another and to the text. This relationship should be represented in both the structure of the tables and the use of language. Tables and figures should use similar formats, and results should be organized similarly. If a table refers to a measure or scale using a particular designation, the same designation should be used in all tables and figures as well as in the text. The author's familiarity with the scales and measures used in a dissertation will not be shared by most readers. If something is referred to as an "inventory," it should be referred to as an inventory throughout, not as a scale, battery, or subscale. If one refers to "reaction time" in the text, this should not become "response latency" in a table.

6. Finally, avoid the use of computer-based variable names. Tables that contain labels such as *CHTOT* or *ABANY* are obtuse. Sometimes it is necessary to use shortened labels in a table to save space in columns, but try to create labels that describe the variable. For example, *CHTOT* stands for "Child's Health Total Score." Although this is a long label, it could be represented in a table with a label such as *Child's Health*.

Parts of a Table

Tables typically contain five major parts: number, title, headings, body, and notes. Each of these is described briefly in this section. More detailed discussion directed toward specific types of tables, such as frequency distributions, cross-tabulations, and analysis of variance, is presented in the following sections.

Table Numbers

Every table must be numbered. The APA suggests that all tables be numbered with Arabic numerals in the order in which they are first mentioned in the text. Begin with Table 1 and continue throughout. Do not use Table A, Table B, and so forth, and do not use Roman numerals (Table I, Table II, etc.). Do not number tables within chapters (Table 3.1, Table 3.2, etc.), and do not number tables containing related or similar information with letters (Table 5a, Table 5b, etc.). Instead, consider combining the tables. The only exception to these rules concerns the numbering of tables within appendices. The third table in Appendix B is Table B-3, and the first table in Appendix A is Table A-1.

Table Titles

Every table must have a title. Generally, a good title presents the name of the major variable or variables and the type of analysis but does not contain information that unnecessarily lengthens the title. Information that can be presented in table headings does not have to be in the title. Good table titles often take considerable trial and error to construct. The following sections, which highlight specific types of analysis, provide many examples of clear table titles, as well as completed tables to use as guidelines or templates. The APA suggests that all table titles be left justified and italicized and that major words be capitalized.

Table Headings

Headings tell the reader which variables and statistics are being presented and establish the organization of the table. It is considered legitimate to use abbreviations for headings, including f for frequency and % for percent, but the meaning of the abbreviation should be obvious. Do not use computer mnemonics or variable names, and do not use scale acronyms without including a note as to their meaning. For example, a mnemonic used with the National Opinion Research Center General Social Survey is XMARSEX. Most people would not realize that this refers to the respondent's attitude regarding extramarital sex, and it is not advisable to use such mnemonics as labels in tables. Similarly, many persons might assume that BDI refers to the Beck Depression Inventory, but a note to this effect must be included in a table that uses BDI as a heading.

Table Body

The table body contains the numbers, or data. As indicated earlier, do not clutter the table with unnecessary numbers, and round numbers to improve readability. When cells of the table are empty, it is customary to enter a dash (–) to indicate that no data are contained within the cell. This prevents the reader from thinking that a number was excluded inadvertently.

Table Notes

There are three kinds of table notes: general notes, specific notes, and notes indicating the statistical significance of findings, or probability notes. A general note is indicated as follows: *Note.* APA format requires that the word *note* be italic and followed by a period. General notes are used to provide information referring to the table as a whole, including the meaning of symbols or abbreviations. For example, one would use a general note to indicate that BDI referred to the Beck Depression Inventory. Notes are relevant to only one table. Thus, just because you used a note to define BDI in one table, it is not appropriate to assume that it need not be defined in future tables. Specific notes are used to refer to the content of a specific cell and are given superscript lowercase letters, beginning with the letter *a*. Specific notes should begin in the upper left of a table and be lettered from left to right across table rows. Probability notes indicate the outcome of significance tests. Asterisks are used to indicate the probability levels, one asterisk being used for the lowest level, two for next lowest, and so on. Probability notes usually appear at the bottom of tables as follows:

$$*p < .05. **p < .01. ***p < .001.$$

A one-tailed test may be distinguished from a two-tailed test by using an alternative symbol in the probability notes:

$$*p < .05, \text{two tailed.} +p < .05, \text{one tailed.}$$

Note that we recommend you not use probability notes in favor of providing the exact probability level (i.e., p value) available from a computer printout; however, you may use these when including exact probability levels might clutter the table unnecessarily. It is reasonable to inquire of your committee regarding the use of probability notes as opposed to the presentation of exact probability values as a separate row or column of a table. If you do choose to use probability notes, remember that these notes should be consistent across all tables. Thus, if one asterisk indicates $p < .05$ in one table, it should also indicate $p < .05$ in the next, not $p < .01$ or some other level.

Many of the major critics of the null-hypothesis-significance-test approach to data analysis also call for the inclusion of confidence intervals or measures of effect size, or both, in all tables presenting the results of statistical tests. This issue is too complex to be fully addressed here, but you should know that null hypothesis significance testing has come under attack during the past few years. Critics range from those who wish to condemn the entire tradition to those who recommend relatively modest changes in the way that results of hypothesis-testing research studies are presented. The arguments behind these positions are summarized in

Newton and Rudestam (1999) and fortified by a set of articles published in Harlow, Mulaik, and Steiger (1997). The primary implication for students who continue to draw on the hypothesis-testing tradition of quantitative research—and that includes most graduate students in the social sciences—is to be aware of the limited information conveyed by only reporting whether or not group differences or relationships between variables are statistically significant at some predetermined level of significance (alpha level).

Statistical significance is merely a statement about the likelihood of the observed result, that is, the probability of making an error in generalizing findings from a sample to a population. In research terms, this refers to maintaining reasonable control over Type I error. What statistical significance does not deal with is the size or strength of a relationship between variables (called the effect size). The clearest demonstration of this distinction is to note that many findings that are not statistically significant at the .05 level, let's say, would be statistically significant at the .05 level if a greater number of subjects had been included in the study. For instance, a simple product-moment correlation of .179 is statistically significant at the .05 level with a sample size of 120. To achieve the same level of significance with a sample size of 15 would necessitate a corresponding correlation of .512. One implication of this phenomenon is the wisdom of including a sufficient number of participants in a quantitative study to give yourself a fair chance of obtaining statistically significant results. (This is what Cohen, 1988, refers to as power and is directly related to reducing Type II error. Power is discussed in Chapter 5.) Another implication particularly relevant to this book is that you should augment your presentation of data to include enough useful information so that the reader (as well as the researcher) can learn more about your empirical findings than merely whether or not they are statistically significant. The types of information to be considered include precise p values, effect sizes, and confidence intervals.

In the following exposition of tabular presentation, we offer some alternatives for the presentation of findings from the most common statistical tests.

Preparing the Data for Analysis

The first type of results information likely to be presented in a dissertation is a description of the sample. The researcher is likely to present a number of one-variable (or univariate) tables called frequency distributions. Some standard guidelines for the presentation of frequency distributions are discussed later. The first consideration, however, is to guarantee that the data have been tabulated correctly. Whether working by hand or with a computer, correct tabulation of the results is a necessity. The following steps outline the process leading to the production of both meaningful tables and reasonable statistical analysis.

Step 1: Formatting the Variable?

Mutually Exclusive Categories. The variable must be constructed so that each observation may be placed in only one category. For example, demographic descriptions often include an item labeled "Marital Status," which includes the categories single, married, divorced, and widowed. It is possible that a person could check both the single and divorced categories. This pattern may be reduced or eliminated by wording the question to read as follows: "Are you *currently* never married, divorced," and so on. When questions assume the "Check all that apply" character, each response must become a separate variable. For example, when assessing a respondent's feelings, behavior, and experience related to a parent's alcohol use, a checklist of items is presented and instructions are to "Check all that occurred in your family." Responses include "Lost sleep because of a parent drinking," "Heard parents fight when one was drunk," and "Wish parent would stop drinking." Items in the checklist each become a separate variable, with a "Yes" and "No" value. When the Yes values are assigned or coded as 1 and the No values are coded as 0, the sum of the Yes codes becomes a new variable that can be used to assess the extent of the damage from alcoholism within the family.

Exhaustive Categories. Every item in a questionnaire, scale, or instrument must have a response for every case, even if the response is "Not Applicable." Thus frequency distributions and their tables must include the percentage of valid responses, those for which meaningful answers were obtained, and the number of invalid responses, often called missing values, for which irrelevant or meaningless answers occurred. When working with frequency distributions, check to make sure that you can account for (i.e., exhaust) the entire sample for every distribution. (This prevents having to figure out after the fact where some of your data went.)

Missing Values. Observations that do not fit logically into a variable's meaningful categories also must be accounted for to produce a set of exhaustive categories. Those that do not fit into these "meaningful" categories are called missing values. Missing values may occur for a variety of reasons.

1. Not applicable (the question does not apply to the respondent)

2. No response, no answer

3. Uncodable responses

4. Incorrect measurements or broken equipment

5. Lost data, subjects who cannot be located

Most computer programs permit special codes, called missing value codes, to allow the program to separate the meaningful responses from the missing values. The number of missing values is usually reported in a table note. When the number of missing values is added to the number of valid responses, the entire sample should be accounted for.

Step 2: Grouping the Data

The second step is to place the data for each observation (i.e., each case or subject) into one of the variable's categories. Although this is often done with a computer, it may also be done by hand tally of the frequencies in each category of the variable in question. Some examples are presented at the end of this section.

Step 3: Creating a Correctly Labeled Table

Creating a frequency distribution does not complete the process of making the distribution presentable and easily understood. The table that you create must be correctly labeled and identified. In addition, you may need to satisfy the requirements of the library or publication that will receive the information. Some general rules, consistent with APA guidelines, are presented in the next section.

Guidelines for Creating Correctly Constructed and Labeled Tables

The Contents of a Complete Table

1. A table number

2. A table name or title that includes the name of the variable and some information about the sample or population

3. The set of mutually exclusive and exhaustive categories you have developed (the headings)

4. Frequencies, percentages, and totals (the body)

5. Notes, including the source, if the data are not original

Dealing With Missing Values

Sometimes missing data may create a problem when constructing tables. These problems may be dealt with in a number of ways:

1. Create a category to contain the missing data
2. Create a footnote delineating the number of missing values
3. Create a residual category for all unimportant values

Line Spacing in Tables

APA guidelines require that every line in a table be double-spaced; however, we have never seen a dissertation that follows this requirement to the letter. This is because the requirement is primarily for journal articles being submitted for publication. We recommend that our students use spacing to make the tables readable, and we follow that guideline in the materials presented in this chapter.

Models for the Tabular Presentation of Common Descriptive and Inferential Statistical Analyses

The next several pages provide examples of correctly labeled tables using the data from computer printouts of different statistical analyses likely to appear in dissertations. We present univariate (one-variable), bivariate (two-variable), and some multivariate examples. These examples may be used as guidelines or templates for your own analyses. For each type of example, we begin with a table that displays the options, based on whether the independent variables are discrete or continuously distributed (see Table 6.1). In addition, we consider the presentation of both the descriptive and inferential statistical material, often working directly from computer printouts. Although the number and variations of such tables are far too numerous to include all situations, we present a set of tables that covers the vast majority of dissertation presentations.

Constructing One-Variable (Univariate) Tables and Statements That Describe Them From Computer Printouts

The two examples that follow are both taken from the 2003 National Opinion Research Center General Social Survey (GSS). The GSS draws

Table 6.1   Models for the Tabular Presentation and Analysis of
Univariate Data

	Type of Data	
Type of Statistics	**Discrete (Nominal and Ordinal Data)**	**Continuous (Interval and Ratio Data)**
Descriptive	Proportions, percentages, ratios, modal values	Central tendency (mean, median, mode); variability (standard deviation, range) and shape (skew, kurtosis)
Inferential	Confidence interval for *p*; one-sample *Z* test	Confidence interval for mean; one sample *Z* or *t* tests; normality tests.
Tables Contain	Frequency and % of categories	F and % of class intervals
Examples	Tables 6.2 (printout) and 6.3 (dissertation ready)	Tables 6.4 and 6.5 (printout) and Table 6.6 (dissertation ready)

data from a national sample of all noninstitutionalized adults in the
United States, 18 years of age or older. The data were processed using the
Statistical Package for the Social Sciences Release 14.0 (September, 2005).
Two variables are considered. The first assesses how frequently the
respondent attends religious services. This variable was given the name
Attend by those who developed the survey. The second variable, given
the name Age, assesses the respondent's age. The computer printout for
Attend is presented in Table 6.2, and the correctly labeled table with fre-
quencies and percentages is presented in Table 6.3.[2]

Note that Table 6.2 contains two sections, the first showing the number of
valid and missing cases and the second showing the variable's categories,
frequency, percent, valid percent, and cumulative percent. The difference
between the percent and valid percent columns is that the Percent column
contains all cases, including the missing values, and the Valid Percent column excludes the missing values. In this example, the missing values
include 0.4% or 11 of the total of 2,812 cases. The Cumulative Percent column
sums the valid percentages down the column. Table 6.3 presents the correctly labeled table based on the data in the computer printout (Table 6.2).

Note the differences between the computer printout and the table.
First, a table number, title, and note indicating the data source have been

Table 6.2   SPSS Printout of Variable ATTEND

Statistics

HOW OFTEN R ATTENDS RELIGIOUS SERVICES

N	Valid	2801
	Missing	11

HOW OFTEN R ATTENDS RELIGIOUS SERVICES

		Frequency	Percent	Valid Percent	Cumulative Percent
Valid	0 NEVER	471	16.7	16.8	16.8
	1 LT ONCE A YEAR	198	7.0	7.1	23.9
	2 ONCE A YEAR	396	14.1	14.1	38.0
	3 SEVRL TIMES A YR	371	13.2	13.2	51.3
	4 ONCE A MONTH	191	6.8	6.8	58.1
	5 2-3X A MONTH	255	9.1	9.1	67.2
	6 NRLY EVERY WEEK	169	6.0	6.0	73.2
	7 EVERY WEEK	508	18.1	18.1	91.4
	8 MORE THN ONCE WK	242	8.6	8.6	100.0
	Total	2801	99.6	100.0	
Missing	9 DK,NA	11	.4		
Total		2812	100.0		

Table 6.3   Frequency of Attendance at Religious Services

Attendance	f	%
Never	471	16.7
Less Than Once A Year	198	7.0
Once a Year	396	14.1
Several Times a Year	371	13.2
Once a Month	191	6.8
2 or 3 Times a Month	255	9.1
Nearly Every Week	169	6.0
Every Week	508	18.1
More Than Once a Week	242	8.6
Don't Know, No Answer	11	.4
Total	2812	100.0

NOTE: Data from the 2004 National Opinion Research Center General Social Survey.

added to the table. Second, only the frequency and percent columns have been included. Third, the full labels have been written out. Category labels are often abbreviated within computer programs, such as "More Thn Once Wk" for "More Than Once a Week." When space permits, as it does in this case because there are only two columns of numbers, writing out the category labels helps clarify the table. With many columns of numbers or very long labels, you will often need to arrive at creative labels or provide notes to the meaning of variable names and category labels.

The data do not speak for themselves, so you, the data analyst, will be required to provide a meaningful summary of the content of the table. The following statement might be used to describe Table 6.3:

> Table 6.3 presents the distribution of attendance at religious services. Approximately 27% of the sample stated that they attend church at least once a week, whereas almost 24% stated they almost never attend.

Note that the summary percentages cited here were obtained by adding and slightly rounding the first two (16.7 + 7.0) and last two (18.1 + 8.6) nonmissing categories of Table 6.3. Note also that many numbers have been left out. It is not the goal to restate every number. If you did so, why would you need a table? The goal is to point out what is perceived as notable in the table, which is in part a matter of judgment on behalf of the data analyst. In this case, the point to be made was that about one fourth of the sample almost never attends and another one fourth attends religious services at least every week.

Tables 6.4 and 6.5 both present computer printouts; the difference is that Table 6.5 has been recoded to reduce the large number of variable categories likely to exist with ratio level variables (39 in this example, if we include the "98" code). Note that Table 6.5 becomes the basis for Table 6.6, the correctly labeled table of a continuously distributed variable, the respondents' age when their first child was born.

The method of presentation of Table 6.6 is different from that of Table 6.3 in a number of ways. Some of these differences are optional, and some result from the fact that one variable is continuous (Age at Birth of First Child) and the other discrete but ordinal (Church Attendance). First, note that Table 6.3 includes the missing values, whereas Table 6.6 does not (but indicates these in a table note). This is an optional decision that can be made by the researcher; however, we generally recommend exclusion and note it as in Table 6.6. When missing values are excluded, always use the

Table 6.4   Distribution of Respondent's Age When First Child Was Born
(SPSS printout)

Statistics

R'S AGE WHEN 1ST CHILD BORN

R'S AGE WHEN 1ST CHILD BORN		
N Valid	2036
Missing	776

R'S AGE WHEN 1ST CHILD BORN

		Frequency	Percent	Valid Percent	Cumulative Percent
Valid	12	1	.0	.0	.0
	13	2	.1	.1	.1
	14	6	.2	.3	.4
	15	12	.4	.6	1.0
	16	48	1.7	2.4	3.4
	17	72	2.6	3.5	6.9
	18	132	4.7	6.5	13.4
	19	168	6.0	8.3	21.7
	20	177	6.3	8.7	30.4
	21	181	6.4	8.9	39.2
	22	157	5.6	7.7	47.0
	23	115	4.1	5.6	52.6
	24	131	4.7	6.4	59.0
	25	114	4.1	5.6	64.6
	26	104	3.7	5.1	69.7
	27	119	4.2	5.8	75.6
	28	86	3.1	4.2	79.8
	29	56	2.0	2.8	82.6
	30	87	3.1	4.3	86.8
	31	52	1.8	2.6	89.4
	32	55	2.0	2.7	92.1
	33	33	1.2	1.6	93.7
	34	27	1.0	1.3	95.0
	35	26	.9	1.3	96.3
	36	12	.4	.6	96.9
	37	12	.4	.6	97.5
	38	10	.4	.5	98.0
	39	11	.4	.5	98.5
	40	6	.2	.3	98.8
	41	3	.1	.1	99.0
	42	2	.1	.1	99.1
	43	2	.1	.1	99.2
	44	1	.0	.0	99.2
	45	1	.0	.0	99.3
	46	1	.0	.0	99.3
	47	1	.0	.0	99.4
	49	1	.0	.0	99.4
	50	1	.0	.0	99.5
	51	1	.0	.0	99.5
	98 DK	10	.4	.5	100.0
	Total	2036	72.4	100.0	
Missing	0 NAP	767	27.3		
	99 NA	9	.3		
	Total	776	27.6		
Total		2812	100.0		

Valid Percent column, as this is based on the total, excluding the missing values. This is particularly important in a variable such as this because of the large number of "not applicable" (NAP) responses, those who never had children. Second, Table 6.6 also includes a column of cumulative percentages not contained in Table 6.3. This is also an optional decision, but cumulative percentages should never be included with nominal level data. (Church Attendance is ordinal; Age First Child Born is a ratio variable.) Cumulative percentages help divide the sample into groups and are generally useful when there are a large number of categories. Third, note that the Value column of the printout for age in Table 6.5 contains only the numbers 1 through 5. These were replaced by age categories in Table 6.6. This is because when recoding the age categories, which originally ranged from 12 to 51, into increments, we must supply a number (code) to represent each class interval. To present data for continuously distributed variables with a large number of categories, the data analyst will be required to recode that variable into a smaller number of categories, as we have

Table 6.5   Distribution of Respondent's Age When First Child Was Born (recoded SPSS printout)

Statistics

R'S AGE 1ST CHILD BORN (recoded)

N	Valid	2026
	Missing	786

R'S AGE 1ST CHILD BORN (recoded)

		Frequency	Percent	Valid Percent	Cumulative Percent
Valid	1.00	441	15.7	21.8	21.8
	2.00	761	27.1	37.6	59.3
	3.00	479	17.0	23.6	83.0
	4.00	254	9.0	12.5	95.5
	5.00	91	3.2	4.5	100.0
	Total	2026	72.0	100.0	
Missing	System	786	28.0		
Total		2812	100.0		

NOTE: This table represents a "recode" of Table 6.4. The category values (1 to 5) represent the class intervals for the Distribution of Respondent's Age When First Child Was Born.

Table 6.6   Distribution of Respondent's Age When First Child Was Born

Age	f	%	Cum %
Under 20	441	21.8	21.8
20–24	761	37.6	59.3
25–29	479	23.6	83.0
30–34	254	12.5	95.5
35 & Older	91	4.5	100.0
Total	2026	100.0	

NOTE: 786 cases were missing; the majority of these (767) did not have children.

done here. The number of categories is up to the researcher, but remember these six general principles:

1. The larger the width of the categories, the more data information is lost. In other words, there is more information lost in an age category of 26–45 years than in the two categories 26–35 and 36–45 years.

2. Remember to label your tables with the range of values, not the code value used to represent that range. In other words, use "Under 20," "20–24," and so on, not 1, 2, and such.

3. Means, standard deviations, and other descriptive statistics for interval and ratio variables generally are based on the unrecoded data, which contain the most information.

4. Do not destroy the original (i.e., unrecoded) data. You may want to code the data differently at some other point in your analysis.

5. Always compare the recoded and unrecoded data to make sure that no mistakes were made and that the missing values were not included in one of the valid groupings (an extremely common error).

6. Try to keep each class interval (e.g., 20–24) the same width. The exceptions typically are made with regard to the first or last categories, as illustrated in Table 6.6. Graphs based on recoded or grouped distributions containing unequal class intervals can be highly misleading and should be avoided.

The reader may wonder why we have spent this much time discussing simple univariate tables. The answer is that table construction principles apply across a wide range of table types, and improperly constructed and misleading tabular presentation is an area that almost always creates problems with early dissertation drafts.

How to Construct and Interpret Two-Variable (Bivariate) Tables

Bivariate distributions, usually presented in the form of tables, are the basic ingredients of many dissertations in the social sciences, education, and business. It is therefore important to understand clearly the information these tables contain and how to construct the tables in such a way as to extract information correctly. This section concentrates on the general principles involved in constructing bivariate tables and interpreting bivariate relationships. We discuss three types of bivariate distribution in this section. We begin with tables in which both the independent and dependent variables are categorical and contain a small number of categories. These distributions are usually summarized by using percentages, and the tables are called cross-tabulations. Second, we discuss tables of means and standard deviations that summarize bivariate relationships in which the independent variable is categorical and the dependent variable a score or interval/ratio variable. For example, consider gender differences in depression or differences between an experimental group and a control group on a measure of performance. Finally, we discuss tables showing the relationship between two variables, both of which are continuously distributed, such as the relationship between the amount of family violence and depression in children.

The General Form of a Bivariate Table I: Cross-Tabulations

A bivariate table (also called a cross-tabulation or contingency table) contains the joint distribution of two categorical variables. The categories of each variable are laid out in the form of a square or rectangle containing rows (representing the categories of one variable) and columns (representing the categories of the other variable). The general form of a bivariate table containing two variables is presented in Table 6.7 for two variables X and Y.

In this example, the letter X represents the variable whose categories form the columns, and the letter Y refers to the variable whose categories represent rows. Thus, if X represents the response to a question indicating

Table 6.7

| | X | |
	x_1	x_2
Y y_1		
y_2		
y_3		

whether or not the respondent has ever had children and Y represents attitudes toward abortion, our table might appear as follows:

Table 6.8

| | | Ever Had Children? | |
		Yes	No
Attitudes Toward Abortion	Always Wrong Almost Always Wrong Never Wrong		

Cell Entries and Marginal Totals

The entries that occur in each cell will be the frequencies representing the number of times that each pair of values (one from each variable) occurs in the sample. These are called cell frequencies. The entries that occur at the end of each row or column are called marginal frequencies and represent the total number of times the category of the row variable or column variable occurred. By adding either the row marginal frequencies or the column marginal frequencies you obtain the total N (total sample size).

How to Determine the Row Variable and the Column Variable

The conventional way to construct a table is with the independent variable at the top and the dependent variable at the side of the table. Thus, as in our example, the letter X is used to identify the independent variable and the letter Y the dependent variable. An independent variable is presumed to cause or determine a dependent variable. If we discover that attitudes toward abortion are partly a function of parenthood (i.e., parents are more opposed to abortion than nonparents are), then parenthood is the independent variable and attitudes toward abortion is the dependent variable. A dependent variable is the variable that is assumed to depend on or be caused by the independent variable. For example, if you believe that income is partly a function of amount of education, income is being treated as a dependent variable.

Summarizing the Information in a Bivariate Table

Table 6.9 includes frequencies for the Attitudes Toward Abortion by Parenthood table described earlier. What we want to do is examine Table 6.9 in such a way as to summarize the information meaningfully and to explore the hypothesis that parenthood influences attitudes toward abortion. Notice, however, that we have a different number of parent (Yes) and nonparent (No) respondents. Thus, we cannot compare the Yes with the No distributions (across the different columns) unless we standardize these distributions. The most frequently used standardizing measure is the percentage, but what is the most sensible way to form percentages from this table?

To calculate percentages, we may work within columns, within rows, or with the total sample of 1,000 observations (i.e., total N). Thus Table 6.9 may be percentaged in three different ways. Depending on how a table is constructed, only one of these ways may provide meaningful answers to the question of the relationship between the two variables. Given our recommendation to place the independent variable as the column variable, the appropriate method of percentaging is within the columns (i.e., up and down each column).

When working within columns, the column marginal total becomes the base number used for the total. For example, to find the percentage of

Table 6.9   Bivariate Table Showing the Relationship Between Attitudes Toward Abortion and Parenthood (cell frequencies only)

		Ever Had Children?	
		Yes	No
Attitudes	Always Wrong	330	180
Toward	Almost Always Wrong	180	120
Abortion	Never Wrong	90	100

"Always Wrong" answers among those with children, we take the number of "Always Wrong" responses in that column and divide it by the total number in that column and then multiply the total by 100: (330/600 × 100 = 55%). Some texts and dissertation manuals may recommend placing the independent variable in the rows of the table. If this is the case, remember to calculate percentages within the rows (i.e., across each row). Table 6.10 presents the data from Table 6.9 correctly labeled and percentaged.

The Concept of Association Based on Subgroup Comparisons

The final step is to compare the conditional distributions with one another after the percentages are computed within each column. This allows us to compare the percentage responding "Always Wrong," "Almost Always Wrong," and "Never Wrong" across the Yes and No, or Parent and Nonparent, categories. In doing this, notice that we have a definite routine in mind. We calculate percentages in one direction and make our comparisons in another direction. Because we compute percentages up and down the columns, we compare across the columns.

To examine the hypothesis that parenthood influences attitudes toward abortion, we can use a few simple rules. If each conditional distribution is identical to each other conditional distribution, then we say that the two variables involved are independent of each other or are not related to each other. If the conditional distributions are different, then the two variables are said to be related. To make this more clear, examine Table 6.10, which has been percentaged appropriately and relabeled for clarity. One easy method of making a statement about the degree or amount of relationship in a table is to compare the percentages in the conditional distributions.

Table 6.10   Correctly Labeled and Percentaged Bivariate Table Showing the Relationship Between Attitudes Toward Abortion and Parenthood (Column %)

		Ever Had Children?	
		Yes	*No*
Attitudes	Always Wrong	55%	45%
Toward	Almost Always Wrong	30%	30%
Abortion	Never Wrong	15%	25%
		100%	100%
		(600)	(400)

This measure is called a percentage difference and is most appropriate for small tables such as Table 6.10. As an example of how this measure might be calculated and used, compare the 55% of the parents who believe that abortion is always wrong with the 45% of nonparents who believe that abortion is always wrong. The difference is 10%. You can now state that 10% more parents than nonparents believe that abortion is always wrong. A similar comparison can be made between the parents and nonparents with regard to the belief that abortion is never wrong. The percentage difference in this comparison is also 10%. An appropriate statement would be "Ten percent more parents than nonparents believe that abortion is always wrong."

General Form of a Bivariate Table II: Presenting Tables of Group Means and Other Groups Descriptive Statistics

In addition to the presentation of tables containing frequency counts and percentages, many analyses examine group differences on continuous variables. Continuous variables are those that can be scaled along a continuum from highest to lowest, most favorable to least favorable, healthy to unhealthy, and the like. These are generally described as interval/ratio variables, but ordinal variables with many categories might also be considered continuous. Most psychological, sociological, political, and educational measures can be considered continuous variables. Examples are self-efficacy, alienation, political conservatism/liberalism, verbal reasoning ability, and a host of attitudes representing agreement-disagreement or approval-disapproval on a variety of issues. We have already discussed how to present the univariate distribution of such variables by recoding, as shown in Tables 6.4, 6.5, and 6.6. Although some may argue that many of these variables constitute ordinal measurement, and thus pose problems for the computation of means and inferential statistics requiring at least interval measurement, standard practice is to use the techniques we suggest in this section with these variables. This topic is discussed further in Newton and Rudestam (1999). The logic underlying our position is that these variables are continuous at the latent level and thus, when other assumptions are met, do not pose serious problems for the social sciences.

When your goal is to compare groups on these variables, the first task is to present the group descriptive statistics in tabular form. For example, Sangster (1991) examined the ability of a training course to improve managers' decision-making ability under conditions of uncertainty. The means and standard deviations for training type and level of management experience are presented in Table 6.11.

Table 6.11   Means and Standard Deviations for Manager's Decision-Making Ability at Posttest by Levels of Training Type and Management Experience

Independent Variable	Decision-Making Ability (Posttest)	
	Mean	SD
Training type		
Descriptive (N = 42)	5.38	1.79
Prescriptive (N = 32)	3.75	1.85
Management experience		
Low (N = 33)	4.70	2.07
High (N = 41)	4.67	1.92

NOTE: Maximum possible score = 10.0; N = 74.

Note that Table 6.11 is simple and easy to understand. The independent variables are Type of Training and Management Experience; the dependent variable is Decision-Making Ability as measured at posttest. Management experience appears to make little difference (.03), and descriptive training appears to result in higher posttest scores than prescriptive training.

This strategy for presenting group means may be extended to a larger number of groups and a larger number of dependent variables. For example, in Richards's dissertation (1991), 16 variables believed to discriminate drug users from nonusers within secondary schools were examined. For each variable, the mean and standard deviation for users and nonusers was presented (see Table 6.12). (We have shortened this table to present only the first 8 variables; the full table contains all 16 variables of interest.)

General Form of a Bivariate Table III:
Presenting Tables of Continuously Distributed Variables

When both the independent and dependent variable are continuously distributed and there is only one such relationship, a correlation coefficient, presented in the text, would typically suffice. Rather than a table, a scatter plot, which is a graph, not a table, would most likely be the best way to display the joint distribution of the two variables. Such relationships can be described in the text by statements of the following type: "The relationship between age of youngest child and number of hours worked by all women in the sample was negative and statistically significant, $r(75) = -.21, p = .004$."

Table 6.12   Means and Standard Deviations of Variables Discriminating Drug Users From Non-Users by Drug Use Category

	Drug Use			
	Users		Non-Users	
Discriminating Variables	X	SD	X	SD
No. of "Ds" and "Fs"	1.57	2.67	0.27	0.85
Grade level	8.37	1.50	7.69	1.40
Importance of grades	3.16	0.83	3.41	0.75
Arguing with teachers	2.16	0.83	1.52	0.73
Absent when not sick	2.53	1.07	1.68	0.86
Ever suspended	0.37	0.50	0.08	0.27
How often angry	2.84	1.01	2.24	0.52
Fight or argue with family	2.63	1.01	2.20	0.71

The statistical statement indicates both the strength of the relationship (.21, a weak to moderate relationship) and its significance (.004, a statistically significant finding). The "75" in parentheses following the italicized *r* is the degrees of freedom (*df*) associated with the statistical test and is one less than the sample size (i.e., $N - 1$).

When a large number of relationships is examined simultaneously it may be necessary to present the correlation matrix in a table. Two examples are given. The first represents a hypothetical analysis examining the relationship between three variables, X, Y, and Z. Note that it is standard to present the means, standard deviations, and sample sizes of all variables in an analysis along with their correlations. We have included these with the correlation matrix of X, Y, and Z in Table 6.13.

Note that Table 6.13 contains only the correlations below the diagonal of 1.00s. This is because correlations are symmetrical—that is, the correlation of X with Z is identical to the correlation of Z with X. Thus, there is no need to present both the lower and upper diagonal. Note also that the 1.00s on the main diagonal each represent the correlation of a variable with itself.

A second example is derived from an article by Rogers, Parcel, and Menaghan (1991) examining the relationship between mother's work and child behavior problems. Rogers et al. presented the correlation matrix of 23 variables (253 unique correlations) in a single table. We present only the first five of these variables in Table 6.14.

A number of variations of the tables discussed earlier may be encountered in the literature and used by the student. First, the decimal points

Table 6.13   Means, Standard Deviations, and Correlations of Variables X, Y, and Z

	X	Y	Z
X	1.00		
Y	0.25	1.00	
Z	0.01	0.35	1.0
$\bar{X}$	3.61	2.74	4.10
S	1.23	1.66	0.93

Table 6.14   Means, Standard Deviations, and Correlations for Mother's Work and Child Behavior Problems (Rogers, Parcel, & Menaghan, 1991)

	1	2	3	4	5
1 Behavior problems	1.0				
2 Mastery	−.18	1.0			
3 Maternal education	−.08	.21	1.0		
4 Child's age	−.05	−.03	−.11	1.0	
5 Hourly pay	−.10	.19	.24	.02	1.0
$\bar{X}$	−.80	.27	2.07	62.51	5.58
S	11.41	12.38	1.48	10.15	2.87

NOTE: Correlations of .08 or greater are significant when one-tailed tests are used.

may be eliminated, as they are usually assumed to exist with correlation coefficients. Second, the main diagonal of 1.0s is sometimes used to present the standard deviations, as opposed to presenting these in a separate row below the correlations as has been shown here. Third, the correlations may be noted with asterisks, and probability notes may be used. Fourth, the number of cases may be included in a note, or, when there is much variation from value to value, may be placed in parentheses below each correlation or may be placed above the main diagonal.

Tabular Presentation of the Results of Inferential Statistics

The materials earlier refer primarily to descriptions of results as contained in contingency tables and tables containing means or other descriptive statistics, but they have not addressed the question of statistical inference. The question of inference considers whether or not the results can be generalized to the population from which the sample was drawn.

In other words, this is the question of whether or not the results are statistically significant. Questions regarding whether or not the results are statistically significant usually follow tables describing the results, or are contained within them, but generally do not precede descriptive summaries. For example, in the bivariate table (Table 6.10), the results seem to indicate that parents are more opposed to abortion than those who are not parents; however, this table does not address the question of whether or not these results are statistically significant. This question would be addressed with a chi-square test. These results would be added to Table 6.10 as a note and also included within the text.

To facilitate our understanding of tests of statistical significance and how to present them in tabular form, we follow Newton and Rudestam (1999) and conceptualize most dissertations as fitting one of four major types of research question. Each of the four questions leads directly to a choice of descriptive and inferential statistical technique, which in turn leads to a particular type of tabular display. We recommend Newton and Rudestam (1999), Chapter 6, for a detailed discussion of how to select these different statistical techniques and models for doing so. In this section, we present each question followed by our recommendations for appropriate descriptive and inferential statistics and tabular display.

Research Question 1: What is the degree or strength of relationship between the independent variable(s) and dependent variable(s)?

Independent variable: Continuously distributed.

Dependent variable: Continuously distributed.

Descriptive statistics: Means and standard deviations for all variables, possibly assessments of normality of distributions. Bivariate relationships are expressed as Pearson or Spearman correlation coefficients. Multivariate relationships are expressed as multiple R and R^2 and standardized regression coefficients. Canonical correlation is less typically used to express relationships between many independent and dependent variables.

Inferential statistics: Bivariate regression analysis and multiple regression analysis. Canonical correlation analysis is less typically used. Analyses may include both statistical tests and confidence intervals.

Tabular displays: Present univariate and bivariate statistics in a correlation matrix table (see Tables 6.13, 6.14, and 6.23) followed by multiple regression analysis summary table (see Tables 6.18, 6.21, and 6.24 and accompanying explanation).

Research Question 2: Are there significant group differences between the groups formed by the independent variable(s) and scores on the dependent variable(s)?

Independent variables: Categorical.

Dependent variables: Continuously distributed.

Descriptive statistics: Means and standard deviations for all variables, within categories of independent variables(s). Bivariate relationships are expressed as mean differences and measures of effect size, including eta, eta^2, and Cohen's *d*.

Inferential statistics: *t* tests and one-way analysis of variance (ANOVA). Factorial design ANOVA is used for multiple independent variables. Factorial MANOVA is used for multiple independent and dependent variables.

Tabular displays: Present descriptive statistics within independent variable categories (see Table 6.11, 6.12, and section on presenting tables of group means) followed by analysis of variance summary table (see Tables 6.15, 6.16, and accompanying explanation). When many analyses exist, present descriptive statistics and ANOVA summary in the same table (see Table 6.20).

Research Question 3: Are the scores on the independent variable(s) significantly related to the categories formed by the dependent variable(s)?

Independent variable: Continuously distributed.

Dependent variable: Categorical.

Descriptive statistics: Means and standard deviations for independent variables, possibly assessments of normality of distributions. Bivariate and multivariate relationships are expressed as odds ratios. Other multivariate relationships include statistics associated with logistic regression or discriminant function analysis.

Inferential statistics: Logistic regression or discriminant function analysis. Analyses may include both statistical tests and confidence intervals, particularly around odds ratios in logistic regression.

Tabular displays: Present table of means and standard deviations of continuously distributed independent variables within categories of dependent variable (see Table 6.12 and section on presenting tables of group means) followed by logistic regression or discriminant function analysis summary table. (We do not present examples of these analyses because of their complexity and space limitations.)

Research Question 4: Are differences in the frequency of occurrence of the independent variable(s) related to differences in the frequency of occurrence of the dependent variable(s)?

Independent variable: Categorical.

Dependent variable: Categorical.

Descriptive statistics: Measures of association for nominal and ordinal-level variables: percent difference, phi, contingency coefficient, Cramer's V, Somer's D, uncertainty coefficient, and others.

Inferential statistics: Chi-square test and other nonparametric measures as conditions dictate.

Tabular displays: Cross-tabulation tables (see Tables 6.7, 6.21, and the section on cross-tabulation tables).

Of course, there are other types of research questions, but the purpose here is to present analyses that are likely to examine two of these major research questions, the examination of relationships and the comparison of groups. For example, research that tests the hypothesis that "the greater the amount of academic self-esteem, the higher one's grade point average" would constitute an examination of relationships, whereas research that examines the hypothesis that "dropouts have lower academic self-esteem than those who complete their education" would constitute a comparison of group differences. It is likely that both hypotheses would be examined within the same dissertation, and each hypothesis would be addressed using a different statistical procedure and presented using a different tabular structure.

As indicated earlier, for each research question there is a general class of analyses or analytic strategy that is typically used. For Research Question 1, correlation and regression are used; for Research Question 2, analysis of variance and its many extensions are typically used; for Research Question 3, logistic regression analysis or discriminant function analysis is typical; and for Research Question 4, cross-tabulation or multi-way contingency table analysis is typical. For each type of analysis, a table or set of tables usually is required, and sometimes a single table will contain a number of such analyses. In the following sections, we present additional examples directed to specific types of analyses not illustrated earlier, beginning with the use of confidence intervals as an alternative to typical hypothesis testing procedures.

The Use of Confidence Intervals in Tables

A confidence interval is a boundary placed around an estimate of a population parameter indicating the range within which a population parameter is likely to fall. A confidence interval is always expressed relative to a given confidence level. This confidence level is typically expressed as a percentage and gives the probability associated with the confidence interval estimate. Thus, a 95% confidence interval expresses the range within which 95% of the sample estimates are likely to fall. Said less technically, we generally take this to mean that the interval will contain the true value of the population parameter 95% of the time, or is 95% accurate. Most people are familiar with confidence intervals because of their use in political polling. For example, if the Gallup Organization estimates that 40% of likely voters will approve a ballot initiative, Gallup also provides the likely accuracy, or margin of error, of that estimate, typically +/−3% or +/−5%. A confidence interval with a +/−5% margin of error would be referred to as a 95% confidence interval.

Confidence intervals represent inferential statistical procedures that are directly analogous to statistical hypothesis testing and are often constructed around measures of effect size, or strength of relationship, such as mean differences and correlation coefficients. In this context, confidence intervals act in lieu of hypothesis tests. Some researchers prefer this method of assessing population parameters because it provides additional information not available from examination of a hypothesis test. We illustrate this point with three tables, all presenting the results of a two-tailed t test.

What are the differences between these three tables? Although all present the means and standard deviations of the two groups and all present the results of an inferential procedure, the tables represent different strategies for presenting conclusions based on inferential statistics. Table 6.15 presents the t -test results via a probability note indicating that the result is significant at less than the .01 level of probability. Table 6.16 provides additional information by indicating the exact level of probability (.004). Finally, in Table 6.17, a 99% confidence interval has been placed around the mean difference. By examining this interval, the reader knows first that a hypothesis test at the .01 level of significance would be significant because the interval excludes the value of zero. (The null hypothesis in a t test indicates that the mean difference is zero; because the confidence interval excludes this value we can reject this hypothesis.)

Table 6.15   Descriptive Statistics and Independent Groups Design t Test for Experimental and Control Groups

Group	N	X	S	t
Experimental	5	15.0	3.87	4.025*
Control	5	6.00	3.16	

*$p < .01$

Table 6.16   Descriptive Statistics and Independent Groups Design t Test for Experimental and Control Groups

Group	N	X	S	t	p
Experimental	5	15.00	3.87	4.025	.004
Control	5	6.00	3.16		

Table 6.17   Descriptive Statistics and 99% Confidence Interval for Mean Differences Between Experimental and Control Groups

Group	N	X	S	Mean Difference (99% CI)
Experimental	5	15.00	3.87	9 (4, 14)
Control	5	6.00	3.16	

Second, the confidence interval indicates that the difference, in the population, could be as small as 4 or as large as 14, thus giving the reader additional information about the nature of the effects of the study. Thus, using a confidence interval in lieu of a hypothesis test shifts some of the emphasis from simply finding significance to an additional consideration of the probable size of the effects observed in the study.

Although each dissertation committee is likely to have a different opinion regarding the manner in which the results of your inferential statistics are displayed, it is quite likely that you will encounter journals that use all three of these strategies.

How to Interpret and Present the Results of an ANOVA

A frequently presented type of statistical analysis is the analysis of variance, or ANOVA, which is typically used when the independent variable or variables form categories and the dependent variable is continuously distributed. These represent questions of the type identified as Research Question 2: Are there significant group differences between the groups formed by the independent variable(s) and scores on the dependent variable(s)? This section presents an example of an ANOVA performed by the Statistical Package for the Social Sciences. The printout is reviewed and converted to dissertation-ready tables, and an example of how this information might be presented and discussed in a Results section is provided. This is particularly important because the tables are intended to elaborate on the text, not act as a substitute for it. The text needs to stand on its own as a focus for the reader in summarizing the results of the research. We use the sample statement types discussed earlier in the section "The Nuts and Bolts of Describing Quantitative Results" to describe Tables 6.19 and 6.20.

Table 6.18, in its multiple parts, presents the results of an ANOVA with two independent variables, Treatment Group and Race/Ethnicity, and one dependent variable, a measure of depression. The Treatment Group variable represents a dichotomy, one group receiving an intervention, the second group (the control group) not receiving the intervention. The Race/Ethnicity variable contains five groups: Hispanic-English, Hispanic-Spanish, Caucasian, African American, and Asian/Other.

Table 6.18   Analysis of Variance of Depression by Treatment Group and Race/Ethnicity

Between-Subject Factors

		Value Label	N
GROUP	1	A-Comparison	241
	2	B-Interv	247
RACE/ETHNICITY	1	Hispanic/English	131
	2	Hispanic/Spanish	94
	3	Anglo	118
	4	African Am	95
	5	Asian/Other	50

Descriptive Statistics

Dependent Variable: BL CESD TOTAL

GROUP	RACE/ETHNICITY	Mean	Std. Deviation	N
A-Comparison	Hispanic/English	18.17	8.89	65
	Hispanic/Spanish	15.28	11.63	40
	Anglo	14.85	8.80	62
	African Am	17.43	10.52	47
	Asian/Other	18.26	8.02	27
	Total	16.70	9.65	241
B-Interv	Hispanic/English	17.23	9.37	66
	Hispanic/Spanish	17.80	9.74	54
	Anglo	16.52	12.15	56
	African Am	18.77	9.62	48
	Asian/Other	18.04	10.01	23
	Total	17.57	10.19	247
Total	Hispanic/English	17.69	9.11	131
	Hispanic/Spanish	16.72	10.60	94
	Anglo	15.64	10.51	118
	African Am	18.11	10.04	95
	Asian/Other	18.16	8.90	50
	Total	17.14	9.93	488

Tests of Between-Subjects Effects

Dependent Variable: BL CESD TOTAL

Source	Type III Sum of Squares	df	Mean Square	F	Sig.
Corrected Model	761.275[a]	9	84.586	.856	.565
Intercept	128761.632	1	128761.632	1303.066	.000
GROUP	82.861	1	82.861	.839	.360
ETHNIC	460.814	4	115.203	1.166	.325
GROUP*ETHNIC	208.687	4	52.172	.528	.715
Error	47233.250	478	98.814		
Total	191348.000	488			
Corrected Total	47994.525	487			

NOTE: a. $R^2 = .016$ (Adjusted $R^2 = -.003$).

In ANOVA language, the design can be described as a 2 × 5 factorial design. In such a design, three effects can be examined for statistical significance: the main effect of the treatment, the main effect of race/ethnicity, and the interaction of treatment with race/ethnicity. The dependent variable,

Table 6.19   Means and Standard Deviations of Depression Scores by
Treatment Group and Race/Ethnicity

| | Treatment Group | | | | | | | | |
| | Intervention | | | Control | | | Total | | |
Race/Ethnicity	N	Mean	SD	N	Mean	SD	N	Mean	SD
Hispanic-Eng.	17.2	66	9.4	65	18.2	8.9	131	17.7	9.1
Hispanic-Span.	17.8	54	9.7	40	15.3	11.6	94	16.7	10.6
Anglo	16.5	56	12.2	62	14.9	8.8	118	15.6	10.5
African-Am.	18.8	48	9.6	47	17.4	10.5	95	18.1	10.0
Asian/Other	18.0	23	10.0	27	18.3	8.0	50	18.2	8.9
Total	17.6	247	10.2	241	16.7	9.7	488	17.1	9.9

Table 6.20   Analysis of Variance Summary Table of Levels of Depression by
Treatment Group and Race/Ethnicity

Source	SS	df	MS	F	p
(A) Treatment Group	82.9	1	82.9	.84	.360
(B) Race/Ethnicity	460.8	1	115.2	1.12	.325
A × B	208.7	4	52.2	.53	.715
Error	47233.3	478	98.8		
Total	47985.7	487			

labeled CESD TOTAL, represents the Center for Epidemiological Studies
Depression Scale. The SPSS printout shown in Table 6.18 contains three
parts: The first part shows the distribution of the number of cases in each
category of each variable ("Between-Subjects Factors"), the second part
presents the descriptive statistics for each treatment by race/ethnicity
combination ("Descriptive Statistics"), and the third part presents the
ANOVA summary table ("Tests of Between-Subjects Effects"). Our goal
is to use the statistical information to provide dissertation-ready tables.
In this example, we use the two-table approach, beginning with a table
of descriptive statistics (Table 6.19) and following with the ANOVA
Summary Table (Table 6.20). With one analysis, this approach works well.
In a later section, we offer a one-table approach with a different analysis,
one that combines both descriptive and inferential information into a single
table of multiple analyses (Table 6.23).

What would one say about this analysis? Clearly many numbers are presented, but what is meaningful about these numbers? The numbers are very similar, particularly in the light of an overall standard deviation (*SD*) of nearly 10 (i.e., 9.9), the smallest mean value being 15.3 (Hispanic-Spanish in the control group) and the largest being 18.8 (African Americans in the treatment group). Both these numbers are close to the average for all 488 cases (17.1). In addition, the *F* and associated *p* values shown in the ANOVA summary table indicate that none of the main or interaction effects is statistically significant. (This is evident because none of the *p* values in the far right column of the last part of Table 6.18 is less than .05, other than that for the intercept.) A short and reasonable summary of these findings might appear as follows.

> Table 6.19 presents the means and standard deviations for level of depression by treatment group and race/ethnicity. The mean differences in these tables are quite small, varying by only one or two points from the grand mean of 17.1 (*N* = 488, *SD* = 9.9). The ANOVA summary table for these data (Table 6.20) indicates that there were no statistically significant main or interaction effects.

Statements summarizing tabular results do not need to be as brief or general as those presented here. For example, imagine that you were testing a specific hypothesis that the control group would be more depressed than the intervention group. This hypothesis would be statistically evaluated through an examination of the direction of the mean differences shown in Table 6.19 and the main effect of treatment group in Table 6.20. You might address this hypothesis with a statement such as the following:

> Hypothesis 1 predicted that mean depression scores in the control group would be higher than those in the intervention group. As shown in Table 6.19, mean differences, though small, were in the opposite direction from those predicted (Control, *M* = 16.7, *SD* = 9.7; Intervention, *M* = 17.6, *SD* = 10.2). As shown in Table 6.20, these differences were not statistically significant: $F(1, 478) = .84, p = .360$.

Presenting the Results of Multiple Regression Analysis

Multiple regression analysis (MRA) is a multivariate statistical technique that examines the relationship between continuously distributed independent variables and one continuously distributed dependent variable. As such, you may recognize this as a technique appropriate for the examination of questions of the type of Research Question 1 presented earlier: What is the degree or strength of relationship between the independent variable(s) and dependent variable(s)? In contrast to ANOVA presentations, there appears to be no standard, universally agreed-on format in which to present the results of MRA. This is not particularly surprising, given the many variations of MRA available and the complexity of the models being tested. Many of our students have used MRA in recent dissertations, and all have struggled with both the interpretation and the presentation of the results. In this section, we make some suggestions and present a few examples that may be used as guides.

A wide variety of output may be generated by multiple regression analysis programs. This includes, but is not limited to, unstandardized and standardized regression coefficients (also known as beta weights), multiple correlations and their square (R squared or R^2), and changes in the values of R and R^2 in stepwise regression procedures. An extremely large amount of output may also be generated with which to examine the assumptions underlying the regression procedure and to address issues of multicollinearity, homoscedasticity, and multivariate normality. In addition to these statistics, there will usually be t and F statistics indicating the statistical significance of these various coefficients. We offer Table 6.21 as a model table to be used in describing the results of MRA.

Table 6.21 presents the independent variables in the rows and the regression coefficients, unstandardized (B), standard error of the B, and standardized (beta) in the columns. The t values associated with the regression coefficients are also presented in the columns. The R^2 value is presented at the bottom of the column, with its associated F ratio. The t values and F value are accompanied by their associated p values, as we show in Table 6.21. An alternative method, one that we no longer recommend, would be to place an asterisk on these values (F and t) if they are statistically significant at the specified level and to include probability notes at the bottom of the table in lieu of the column of p values.

Table 6.21   Sample Table Template for Presenting the Results of Multiple Regression Analysis (Three Independent Variables)

Independent Variable	B	SE_b	Beta	t	p
Variable 1 Variable 2 Variable 3					

NOTE: $R^2 = .xxx$, $F(x, xxx) = xx.x$, $p = .xxx$

An Example of Multiple Regression Analysis

Imagine a study examining the effects of education, age, and frequency of church attendance on attitudes toward premarital sex. (Clearly, other variables could also influence these attitudes, but we want to keep this example simple.) Table 6.22 presents the results of a number of SPSS procedures that might accompany a multiple regression analysis and the results of an MRA examining the effect of these variables. The results are based on data from the 2003 National Opinion Research Center General Social Survey. (These data may be downloaded from http://csa.berkeley .edu:7502/ or http://webapp.icpsr.umich.edu/GSS/. This analysis can also be replicated while online at either site.)

Table 6.22 is composed of the following parts of the SPSS printout:

I. Descriptive statistics: This section presents the means, standard deviations, and number of cases for each independent and dependent variable.
   A. Note that the number of cases is different for the different variables because cases are only deleted if there are no data for a specific variable.
   B. Note the "Valid N (listwise)" row indicating that there are only 877 cases in the data file that have valid (nonmissing) data for all variables.

II. Correlations: This section contains the correlation matrix of all variables, with significance level and number of cases.
   A. This correlation matrix uses pairwise deletion of missing values.
   B. Note that the N varies for each correlation coefficient.

III. Descriptives and correlations: These two sections of output represent the correlate procedure with a request for descriptive statistics.
   A. Note that the valid N for all procedures is 877, representing the number of cases with complete data on all variables.
   B. This is the same N that will be used in the multiple regression procedure.

IV. Model summary: Provides the R, R^2, adjusted R^2, and standard error for the overall regression model. The R^2 indicates that 23.9% of the variance in attitudes toward premarital sex can be explained by the combined influence of the three independent variables.
   A. The adjusted R^2 adjusts for the number of cases relative to the number of variables in the equation. The adjustment is small because the number of cases is large.

V. ANOVA: This section presents the ANOVA summary table. This table indicates that the amount of variance explained by the regression equation is statistically significant, as shown by an F value and its associated p value.
   A. The p value, sometimes called Sig. (for significance), is .000.
   B. This does not mean no significance. It means that the probability that the results are due to chance (i.e., random) is less that .001 or 1 in 1,000.

VI. Coefficients: This section presents the standardized and unstandardized regression coefficients and their accompanying t values and level of significance.

A. Note that, as indicated by the probability notes, all t values are statistically significant at $p = .001$ or less.
B. The beta weights provide an indication of the relative contribution of the variables to the prediction of attitudes toward premarital sex, when the other variables are controlled. Clearly, church attendance has the greatest influence, followed by age and education.
C. The negative sign on the B and beta for church attendance indicate that as church attendance increases, approval of premarital sex becomes less likely.

As researchers, we once again face the question of how to present these data, and as with analysis of variance, we suggest a two-table approach. The first table (Table 6.23) presents the correlation matrix and descriptive statistics. The second (Table 6.24) presents the multiple regression analysis results.

Before presenting a sample interpretation of these two tables, we return to the printout to examine how and where the information from the printout was included in the two tables. Both tables include descriptive and inferential statistics; however, the first provides only univariate and bivariate descriptive statistics and notes the significance of the correlation coefficients. This information provides the foundation on which a multiple regression analysis is based and should always be included. The second table contains the MRA results that relate to the full regression equation. Note that exact probability values are not presented because these are extremely small and displayed as .000 by SPSS. Under these conditions, we recommend using $p < .001$, not $p = .000$, which implies a zero probability. Space does not permit discussion of the complexities or variations of MRA.

Table 6.22   SPSS Procedures: DESCRIPTIVE, CORRELATE AND REGRESSION: Multiple Regression Analysis of the Effects of Education, Age, and Church Attendance on Attitudes Toward Premarital Sex (SPSS V14 Printout)

I: Descriptive Statistics: DESCRIPTIVES PROCEDURE

	N	Minimum	Maximum	Mean	Std. Deviation
SEX BEFORE MARRIAGE	883	1	4	2.83	1.267
AGE OF RESPONDENT	2803	18	89	45.96	16.804
HIGHEST YEAR OF SCHOOL COMPLETED	2810	0	20	13.70	2.889
HOW OFTEN R ATTENDS RELIGIOUS SERVICES	2801	0	8	3.80	2.708
Valid N (listwise)	877				

II: Correlations: CORRELATE PROCEDURE

		SEX BEFORE MARRIAGE	AGE OF RESPONDENT	HIGHEST YEAR OF SCHOOL COMPLETED	HOW OFTEN R ATTENDS RELIGIOUS SERVICES
SEX BEFORE MARRIAGE	Pearson Correlation	1	−.151(**)	.099(**)	−.462(**)
	Sig. (2-tailed)		.000	.003	.000
	N	883	879	882	880
AGE OF RESPONDENT	Pearson Correlation	−.151(**)	1	−.104(**)	.113(**)
	Sig. (2-tailed)	.000		.000	.000
	N	879	2803	2802	2793
HIGHEST YEAR OF SCHOOL COMPLETED	Pearson Correlation	.099(**)	−.104(**)	1	.051(**)
	Sig. (2-tailed)	.003	.000		.007
	N	882	2802	2810	2800
HOW OFTEN R ATTENDS RELIGIOUS SERVICES	Pearson Correlation	−.462(**)	.113(**)	.051(**)	1
	Sig. (2-tailed)	.000	.000	.007	
	N	880	2793	2800	2801

** Correlation is significant at the 0.01 level (2-tailed).

III: Descriptive Statistics and Correlation Matrix: Correlate Procedure with Descriptive Statistics and Listwise Deletion of Cases

	Mean	Std. Deviation	N
SEX BEFORE MARRIAGE	2.83	1.266	877
AGE OF RESPONDENT	45.65	17.187	877
HIGHEST YEAR OF SCHOOL COMPLETED	13.68	2.907	877
HOW OFTEN R ATTENDS RELIGIOUS SERVICES	3.77	2.742	877

(Continued)

Table 6.22 (Continued)

Correlations(a)

		SEX BEFORE MARRIAGE	AGE OF RESPONDENT	HIGHEST YEAR OF SCHOOL COMPLETED	HOW OFTEN R ATTENDS RELIGIOUS SERVICES
SEX BEFORE MARRIAGE	Pearson Correlation	1	−.152(**)	.096(**)	−.464(**)
	Sig. (2-tailed)		.000	.004	.000
AGE OF RESPONDENT	Pearson Correlation	−.152(**)	1	−.136(**)	.086(*)
	Sig. (2-tailed)	.000		.000	.011
HIGHEST YEAR OF SCHOOL COMPLETED	Pearson Correlation	.096(**)	−.136(**)	1	.054
	Sig. (2-tailed)	.004	.000		.113
HOW OFTEN R ATTENDS RELIGIOUS SERVICES	Pearson Correlation	−.464(**)	.086(*)	.054	1
	Sig. (2-tailed)	.000	.011	.113	

** Correlation is significant at the 0.01 level (2-tailed).
* Correlation is significant at the 0.05 level (2-tailed).
a. Listwise $N = 877$

IV: Model Summary: MULTIPLE REGRESSION PROCEDURE

Model	R	R Square	Adjusted R Square	Std. Error of the Estimate
1	.489(a)	.239	.236	1.107

a. Predictors: (Constant), How Often R Attends Religious Services, Highest Year of School Completed, Age of Respondent

V: ANOVA(b): MULTIPLE REGRESSION PROCEDURE

Model		Sum of Squares	df	Mean Square	F	Sig.
1	Regression	335.861	3	111.954	91.413	.000(a)
	Residual	1069.165	873	1.225		
	Total	1405.026	876			

a. Predictors: (Constant), How Often R Attends Religious Services, Highest Year of School Completed, Age of Respondent
b. Dependent Variable: Sex Before Marriage

VI: Coefficients(a): MULTIPLE REGRESSION PROCEDURE

Model		Unstandardized Coefficents		Standardized Coefficients	t	Sig.
		B	Std. Error	Beta		
1	(Constant)	3.326	.221		15.064	.000
	AGE OF RESPONDENT	−.007	.002	−.098	−3.269	.001
	HIGHEST YEAR OF SCHOOL COMPLETED	.047	.013	.108	3.599	.000
	HOW OFTEN R ATTENDS RELIGIOUS SERVICES	−.213	.014	−.461	−15.527	.000

a. Dependent Variable: Sex Before Marriage

For a more complete discussion of this technique and the major issues surrounding its use, we suggest consulting Newton and Rudestam (1999). For a detailed statistical treatment, we suggest Tabachnick and Fidell (2006). Returning to the issue of discussing the tabular results within the dissertation text, we suggest the following as a reasonable, but not the only, approach:

Table 6.23 presents the correlation matrix and descriptive statistics for the regression of attitudes toward premarital sex on education, age, and church attendance. Note that the correlations for both age and church attendance are negative (−.152 and −.264, respectively). Thus, as both age and church

Table 6.23 Correlation Matrix and Descriptive Statistics for Education, Age, Church Attendance, and Attitudes Toward Premarital Sex (dissertation ready)

	1	2	3	4
Premarital Sex[a]	1.0			
Age	−.152	1.0		
Education (Years)	.096	−.136	1.0	
Church Attendance[b]	−.264	−.086	.054	1.0
Mean	2.83	45.65	13.68	3.77
Standard Deviation	1.27	17.19	2.91	2.74

NOTE: $N = 877$. Premarital sex is the dependent variable. All correlations are statistically significant at $p < .001$, except the relationship between education and church attendance, which is not statistically significant. Data source is National Opinion Research Center General Social Survey, 2004.

a. Values for premarital sex range from 1, *always wrong,* to 4, *not wrong at all.*
b. Values for church attendance range from 0, *never,* to 8, *more than once per week.*

Table 6.24 Multiple Regression Analysis of Attitudes Toward Premarital Sexual Relations[a] by Education, Age, and Frequency of Church Attendance[b] (dissertation ready)

Independent Variable	B	SE_b	Beta	t	p
Age	−.007	.002	−.098	−3.27	.001
Education (Years)	.047	.013	.108	3.60	< .001
Church Attendance	−.213	.014	−.461	−15.53	< .001

NOTE: $R^2 = .239$, $F(3, 873) = 91.4$, $p < .001$.

a. Values for premarital sex range from 1, *always wrong,* to 4, *not wrong at all.*
b. Values for church attendance range from 0, *never,* to 8, *more than once per week.*

attendance increase, respondents are more likely to oppose premarital sex. As education increases, people become more favorably disposed toward premarital sex, but this relationship is small (.096). Table 6.24 presents the results of the MRA. Although all variables are statistically significant due to the large sample size, it is clearly church attendance that plays a major role in predicting attitudes: beta = −.461, $t(876) = −15.53$, $p < .001$. Almost 24% of the variability in attitudes toward premarital sex can be explained by reference to age, education, and church attendance ($R^2 = .239$, $F(3, 873) = 91.4$, $p < .001$).

Streamlining Your Results:
Presenting Multiple Analyses in a Single Table

It is frequently the case that many similar analyses need to be presented in a Results section. For example, if the study using analysis of variance described in the previous section had also examined the relationship of treatment group and race/ethnicity to locus of control and four dimensions of life satisfaction, each of these analyses would also need to be presented in tabular form. If each set of means and each ANOVA summary table were presented in separate tables, an additional 10 tables would be necessary. When such a situation arises, we strongly recommend that you seek a means by which the results may be combined into a single table. For example, a student of ours (Ferguson, 2006) examined race/ethnic differences in the Zimbardo Time Perspective Inventory (ZTPI), the Consideration of Future Consequences Scale (CFC), and the Barratt Impulsiveness Scale (BIS). In this study, one-way analysis of variance was used to examine the differences between the two ethnic groups on the six subscales of the ZTPI and the CFC and the four subscales of the BIS. Rather than present each of the 11 analyses in a separate table, Ferguson decided to combine them into a single table, as shown in Table 6.25.

Note that Table 6.25 presents the mean, standard deviation, and number of cases for each variable for each ethnic group, but it does not present the complete ANOVA summary table for each analysis. It is sufficient to present only the F ratio and either the accompanying probability notes or exact probability values, as in this case, to indicate the statistical significance of each analysis. Such a presentation enables the reader to examine all of the results related to specific research questions in a single table, facilitating discussion and comprehension of the results.

As a second example, consider the situation in which one or more groups are asked a number of questions in conjunction with follow-up questions. You may want to present the answers to both the main questions and the follow-ups for each group in the study. An efficient way to do this is to present the results in a table that facilitates the examination of the questions and comparisons between groups. For example, in a study of psychologists and marriage, child, and family counselors, Neighbors (1991) asked each to rate the courses they had taken in the diagnosis, etiology, and physiology of mental disorder. Each area was rated as *not adequate, adequate,* or *very adequate.* Following these ratings, the same groups were asked to rate their need for additional education in each area. Ratings were coded "yes" to indicate the perceived need

Table 6.25   Oneway ANOVA of The Zimbardo Time Perspective Inventory (ZTPI), Consideration of Future Consequences Scale (CFC), Future Time Perspective Scale (FTP) and the Barratt Impulsiveness Scale, Version 11 (BIS) by Respondent Race/Ethnicity

Scale Name		N	Mean	SD	F	Sig.
BIS Attention Key	African-American	34	15.5000	3.24037	.003	.957
	White/Anglo	102	15.4608	3.75400		
BIS Motor Key	African-American	38	13.9737	3.69431		
	White/Anglo	101	14.8416	4.23493	1.240	.267
BIS Non-Planning Key	African-American	37	22.7568	4.43725		
	White/Anglo	101	21.8713	4.99933		
BIS Total Score	African-American	31	52.5161	10.33722	.900	.344
	White/Anglo	100	52.2500	11.12498		
CFC Total	African-American	40	37.3250	7.63053		
	White/Anglo	102	38.9510	7.90335	.014	.906
FTP Total	African-American	40	48.7250	8.94997		
	White/Anglo	101	53.1188	11.12141		
ZTPI Past Negative	African-American	41	32.6341	7.45237	1.240	.267
	White/Anglo	102	31.7549	6.77274		
ZTPI Present Hedonistic	African-American	40	45.8750	8.74478		
	White/Anglo	103	47.0971	7.15037	4.963	.028
ZTPI Future	African-American	40	45.2750	7.36585		
	White/Anglo	101	46.3168	6.70064		
ZTPI Past Positive	African-American	39	29.2308	5.21365	.465	.496
	White/Anglo	100	30.1500	5.52931		
ZTPI Present Fatalistic	African-American	40	21.9250	5.35119		
	White/Anglo	103	21.4854	5.24098	.740	.391

NOTE: From Ferguson, 2006.

Table 6.26   Self-Ratings of Adequacy of Education and Need for More Education by Type of License

Type of Course	Adequacy of Education (%)			Need More	
	Not Adequate	Adequate	Very Adequate	% "Yes"	$x^2(df, N)$
Diagnosis					
Psychologists	48.2	25.9	25.9 (27)	35.9 (40)	6.9 (2, 76)*
MFCCs	26.5	57.2	16.3 (49)	29.8 (57)	0.3 (1, 97)
Etiology					
Psychologists	38.5	42.3	19.2 (26)	30.0 (40)	3.9 (2, 73)
MFCCs	21.3	65.9	12.8 (47)	24.6 (57)	0.4 (1, 97)
Physiology					
Psychologists	36.0	28.0	36.0 (25)	42.5 (40)	3.5 (2, 72)
MFCCs	40.4	42.6	17.0 (47)	42.1 (57)	0.0 (1, 97)

NOTES: Cell percentages for"Adequacy of Education" sum to 100 across columns. Ns in parentheses. The first chi-square value represents "Adequacy of Education" and the second represents "Need for More Education."

*$p < .05$

for more education. A "no" response indicated no perceived need for additional training. Tables that present bivariate distributions such as these were discussed in an earlier section. A bivariate distribution could be presented for each area of training and each assessment of the need for more training, making a total of six tables. The statistical significance of each relationship was assessed with a chi-square test, creating a need to present the results of these tests as well. Table 6.26 presents the results of the analyses in a single table. Note that Table 6.26 presents the data for both questions, for each group, in a single row. Only the percentage that gave a positive (yes) response to the question regarding the need for more education is presented because the percentage that stated "no" is redundant, obtained simply by subtracting the percentage that said yes from 100. The chi-square tests, one for each question, are presented in the column labeled $\chi^2(df, N)$. A general note indicates that the first chi-square value represents the test for the adequacy of education question, whereas the second presents the test for the need for more education question.

As a final caution, it is important to point out that one can carry the quest to streamline tables too far. The result may be considerable confusion rather than clarification and ease of comparison. Table 6.26 may be approaching the limits in this regard, but we believe that it presents a strategy for approaching table construction that you will find useful when composing your dissertation tables.

Some Guidelines for the Presentation of Figures in a Dissertation

Much of what we have said in this chapter also applies to figures; however, figures are much broader in scope because they encompass anything not put in a table. Thus, a figure might be a causal diagram, a photograph, an organizational chart, a map, a line drawing, a flowchart, a timeline, or any number of other things. Figures can be particularly helpful in presenting an overall pattern. In this sense, they might be used to illustrate a relationship in a table that isn't obvious from simply examining the tabulated numbers. Therefore, figures are often used to augment tables, but because figures require the reader to estimate values, they generally should not be used instead of a table. Figures that augment tables are particularly helpful when interaction effects or nonlinear relationships, such as those found in survival analysis, need clarification.

For example, we present data from a study of foster children. This study sought to explore the effect of type of placement (with a relative or a nonrelative), sex, and ethnicity (White, African American, or Hispanic) on the number of behavior problems exhibited by the child. The results of a $2 \times 2 \times 3$ ANOVA revealed two statistically significant two-way interactions; however, the nature of these interactions is difficult to discern from an examination of either the table of cell means (Table 6.27) or the ANOVA summary table (Table 6.28).

We used a classification plot to graph the two-way interaction between gender and type of placement (Figure 6.1).

Note that when examining the figure the nature of the interaction effect is easily interpretable. For both males and females there are fewer behavior problems when placed with a relative, as compared to placement with a nonrelative (foster home); however, for females placement with a relative produces fewer problems than evidenced by males and placement in a foster home produces more problems than evidenced by males, thus creating the significant interaction shown in Table 6.28.

Table 6.27 Mean Scores on Total Behavior Problems by Gender, Ethnicity, and Type of Placement

	Relative Placement by Ethnicity			Foster Home Placement by Ethnicity		
	White	Black	Hispanic	White	Black	Hispanic
Male	58.81 (37)	56.59 (22)	55.95 (44)	58.51 (82)	56.82 (34)	58.08 (60)
Female	57.40 (43)	53.76 (21)	50.90 (40)	58.98 (133)	58.27 (44)	61.93 (61)

Table 6.28 Analysis of Variance of Total Behavior Problems by Gender, Ethnicity, and Type of Placement

	SS	DF	MS	F	p
Main Effects					
Gender, A	.173	1	.173	.001	.973
Ethnicity, B	219.753	2	109.876	.726	.484
Placement, C	1375.253	1	1375.253	9.089	.003
Interaction Effects					
A × B	23.263	2	11.974	.079	.924
A × C	826.924	1	826.924	5.465	.020
B × C	1000.307	2	500.154	3.306	.037
A × B × C	331.368	2	165.684	1.095	.335
Error	92146.001	609	151.307		
Total	95934.573	620			

The APA lists seven general principles underlying a good figure (2001). A good figure:

- Augments rather than duplicates the text;
- Conveys only essential facts;
- Omits visually distracting detail;
- Is easy to read—its elements (type, lines, labels, symbols, etc.) are large enough to be read with ease in the printed form;
- Is easy to understand—its purpose is readily apparent;

- Is consistent with and is prepared in the same style as similar figures in the same article; that is, the lettering is of the same size and typeface, lines are of the same weight, and so forth; and
- Is carefully planned and prepared. (p. 177)

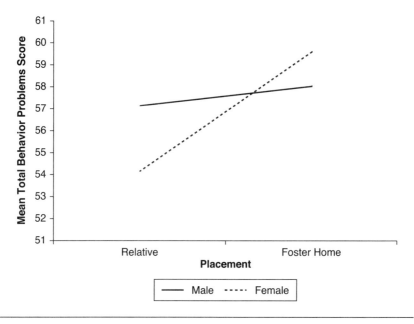

Figure 6.1   Classification plot demonstrating the interaction between gender and type of placement

Notes

1. The four statements for describing quantitative results were suggested by Dr. David Perkins, Department of Psychology, California State University, Fullerton.

2. The interested reader can access the NORC General Social Survey and either download this data into SPSS or analyze the data while online. Two excellent sites for doing this are http://webapp.icpsr.umich.edu/GSS/ and http://csa.berkeley.edu:7502.

The Results Chapter Toolkit

The Results chapter toolkit contains three tools for presenting your results: text, tables, and figures (e.g., charts, graphs). These are the basic tools for presenting quantitative findings. The better job you do of selecting the correct tool, the better your overall presentation of the results will be.

It does not make sense to produce a table or figure for every analysis. Try to use these as visual aids to present a large amount of information in a small space (tables) or to illustrate relationships that might be difficult to discern just by observing rows or columns of numbers (graphs).

The distribution of sex as produced by SPSS would look something like this:

Respondent's Gender					
		Frequency	*Percent*	*Valid Percent*	*Cumulative Percent*
Valid	Male	156	47.3	47.3	47.3
	Female	174	52.7	52.7	100.0
	Total	330	100.0	100.0	

An APA format table presenting these results might look as follows:

Table 1 Distribution of Respondent's Gender		
Gender	*f*	*%*
Male	156	47.3
Female	174	52.7
Total	330	100.0

Similarly, a graph of these findings might look as follows:

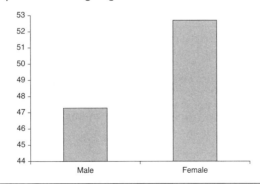

Figure 6.1   Percentage distribution of respondent's gender

The Results Chapter Toolkit (Continued)

Both of these strategies for presentation of these data are unnecessary and ill advised. Moreover, the figure distorts the size of the gender difference in the sample by stretching the vertical axis, and neither the vertical nor the horizontal axis is fully labeled. A better method would be to simply describe the gender distribution as follows: "Of the 330 participants in the sample, 52.7% were female."

The APA publication manual (2001, p. 137) provides the following three general guidelines, which we endorse:

1. If you have 3 or fewer numbers, use a sentence.

2. If you have 4 to 20 numbers, use a table.

3. If you have more than 20 numbers, consider using a graph or figure instead of a table.

Our fourth guideline is:

4. Remember, there are always exceptions.

Types of Hypotheses in the Results Section

The Two Major Types of Hypotheses		
	Research	*Statistical*
Where First Presented	End of problem statement	Results section
Source	Research & theory	Statistical test
Example: General	I hypothesized that women's recent experiences of abuse would be positively related to their levels of depression.*	There will be a significant positive Pearson product-moment correlation between women's recent experience of abuse and depression.
Example: Specific	I hypothesized that women's recent experiences of abuse as measured by the Conflict Tactics Scale would be positively related to their levels of depression as reported on the Beck Depression Inventory.	Null: H_0: $\rho \leq 0$ Alternative: H_1: $\rho > 0$ Null: The Pearson product-moment correlation will be equal to or less than zero. Alternative: The Pearson product-moment correlation will be greater than zero.

*Wording modified from "The Long-Term Effects of Battering on Women's Health," by C. Sutherland, D. Bybee, and C. Sullivan, 1998, *Women's Health: Research on Gender, Behavior, and Policy, 4*(1), p. 41. Adapted with permission.

Note the following characteristics of the statistical hypotheses:

1. The null and alternative hypotheses are mutually exclusive. They cannot both be true.

2. The null and alternative hypotheses are directional; they specify the relationship as positive. Thus, a one-tailed test is specified.

3. The hypotheses are written using Greek letters. These represent the population parameters. The Greek letter rho (ρ) refers to the population correlation, not the value of the correlation observed in the sample.

4. Rejecting the null hypothesis results in support for the alternative hypothesis. Never accept the null hypothesis; however, you may fail to reject it.

5. Supporting the alternative hypothesis should not be taken to "prove" your research hypothesis and should not be reported as such. It does, however, provide statistical evidence in support of the research hypothesis.

6. Supporting the alternative hypothesis should not be taken to mean that your results are substantively meaningful or important.

7. If you "reject" the null hypothesis, you may report the relationship as statistically significant at a given level of probability (i.e., the level of significance, typically .01 or .05).

Software Suggestions: Quantitative Data Analysis: A Sampling of Programs

Name	Distributor	Web Site	Download Demo Available?	Comments
Statistical Package for the Social Sciences (SPSS)	SPSS Inc.	www.spss.com	Yes. http://www.spss.com/downloads/	Grad pack inexpensive and contains full program but must be purchased through university member. Many stat texts and user guides from other publishers. Most widely used in world. User-friendly pull-down menu structure.
Statistical Analysis System	SAS Institute	www.sas.com	No.	Not recommended unless departmental standard. Not generally the program of choice for general social science analysis and students. Large company with many software titles, complex Web site.
MicroCase	Wadsworth Publishing Company	www.microcase.com	Yes. Download a 45-day fully functional trial version. http://www.microcase.com/ancilinfo2.html	Very user friendly; student version free with text.
GB Stat	Dynamic Microsystems Inc.	www.gbstat.com	Yes. Click Demo button on home page.	No longer distributed by Scolari.

Stata	Stata Corporation	www.stata.com	Yes.	Great user support. Known for exploratory data analysis (EDA) capabilities.
Systat	Systat Software Inc.	http://www.systat.com/	Yes. http://www.systat.com/downloads/?sec =d001	Primarily focused on scientists and engineers. Numerous software products for graphics and plotting.
Minitab	Minitab Inc.	www.minitab.com	Yes. Download a fully functional, 30-day demo version of Minitab Release 14. http://www.minitab.com/downloads/	Large and longstanding company. Many stat texts and users guides from other publishers. Widely used in business.
Statgraphics	StatPoint, Inc.	www.statgraphics.com	Yes. Download a 30-day trial copy. http://www.statgraphics.com/download _center.htm	As name implies, very graphics intensive. Designed to be user friendly.
Number Cruncher Statistical System (NCSS)	NCSS Statistical Software	www.ncss.com	Yes. Download a 30-day trial copy of NCSS or PASS. http://www.ncss.com/download.html	Also produces PASS, a power analysis & sample size program: http://www.ncss.com/pass.html
JMP 6	SAS Institute	http://www.jmp.com/	Yes. Click "download jmp" from the home page.	Oriented toward business and product development.

7

Presenting the Results of Qualitative Research

Writing an informative Results chapter of a research dissertation consists of two interrelated skills: choosing and describing the data analysis methods and presenting the results of the analyses. Generally accepted guidelines exist for how to display data and summarize the results of statistical analyses in quantitative studies. This is not the case with qualitative studies. Although some sources (Miles & Huberman, 1994; Richards, 2005; Silverman, 2001) offer very specific advice on how to conduct and report qualitative data analyses, we have found no clear agreement in the literature and our students have, in fact, used a variety of formats and approaches. As with all research, the first priority is to adopt a well-organized strategy that makes sense of your data and presents them clearly and comprehensively.

Qualitative studies are likely to produce large quantities of data that represent words and ideas rather than numbers and statistics. These include, but are not limited to, interview transcripts and field notes, a wide variety of records, documents, video and audio recordings, and unobtrusive measures. The researcher may be the victim of data overload, with no idea of what to present or where to begin. Statistical program packages, such as SPSS, present quantitative data in standardized ways that permit immediate comparisons both within and across groups. Qualitative data analysis programs also exist and are becoming increasingly sophisticated. The explosion of qualitative dissertations has been accompanied by the development and refinement of a group of excellent programs for qualitative data analysis. The most popular qualitative data analysis software programs are shown in the following tip box, along with links to Web sites and downloads of trial versions. Some of these primarily focus on the analysis of text and transcript data, whereas others use a broad net designed to capture photo- and video-based data. Please keep in mind, however, a fundamental fact: All computer-based qualitative data analysis programs are data organizers. As such, they can be tremendous time savers for storing, coding, and manipulating text data. It certainly makes sense to transfer large amounts of written text into a computer if the alternative is index cards that cover every square inch of your office floor. If you are doing complex coding, the software program acts as a personal assistant to help you locate key passages with the click of your keyboard; assign codes to the text, including assigning a unit of analysis to more than one category; and move the segments around for easy categorization, search, and retrieval. It will even help you sort and connect data on the basis of common words and phrases. For that matter, the software can help you test your hunches and hypotheses and present data in the form of content analyses, descriptive statistics, and graphic displays.

A growing market for qualitative data analysis software to match the longstanding market for sophisticated and versatile quantitative analysis is producing new and creative products to make the data management task easier. For example, one of the most time-consuming tasks associated with qualitative data analysis is transcribing data. A new program, Hyper TRANSCRIBE, lets you transcribe almost any audio or video file quickly and easily (visit http://www.researchware.com/ for a free demo version). Another tricky task is the visual presentation of qualitative results in the form of charts, graphs, flow diagrams, and the like. A new program designed to facilitate this task is MAX Maps. Launched in March of 2006, MAX Maps allows you to design graphical models or networks that represent the results of qualitative analyses (see http://www.maxqda.com/index .htm). One example of a MAX Maps presentation is provided in Figure 7.1. This model shows different areas where environmental conflicts exist empirically. The basis for this model was the systematic analysis of corresponding articles from newspapers and magazines (Environmental Awareness in Germany). For copies of these reports, in German, see www.umweltbe wusstsein.de. Visit the MAXqda Web site for further examples of MAX Maps presentations and a trial version.

So with all the new software designed to facilitate the qualitative data analysis process, what's the problem? The limitation is that the software cannot read meaning into the organization of the text or other qualitative

Name	Distributor	Web Site	Download Demo Available?	Comments (All from manufacturer's Web sites.)
ATLAS.ti	Scientific Software Development	www.atlasti.de	Yes. http://www.atlasti.com/download.html	**ATLAS.ti** is a powerful software workbench for the qualitative analysis of large bodies of textual, graphical, audio, and video data. It offers a variety of tools for accomplishing the tasks associated with any systematic approach to "soft" data.
Ethnograph	Qualis Research Associates	www.qualisresearch.com/	Yes. Directly from home page	**The Ethnograph v5.08** for Windows PCs is a versatile computer program designed to make the analysis of data collected during qualitative research easier, more efficient, and more effective. You can import your text-based qualitative data, typed in any word processor, straight into the program. **The Ethnograph** helps you search and note segments of interest within your data, mark them with code words and run analyses which can be retrieved for inclusion in reports or further analysis.
Hyper-RESEARCH	Research Ware	www.researchware.com	Yes. http://www.researchware.com/ht/downloads.html	**HyperRESEARCH's v2.06** ability to work with multiple data types, such as text, graphics, audio, and video sources, provides the flexibility to integrate all of the data necessary to conduct research. This program has a menu-driven "Point & Click" interface. A new program **HyperTRANSCRIBE 1.0** is also available.

(Continued)

A Selection of Qualitative Data Analysis Software Programs (Continued)

Name	Distributor	Web Site	Download Demo Available?	Comments (All from manufacturer's Web sites.)
QSR NVivo	QSR International	http://www.qsrinternational.com/index.htm	Yes. Download trial versions of four different programs. http://www.qsrinternational.com/DemoReg/Demo Reg1.asp	**NVivo 7** was launched in February 2006. It takes the best of QSR's **NVivo 2** and **N6** (formerly NUD*IST) software, and adds innovative new features and tools. It allows qualitative researchers to manage, code, analyze and report on data in ways they never thought possible.
MAXqda2 MAX Maps	MAXqda - Verbi GmbH - Germany	http://www.maxqda.com/index.htm	Yes. http://www.maxqda.com/2_demo.htm	**MAXqda2** is the successor of **winMAX**. **MAXqda** supports qualitative data analysis and helps you systematically evaluate and interpret texts. It is also a powerful tool for developing theories as well as testing theoretical conclusions of your analysis. **MAX Maps** launched in March of 2006 gives a graphical representation of the different elements of a **MAXqda** project. These "objects" can be inserted into the **MAX Maps** drawing pad, and connections can be made in order to visualize a complex graph of relationships. **MAX Maps** also allows you to design graphical models or networks that are completely independent of **MAXqda's** data.

NOTE: The interested reader may want to examine Christine A. Barry (1998) "Choosing Qualitative Data Analysis Software: Atlas/ti and Nudist Compared" *Sociological Research Online*, vol. 3, no. 3, http://www.socresonline.org.uk/socresonline/3/3/4.html.

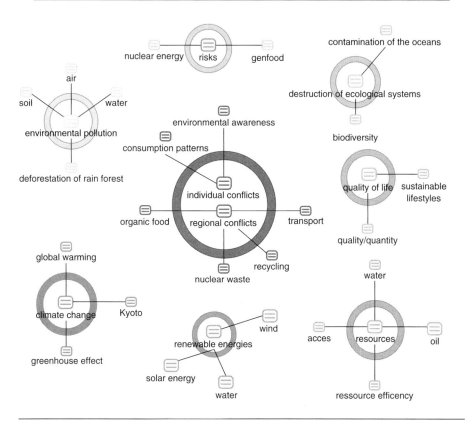

Figure 7.1   Graphic representation of environmental awareness in Germany

SOURCE: Produced by MAX Maps. Reprinted with permission.

materials that constitute the foundation of your project. That responsibility falls to you, the researcher, and if you are not careful, you may end up relying too much on the computer and neglecting the creative meaning making and theory building that is the hallmark of all good qualitative research. We strongly encourage you to read and reflect on your data, take primary responsibility for creating your categories, and draw your own conclusions. Use the software to support your scholarly activity if you wish, but don't rely on it to "do" your data analysis.

There is considerable latitude in analyzing qualitative data, and each qualitative analysis still requires the researcher to devise his or her own method for presenting the results. Most qualitative researchers begin their data analysis by reading and rereading in its entirety all the information they have collected, including interview transcripts and field notes, to get a feel for the whole. They may also summarize the information in the form of memos and reflective notes. Because of the tendency for text data to be overwhelming in scope and quantity, there is almost always a need to reduce the data by developing categories or codes for sorting and refining them. Richards (2005) clarified the important distinctions between qualitative coding and quantitative coding, which is more frequently associated with survey research. An edited summary of these distinctions can be found in Table 7.1. Richards (2005) also recommends a fairly straightforward approach to coding qualitative data: (1) descriptive coding, much like quantitative coding, involves storing and summarizing the attributes that describe each case (age, origin, etc.); (2) topic coding, or labeling text (as categories) with regard to its subject, takes time but can be automated; (3) and analytical coding, or creating new categories based on ideas that emerge as you reflect on the data. This last step is at the heart of qualitative theory building.

Each major qualitative research tradition has its own approach to analyzing textual data. There is even more latitude in how to present the data and the conclusions within the written document. Moustakas (1994), one of the leading representatives of the phenomenological tradition, describes two approaches to analysis. The first is a modification of van Kaam's (1966) method. The second is a variation of methods suggested by

Table 7.1 Quantitative and Qualitative Modes of Coding (Based on Richards, 2005)

	Quantitative	*Qualitative*
Place in research process	Between data collection and analysis	Throughout the study
Relation to categories	Predetermined categories	Generate categories
Relation to original data	Code replaces original data, which are not retained	Code points to original data, which are retained
Revision of categories	Usually no new categories added	New categories continually generated
Process of coding	Coding is a clerical task	Coding involves analytical work

Stevick (1971), Colaizzi (1973), and Keen (1975). The following steps, adapted from Moustakas (1994, p. 122), are taken with the entire transcript from every research participant. Begin with a full description of your own experience of the phenomenon. Then, from this transcript, take the following steps:

1. Review each statement for how well it describes the experience.

2. Record all relevant statements.

3. Remove all statements that are redundant or overlap with others, leaving the key meaning units of the experience.

4. Organize the invariant meaning units into themes.

5. Coalesce the themes into a description of the textures of the experience and augment the description with quotations from the text.

6. Using your imagination and taking multiple perspectives to find possible meanings in the text, construct a description of the structures of your experience.

7. Create a textual-structural description of the meanings and essences of your experience.

Go through these seven steps with the complete narrative transcript of each participant of the study. Then integrate the individual textual-structural descriptions into a composite description of the meanings and essences of the experience of the entire group.

Students who select a phenomenological dissertation need to obtain familiarity with these kinds of data reduction procedures. One of our students, Diane Armstrong (1994), conducted a phenomenological dissertation exploring the dreams of the blind. She relied on data from 36 interviews with congenitally blind (blind from birth) and adventitiously blind (develop blindness after a period of sight) adults. Her approach to data reduction was based on the naturalistic methods of Giorgi (1985) and led to descriptions of the sensory input, the dream setting, the dominant emotional qualities, and the content structure of the dreams. Armstrong began her Results chapter by providing a brief overview of each of her participants (a typical approach in qualitative studies) and then presented the themes that emerged from her interview data across participants, amply illustrated and supported by examples and quotations from the participants.

The results of ethnographic studies include the detailed description of persons and settings. Wolcott (1994) recommended that the Results chapter include (1) a description of the culture and what is occurring with it; (2) an analysis of the findings, including the identification of patterns and comparison of cases, a critique of the fieldwork procedures, and placement of the information within a larger analytic framework; and (3) an interpretation of the culture-sharing group, which includes both theoretical implications and personal experience. As described by Creswell (1998), the description might highlight a day in the life of the group or an individual, focus on a critical event, adopt an analytical framework, or report different perspectives through the eyes of the informants. The analysis might include the use of tables, diagrams, and figures to help clarify and evaluate the written information. The interpretation phase goes beyond the data to the implications of the study to the larger research question. The write-up of results in ethnographic studies can range from taking a highly impersonal and objective approach to favoring a more personal, impressionistic style. If you are conducting an ethnographic study for your dissertation, you need to consult with your dissertation committee to gauge the appropriate approach within your discipline and program.

Anissa Butler's (2006) ambitious ethnographic study about the experiences of people of color living and those working in a predominantly White college town took a personal approach to the topic, abetted by significant data collection and intellectual rigor. Butler conducted an autoethnography, which, in contrast to the more objective orientation of most purely ethnographic studies, included her own experiences and observations as a knowledgeable participant-observer in the town of Boulder, Colorado. The Results section of the dissertation opened with her own lengthy story of being a person of color in this setting. This was followed by a summary of in-depth interviews with 23 other people of color connected with the community, another section dealing with the results of a structured survey, and a section describing the results of a series of focus groups she conducted. The subsequent chapters of her dissertation maintained the autobiographical blend of moving back and forth between the personal and the cultural. She used a triangulation of her data to offer a series of themes, including a description of the acculturation process for people of color living or working in the town, and concluded with a chapter on analyses and implications of the study.

Proponents of grounded theory have a somewhat different way of thinking about and expressing what takes place in the Results chapter of a dissertation. Making sense of naturalistic data means processing the data through a technique of inductive analysis. Grounded theory offers perhaps the most structured and unified procedure for developing categories of information and moving from these categories to construct a narrative to connect them and generate a set of theoretical propositions. Data are systematically coded into as many themes and meaning categories as possible. As the categories emerge and are refined, the researcher begins to consider how they relate to one another and what the theoretical implications are. Gradually the theoretical properties of the meaning categories crystallize and form a pattern. The pattern that emerges is called grounded theory.

The grounded theory approach involves two essential subprocesses that compose the basis of inductive analysis: unitizing and categorizing. Unitizing is a coding operation in which information units are isolated from the text. In the second subprocess, categorizing, information units derived from the unitizing phase are organized into categories on the basis of similarity in meaning. As the number of categories reaches a saturation point, the researcher attempts to write rules that define which units of information may be included or excluded from the category. This process has been called the constant comparative method by Glaser and Strauss (1967). The constant comparative method requires continual revision, modification, and amendment until all new units can be placed into an appropriate category and the inclusion of additional units into a category provides no new information.

The following is Strauss and Corbin's (1998) description of the steps in this inductive process:

1. Open coding involves reviewing the entire text for descriptive categories. Here the constant comparative method is used to refine each category by seeking examples of it until no new information yields additional meaning (saturation of the category).

2. Axial coding involves relating categories to their subcategories according to their properties and dimensions. Here the data are assessed for how major categories relate to each other and to their subcategories.

3. Selective coding involves integrating and refining the theory. Here the single category is chosen as central, and a theoretical model is generated to relate the other categories to it according to how they influence it, are caused by it, provide a context for it, or mediate it.

The resulting theory can be presented in the dissertation as hypotheses generated by the data or proposed as a comprehensive model (or both), perhaps abetted by figures or tables, to understand the phenomenon in terms of both the context of the study and previous research and practice.

Once the theory is written, the research literature is referred to for supplemental validation.

The constant comparative method can be seen in many qualitative studies in the social sciences. Fundamentally, it refers to checking and revising an emerging theory against additional data, whether the new data come from inspecting all data fragments within the same case or from examining data across cases. The qualitative researcher is encouraged to look for other cases through which to evaluate provisional hypotheses. Deviant case analysis is the term used to extend the search for meaning to discrepant data or cases that help to clarify or delimit the conceptual conclusions of the study.

Many qualitative researchers have adopted other coding procedures that deviate somewhat from those of Strauss and Corbin. A dissertation example using the grounded theory approach to work with qualitative data comes from Einhorn's (1993) goal to understand the relational aspects of women's experience in asking help from their friends. Thirty women were interviewed, both individually and in focus groups. The following comments from Einhorn reflect her attempts to cope with the tremendous amount of data she collected:

> I transcribed the interviews as soon after they were conducted as possible, and often listened to the group interview tapes before meeting with members individually so that I would remember specific areas I wanted to explore. I wrote extensive descriptions of my observations and experiences. I also talked extensively with my research consultants. . . . I began with immersing myself in the raw data (all of the interview materials and my notes); then moved to descriptions of the data (summaries of my interviews and my notes), and finally turned to understanding and interpretation—constructing meaning from the data. (p. 116)

> I employed two "subprocesses" for making sense of the data: "unitizing" and "categorizing." Unitizing involved identifying and coding the parts of the interview experiences, content and process, that were to qualify for each of the four types of data. . . . For example . . . a participant's report qualified as a "story" if it had at least two of four characteristics: time, place/situation, identified other person, and an identified kind of help. Participants' concepts about help seeking were identified as interview content that outlined beliefs, "life truths," generalizations, or assumptions *about* asking for help. The thoughts and beliefs were not quantified as units. These two types of data (stories and thoughts) proved quite distinguishable. (pp. 117–118)

> Categorization was the second step. As themes began to emerge a process of sorting began: provisionally labeling categories, noticing the rules for inclusion or exclusion of particular units from one or another category, and revising

categories. Themes and categories were revised until the rules for inclusion and exclusion seemed to be working, and all data "fit" a category. (p. 119)*

The Results chapter of the dissertation reported the outcomes of the 247 stories Einhorn (1993) collected and categorized into the following four themes: whether and how women asked for help and received it, relationship awareness, mutuality, and empowerment. The chapter also goes into detail about the participants' thoughts and beliefs about help seeking, as well as observations about the process among the participants in the focus groups and the process between the researcher and the participants.

Here is another take on the analysis process from Katz's (1995) phenomenologically oriented grounded theory dissertation:

Analysis of the data, following Hoshmond's (1989) description of grounded theory technique and hermeneutic interpretation, utilized constant comparative methods as propounded in the technique of grounded theory data analysis. That is to say, with immersion in the data—listening to the tapes, reading and rereading the transcripts, and reflecting upon the memos—I began to index the natural meaning categories used by the participants, as incidents, analysis units, and shifts of meaning began to stand out that related to the experience of chronic vulvar pain. As these key phrases and constructs accumulated into stabilized meanings, they became the units of analysis. I organized them as issues and themes. Each datum incident was coded into as many categories as possible. As categories emerged and as data emerged that fit existing categories, I began to think in terms of the possible theoretical properties of the category, its dimensions and relations to other categories, and conditions under which it was pronounced or minimized (Hoshmand, 1989).

The analytic process involved deconstructing and reconstructing, going back and forth from text to emergent categories in a hermeneutic circle, "interrogating" the data with imaginative variations, looking for constituents, distinctions, relationships, and themes. This process of data analysis proceeded simultaneously with the collection of new interviews, facilitating a cumulative theoretical sensitivity to meaning units which enabled me to follow up on emergent themes. Thematic categories were coded with brief labels which conveyed something essential about the content and topic of the units that they contain. The coding process was continually refined during the data analysis phase, as I went over the material repeatedly in different levels of analysis. (pp. 98–99)*

Chase (2005) noted that the interpretive process in narrative research is different from the traditional theme-centered approach to analyzing qualitative content. The analysis starts with absorbing the voices and stories of the participants, not deciphering their narratives as if they were

SOURCE: *Reprinted with permission of the author.

responses to questions posted by the interviewer. The researcher first looks for voices within each interview rather than for themes across interviews. In this way, it becomes possible to find relationships between different stories from the same narrative. The experience of grief or letting go, for example, may never be expressed explicitly but serves as a bridge between stories about a parent's crippling disease and not joining the family business. The narrative researcher needs to read the same text many times from different perspectives to obtain an understanding of the overall structure of the narrative, the emotional tone, the developmental trajectory of the narrator, and the conceptual network underlying the themes and events.

Ilana Tal's (2004) dissertation explored the meaning of becoming a woman in a non-Western culture through a narrative analysis of first menstruation stories of 27 Ethiopian Jewish women. Tal collected her data through a combination of individual and group interviews, read and reread her transcripts, and extrapolated seven themes as she viewed the narratives as reconstructions of past experiences in the context of the meaning the participants made of them in the present. Tal introduced her Results chapter in this way:

> In this chapter I would like to present the Ethiopian women's stories of first menstruation. I begin with a three-generational story of the Raffi family which introduces the main themes that appear in most of the other stories. This interview, like the rest of my data, was translated from the Hebrew transcripts in a way that closely represents the language of the teller. Further, I omit my questions in order to let the story unfold following the order in which information was provided and the way in which it was described. Following the Raffi interview, I will identify the main themes as they appear in this and other stories that are part of this project. Although I have organized the material according to these themes, I let the women speak for themselves in a way that makes each story comprehensible. My interpretations and discussion will be presented in the following chapter. (p. 89)

The written organization of the Results chapter in qualitative studies varies widely. Usually there is a section that introduces or provides some descriptive overview of the participants or the setting, or both. Although Tal (2004) elected to introduce her themes through the experiences of each respective participant, most qualitative researchers organize the Results chapter around the themes or, as in the following example, organize the chapters into themes derived from an analysis of the data. Description and clarification of the themes is usually highlighted by ample examples from the data and quotations from the participants, although much more is left on the cutting room floor. Sociologists, for instance, are known for offering liberal quotes with interspersed quotations, whereas psychologists tend to provide long summaries of interviewee responses followed by interpretations (Chase, 2005). Qualitative researchers also differ in terms of how authoritative their own voice is in the rendering of the results versus how visible and privileged the voice of the participants is in the dissertation.

Edwina Haring's (2006) grounded theory dissertation on how business expatriates make sense of their experience of returning to their home culture is noteworthy in several ways. Haring was aware of the criticism of some researchers who claim that grounded theory data analysis can be too structured and rule bound. However, Haring appreciated the elements of structured creativity within these rules. The write-up of her Results chapter is heavily oriented toward an impressive amount of theory building. She reserved three separate chapters for describing and exploring the three core concepts in her theory of repatriate sense making: decisioning, escalation-incoherence, and attenuation. These three concepts are key elements that support her core theoretical variable, Between Worlds Tension. The resulting model, which is generated and linked to existing literature in the Results and Discussion sections of her dissertation, can be found in Figure 7.2.

In another qualitative dissertation, Dumas (1989) examined the relationship between daughters and fathers in 18 family-owned businesses. In contrast to Haring, Dumas felt constrained by the relative formalism of a pure grounded theory approach. Her data analysis is predominantly based on grounded theory principles but her presentation contains more of the personal relationship with the participants exemplified by narrative inquiry. She described her data analysis as follows:

Data analysis for each family-business interviewed consisted of unitizing and categorizing the data collected during 40 in depth interviews averaging 2.5 hours each. I categorized these units in an ongoing manner by provisionally categorizing the cards (units) that seemed to relate to the same content. As I did this, I devised propositional statements to characterize each category's properties. I then combined these properties into rules for inclusion in each category. These rules served to justify the inclusion of each card which ultimately remained assigned to a category, to render each category set internally consistent. I then gave each category a title which was an attempt to capture the essence of the rule for inclusion of units in the category. Finally, I reviewed the entire set of categories I had formulated, including the miscellaneous cards. Some of these were eventually discarded as irrelevant. To determine when it was time to stop collecting and processing data, I used the four criteria proposed by Lincoln and Guba (1985): exhaustion of sources; saturation of categories . . . emergence of regularities . . . and overextension. (pp. 207–209)*

SOURCE: *Reprinted with permission of the author.

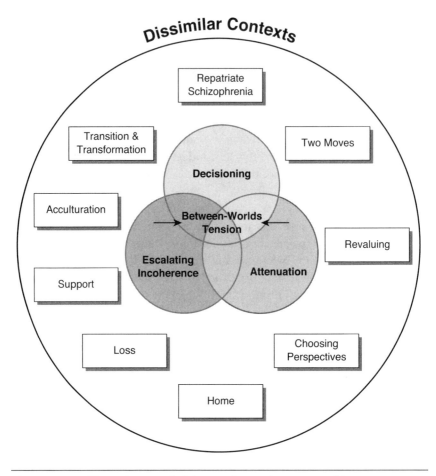

Figure 7.2   Haring's grounded theory of repatriate sense making

SOURCE: Reprinted with permission of the author.

Dumas (1989) found seven constructs that describe the essence of her interviews with fathers and daughters in family-owned businesses. She described these constructs as "intended to portray the situations studied, and to make the complexities of each situation apparent, as well as indicate how these complexities interact" (p. 245). For example, the first construct, Daddy's Little Girl, refers to the "roles assigned to the daughters by their fathers and the daughters themselves" (p. 246):

> These fathers and daughters had no previous point of reference for how to behave when working together. They only had their previous roles of father and daughter as models for how to relate to each other. Therefore the fathers

and daughters interviewed often found working together confusing, unsettling and stressful. As these daughters indicated:

Even though I've been here a long time I still have to kiss him every morning. Otherwise he'll be hurt. I don't think he's made the transition to seeing me as an adult. I'm still his little girl.

I never know whether I'm talking to my dad or my boss! It drives me crazy! My dad too. I just don't know when he expects me to be "daddy's little girl" and when he expects me to be businesslike. That makes it hard on me. (p. 237)

The work of Dumas (1989) illustrates how the results of qualitative analysis may be reported. Following a conceptual definition of the meaning of a category, relevant quotations that illustrate this meaning are presented. Although some authors take the position that a case study report is primarily in written form, others, such as Miles and Huberman (1994), suggest that the use of a wide variety of displays—presenting one's conceptual framework, context of analysis, and results—greatly facilitates the analysis of qualitative data. They provide advice on constructing scatter plots, context charts, causal networks, and causal models. Our students generally choose to use a combination of techniques to present their results, including written, graphic, and tabular displays.

For example, in addition to illustrating the meaning of each construct developed in her analysis, as quoted earlier, Dumas (1989) presented a genogram and organization chart for each family business included in her research. The genogram (see Figure 7.3) presented the family tree as a guide to locating each interviewee's position in the family, and the organization chart (see Figure 7.4) depicted each interviewee's position in the family business.

As a second example, Leon (1991) studied motivation for gang membership among White and Hispanic incarcerated juveniles. Table 7.2 presents a matrix designed to classify descriptions provided by gang members as to reasons for joining a gang. This table is based on the suggestion of Miles and Huberman (1994) to build a matrix display that organizes descriptive data categories around a particular event or experience. This matrix has been completed with a summary statement (an exact quotation could also have been used) that represents the reasons given by each participant, represented by a letter indicating their ethnicity (H or W) and an identification number (1, 2, 3, etc.) that placed the participant in the respective row.

A causal network is a graph displaying the independent and dependent variables in a naturalistic study. Such a graph uses arrows to represent the direction of influence (causality) and makes specific notations regarding

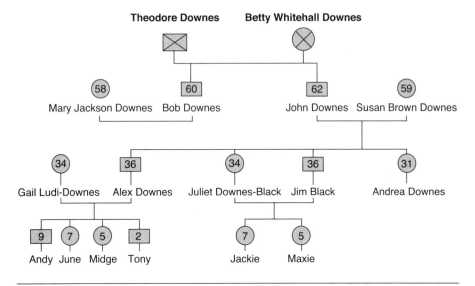

Figure 7.3   Downes' family genogram

SOURCE: From *Daughters in Family-Owned Business: An Applied Systems Perspective* (p. 214), by C. Dumas, 1989, unpublished dissertation, Santa Barbara, CA: Fielding Graduate University. Copyright 1989 by C. Dumas. Reprinted with permission of the author.

the meaning of the connections between the arrows linking the variables in the analysis. This chart may serve as the basis for a conceptual framework or the development of grounded theory. For example, Williams (1989) examined the transition from individualism to social advocacy as experienced by 13 American social advocates. The descriptive model Williams developed from an analysis of interviews contained what Williams called turning points. As Williams stated, "The advocates often reflected upon significant 'markers' in their transitions and how the role of self-directed action at those markers influenced the course of the transition" (p. 240). Figure 7.5 contains Williams's representation of "marking the course," in the transition from individualism to social advocacy.

In sum, both qualitative and quantitative analyses pose the same task for the researcher—making sense of the data. The methods of analyses may differ, the standards on which reliability and validity are judged may not be the same, and the raw data on which analysis is based assumes very different forms; nevertheless, clearly written and documented analytical summaries, the use of tables and graphs, and a careful consideration of the order and logic of presentation serve as the foundation of quality research, regardless of the researcher's method of choice.

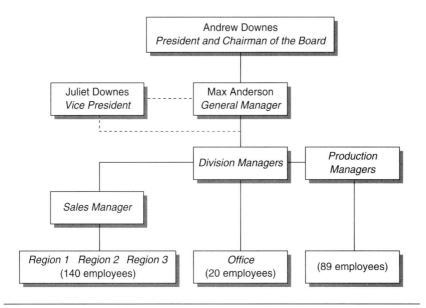

Figure 7.4   Downes, Inc. organization chart

SOURCE: From *Daughters in Family-Owned Business: An Applied Systems Perspective* (p. 214), by C. Dumas, 1989, unpublished dissertation, Santa Barbara, CA: Fielding Graduate University. Copyright 1989 by C. Dumas. Reprinted with permission of the author.

Table 7.2   Reasons for Joining a Gang for White and Hispanic Gang Members

Participants	Reasons
Hispanics	
H1	Grew up with it
H2	All my friends part of it
H3	Grew up with it
Whites	
W1	All my friends part of it
W2	Fun
W3	Hanging out

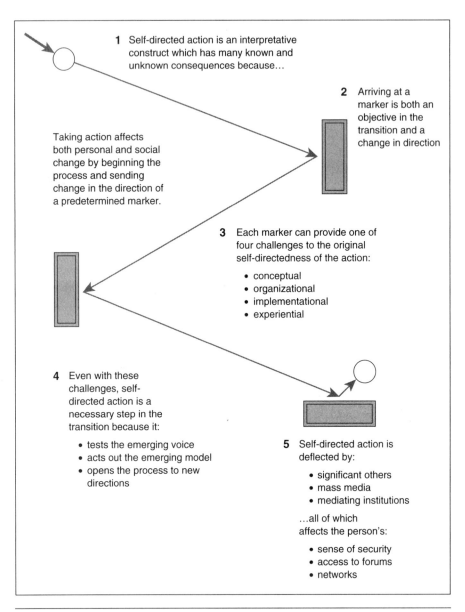

Figure 7.5   Marking the course

SOURCE: From *Finding Voice: The Transition From Individualism to Social Advocacy* (p. 269), by R. L. Williams, 1989, unpublished dissertation, Santa Barbara, CA: Fielding Graduate University. Copyright 1989 by R. L. Williams. Reprinted with permission.

8

Discussion

By the time data have been collected and analyzed and the Results chapter of the dissertation has been completed, proceeding to write the remainder of the dissertation may seem anticlimactic. Consequently, many students do not do justice to the Discussion chapter, and it ends up being less thoughtful and comprehensive than it should be.

The Discussion chapter is an opportunity to move beyond the data and integrate, creatively, the results of your study with existing theory and research. Whereas clear guidelines exist for preparing a Method chapter and Results chapter in terms of content and format, no such formal guidelines exist for writing the Discussion chapter. A good Discussion chapter typically contains the following elements:

1. An overview of the significant findings of the study

2. A consideration of the findings in the light of existing research studies

3. Implications of the study for current theory (except in purely applied studies)

4. A careful examination of findings that fail to support or only partially support the hypotheses

5. Limitations of the study that may affect the validity or the generalizability of the results

6. Recommendations for further research

7. Implications of the study for professional practice or applied settings (optional)

Think back to the research wheel introduced in Chapter 1, which describes how the dissertation process is an evolving shift between deductive and inductive modes of reasoning, from the general to the specific and back again to the general. The Discussion chapter is largely an exercise in inductive thinking, grappling with the specific results of your study and drawing inferences to the world of theory by linking your results with the existing literature. This chapter takes over where the introduction and literature review left off and may be quite similar to them in style and content. Here you are forwarding your conceptual argument on the basis of the obtained data, exploring the meaning of the data from the relationships that have emerged among the variables of the study. You evaluate the extent to which your study answered the questions you posed at the outset, basing your reasoning as much as possible on the data. Look for patterns in the data and see if you can identify multiple lines of evidence toward the same conclusion. As you marshal your own interpretation of the findings, consider the strengths and weaknesses of alternative interpretations from the literature, along with the points of agreement and disagreement between your data and conclusions in comparison with the contributions of others. A good Discussion chapter openly acknowledges and evaluates rival explanations for the results.

It is not sufficient to reiterate the findings of your study, although this is a good place to begin. One popular way of starting the chapter is by reviewing, in turn, the status of each of the hypotheses and research questions of the study now that the data have been collected and examined. Stay focused on a straightforward exposition of what you determined, taking the principal ideas one at a time. In so doing, avoid terminology that is meaningless outside the context of your study, such as referring to "Hypothesis 1" or noting that "the A group scored significantly higher than the B group." Instead, use plain English and refer to the variables by name so that readers unfamiliar with the specific terminology of your study will be able to comprehend the meaning of the results. For example, the following sentence is an accurate restatement of a finding that may have been expressed more technically in the Results chapter: "The teachers who received intensive training in conflict resolution skills were significantly more successful in defusing classroom conflicts than teachers without such training."

Perhaps the most common oversight made in writing the Discussion chapter is a failure to return to the literature to integrate results of the study with other empirical studies examining the same phenomenon. A good discussion embeds each result within the theoretical context that was presented in the literature review. Thus, you need to cite some of the relevant studies that were discussed previously, as well as return to the literature to seek additional ways of understanding your results and to look for confirmatory or disconfirmatory evidence. The kinds of statements that are often found in Discussion chapters are of the following form:

> The results of this study are consistent with Jones's (2003) findings of a nega- tive relationship between learned helplessness and efforts to seek employ- ment and extends his findings to a nonhandicapped population.

> Unlike Smith (2004), who relied on self-report to look for evidence of dissim- ulation, the current study found behavioral evidence that teenagers drink more alcohol than they admit they drink to family members.

Here are some other suggestions for writing an appropriate Discussion chapter, based on common misunderstandings:

1. The data analyses should have been thoroughly presented in the Results chapter. In the same way that the interpretation of findings is not discussed in the Results chapter, secondary analyses of data are not presented in the Discussion chapter.

2. Do not repeat and reformulate points that have already been made. This chapter is frequently regarded as a summary of specific findings. On the contrary, discuss the findings rather than describe them again. Focus on explaining how your data can be used to infer broader conceptual and theoretical statements by analyzing the relationships among your specific variables. The following is an example of such a generalized statement: "On the basis of these findings, it appears that loss of a parent leads to an increased risk of adolescent suicidal behavior only in those families that fail to communicate openly about their grief." Avoid speculation that is not related to empirical data or theory.

3. A common tendency among students is to list all possible criticisms of a study and to do so with an apologetic tone. It is much better to accept the study for what it is. If there are fundamental criticisms, such as attributing negative findings to a major flaw in the design of the study, it is reasonable to question why the study was conducted. At the same time, it is not unrea- sonable to identify flaws that were unintended or were delimitations in the study. Do so only in the context of evaluating the relative trustworthiness of your conclusions.

4. A parallel tendency is to offer a long list of recommendations for future research. This is inadvisable. It is much better to focus on one or two major recommendations. For example, to suggest that a study be extended to males, to brunettes, to 13- to 16-year-olds, and so on is a waste of space. It is preferable to suggest the next reasonable step in forwarding a program of research in a given area of study.

5. Be careful not to offer suggestions for future research that can be addressed easily within your own study. These indicate that you have not done a thorough job of examining your own data.

6. Do not include trivial details or ramble aimlessly around the topic. This is an opportunity to think creatively, but like all other chapters of the dissertation, the Discussion chapter should be logical and focused. One specific way to maintain the balanced perspective of the scientific investigator is to avoid melodramatic or intemperate language, such as the terms *amazing* or even *interesting* or *important*. Allow your data and conclusions to be judged on their own merits and not on your amplification of them.

The mandate to present and discuss significant findings is clear. What do you do, however, when results are not statistically significant or "nearly" significant? One cannot pretend that a nonsignificant finding is significant and, strictly speaking, it should not be treated as such. On the other hand, conventions regarding significance levels (e.g., .05, .01) are somewhat arbitrary, and each field seems to have its own prevailing standards for acknowledging or ignoring trends that do not quite live up to these a priori levels. Our own position is that the size of a finding—expressed, for example, in the percentage of variance accounted for between two variables or the size of a correlation coefficient—ultimately is more informative than the presence or absence of a statistically significant effect. This is another reason not to be blinded by statistics, in terms of either overestimating or underestimating the meaning of a particular result.

Students may become particularly disheartened about nonsignificant results, when hypotheses are not validated. But nonsignificant results need not imply an inferior study. The research enterprise is a treasure hunt with an unknown outcome, and if a study is performed according to acceptable standards, negative results ought not invalidate the legitimacy of the research. Prior to collecting data it is important to anticipate how to explain the full range of empirical outcomes so that no result will be a bad result. Any result should be conceptually informative, in the sense of forwarding knowledge in a field. Negative results should, however, signal the need for a complete inquiry. Such results typically can be attributed to methodological or theoretical shortcomings. An opportunity to challenge commonly understood theory can serve as a major research contribution. Methodological shortcomings may be more difficult to handle because it is presumed that they would have been attended to in designing the study. Nevertheless, there is usually some disparity between the best-laid plans and real-world events. Even the most meticulous researcher may not correctly anticipate mailings that go awry, research assistants who quit, participants who refuse to complete a posttest, and equipment that malfunctions.

A Discussion chapter in a qualitative dissertation performs a similar function: drawing implications from the results of the study to the worlds of theory and practice. As previously discussed, some researchers or some disciplines may choose to incorporate the discussion into the Results chapter, or even into a series of results chapters. Most qualitative dissertations we have seen, regardless of the particular orientation to method, have a separate chapter that is referred to as the Discussion chapter. It could be argued that a discussion of the implications of the findings is even more important in qualitative studies than in quantitative ones. The hypotheses within an experimental or quasi-experimental study are always introduced as emerging from theory and the relevant empirical literature. In most qualitative studies, there are no hypotheses as such, and the link between the research questions and the theoretical and research literature is not always as evident. The theory emerges inductively, after the data have been collected and explored. Thus, there is a compelling need to discuss the implications of new theoretical propositions and place them within the context of the existent empirical and theoretical literature at the conclusion of the study. This, as we indicated, is the precise function of the Discussion chapter.

Dissertations do not typically contain a Summary section, although a subheading titled "Conclusions" is not unusual.[1] This is the place to summarize concisely the principal implications of your findings in a few paragraphs. Resist the temptation to use the final pages of the dissertation as a pulpit to lament the sorry state of affairs in your area of study, your discipline, or the world at large, or, conversely, to rhapsodize about the terrific opportunities afforded to anyone willing or able to capitalize on the significance of your study. An inspired quotation or eloquent turn of phrase can add a nice touch to the conclusion, but there is a difference between forceful writing and gratuitous clichés.

Abstract

Every dissertation requires an Abstract, which is essentially a brief summary of the project placed before the introductory chapter. The clarity of the Abstract should not be overlooked because it is this section of the dissertation that is generally reproduced in computerized databases as well as in *Dissertation Abstracts*. It is also the section of the dissertation that is usually read first, and it may be the only section that is read. The Abstract therefore should accurately reflect the content of the dissertation and be written in a way that makes the study seem articulate and scholarly.

It is relatively easy to put together a good Abstract after a dissertation is completed. You can almost lift two or three key sentences from each chapter of the dissertation to assemble the abstract because the Abstract needs to provide an overview of the study's purpose, method, results, and implications. It is important to be precise and specific and not to include content that is not present in the dissertation itself.

Dissertation abstracts are generally about 150 words in length and include short statements summarizing the research problem, the participants, the method and procedures (avoiding abbreviations and idiosyncratic terms), the results, and the conclusions and implications. Write in the past tense to report specific manipulations and procedures you employed in the study, and the present tense to describe conclusions based on the findings. Here is a sample abstract adapted from a quantitative dissertation (Wegmann, 1992, p. 7):

This study carries forward the exploration of a link between authoritarianism and deficits in cognitive functioning. The subjects were 50 community college students and 29 registered voters recently assigned to jury duty. All participants completed Altemeyer's Right-Wing Authoritarianism Scale and three early-stage information processing tasks: (a) content recognition of a news article 2 minutes after exposure, (b) content recognition of a recorded debate 2 minutes after exposure, and (c) the selection of correct inferential statements in a set of brief paragraphs taken from the Watson & Glasser Critical Thinking Appraisal Test. The experimental setting utilized an interactive computer program that guided and monitored each subject through all phases of the study. When material to be recalled was in written format, authoritarianism interacted with reading skills to limit the recognition and retention of new information. When material was presented orally, retention was significantly affected by authoritarianism. Subjects in both samples who scored high in authoritarianism also made significantly more inferential errors. The data strongly suggest that authoritarianism covaries significantly with a lessened ability to process incoming cognitive information with reasonable care and accuracy.

Here is another example, this one based on a qualitative dissertation (Tal, 2004):

This narrative research explored the meaning making of first menstruation experiences reconstructed by Ethiopian Jewish women in Israel. Narratives of 19 women, aged 19–64, were collected in individual and group interviews.

Psychoanalytic and developmental theories, as well as feminist and anthropological research were used to examine various ways of understanding the place of first menstruation in the transition from girlhood to womanhood. This study made clear that female identity formed at the time of puberty is connected to the meaning made of menarche. An analysis of coming of age in a pre-industrial non-Western culture such as the Beta Israel, demonstrates that the radical (biological) changes a girl goes through at menarche receive much of their meaning from the script offered to her by her culture. In this culture, there is a close association between first menstruation and motherhood; thus, womanhood and motherhood are conflated. Sexuality was expressed indirectly as dangers and fears of violation. It is recommended that a similar approach be used to collect girls' and women's stories about their personal experiences in order to see how they make meaning of becoming and being a woman. (p. 3)

Title

It may seem strange to position a statement about writing the title of the dissertation in the last chapter. Dissertations often have working titles that are amended when the study is completed. We are frequently amazed at how little attention students give to composing a clear and accurate title. This is in spite of the fact that the title is the vehicle that carries the meaning of the dissertation into the professional community. In constructing a title, follow these steps:

1. Include all necessary key words to correctly and fully convey the content of the study.

2. Delete all words that are redundant or do not contribute to the essential meaning.

3. Order the words to reflect accurately the meaning you intend.

Here are some examples of titles that are problematic:

A Study of Information Processing Deficits of the Authoritarian Personality.

The phrase "A study of" is redundant and unnecessary.

Better: Information Processing Deficits of the Authoritarian Personality.

The Effect of Sexually Abused Children Testifying in Court.

The word order makes it unclear who is being affected by the testimony.

An alternative order: The Effect of Testifying in Court on Sexually Abused Children.

An Exploratory Study of the Interrelationship of Loneliness, Obesity, and Other Selected Variables Within Two of Bruch's Obesity Subgroups and a Control Group.

Much too long and cumbersome. Try to reduce your title to no more than 12 to 15 key words that summarize the main idea.

For example: The Role of Loneliness in Bruch's Obesity Subgroups.

Predicting Acting-Out Behavior From the Achromatic-Chromatic HTP.

Do not use abbreviations in the title. Accurate indexing of the dissertation depends on writing out all variables.

Better: Predicting Acting-Out Behavior From the Achromatic-Chromatic House-Tree-Person Test.

Note

1. In some settings, the last chapter of the dissertation is titled Conclusions, although this has not been our personal experience. This chapter would be devoted to summarizing the findings and their implications to theory and to practice.

BOX 8.1   Student Suggestions

1. You can't always rely on standard manuscript and publication guides to give you the exact format needed for your dissertation. Because dissertations are submitted to your graduate school, and not to a journal, you need to consult your program's requirements for preparing the final manuscript. There seem to be departmental differences, for example, on whether or not to include a Summary, whether or not to include applications in the Discussion chapter, and how to format references.

2. It was tempting to think of my dissertation as finished when the data were collected and analyzed. I had to get my second wind to write the Discussion chapter. I recommend allotting sufficient time and energy to think about the meaning and implication of your results. Don't set unrealistic deadlines for completing this chapter! In many ways, it becomes the most important chapter of the dissertation.

3. I used a private journal to process my frustrations, discoveries, and annoyances, and I kept a dated log for each conversation I had with my chair and others on my committee assisting with the process. This empowered me, especially when I needed to get past emotions impeding the process. Sometimes I would jot down things to remember to do later when I had more time. Because anything about my dissertation always went into my journal, I always had a central location where I could find insights when trying to decide my next step.

PART III

Working With Process

What You Need to Know to Make the Dissertation Easier

9

Overcoming Barriers

Becoming an Expert While Controlling Your Own Destiny

T hroughout this book, we intersperse firsthand suggestions from some of our students to streamline the task of completing the dissertation successfully. In this chapter, we take up six specific types of issues that, when unattended, can lead to complications in the dissertation process:

- Working with your committee
- Emotional blocks
- Task blocks
- Organization issues
- Dependence on others for data collection and data analysis
- Dissertation orals

Awareness of these issues can go a long way toward the prevention of subsequent trouble.

Working With Your Committee

Each dissertation committee becomes its own social system. Under the best circumstances, all committee members work together smoothly, communicate frequently, and support the student through the dissertation process. That's the ideal scenario. In real life, things rarely happen so fortuitously. Committee members disagree and squabble, each member has his or her personal axe to grind, and at least one recalcitrant or neglectful member holds up the completion of the dissertation in an inexcusable fashion.

Students in most graduate programs have the opportunity to choose most, if not all, of their committee members. Certainly the rumor mill in most academic departments provides enough data about this selection process. It may be tempting for you to choose "easy" committee members, that is, faculty who may let you get away with an inferior product and not offer much in the way of feedback—helpful or not. In our experience, there is little advantage in avoiding difficult committee members, if by *difficult* one means not obstinate or unreasonable but those who give rigorous feedback and demand the highest quality product. We have found that students who are willing to invite, insist on, and manage thorough, sometimes critical feedback early in the dissertation process end up not only with superior studies but also with proposals that glide smoothly through almost any knowledgeable reader's hands in the later stages. The way to get through many challenging educational hurdles, as well as situations in life, is to manage negative feedback with grace and nondefensiveness. It is a skill worth cultivating.

We would be remiss, however, if we did not note that one can cogently argue for choosing a very competent and supportive chair, working closely with that person, and selecting additional committee members who are not likely to provide much substantive input and, hence, slow down the dissertation process. With this cynical but possibly pragmatic strategy, you would be encouraged to circulate drafts of the dissertation to committee members as infrequently as possible and rely on the wisdom and support of your chairperson for major input and guidance. Whether or not this strategy seems appropriate should depend in part on your assessment of the political climate of your department.

One aspect of the skill of managing feedback is how to deal with instances when committee members differ in opinion and make contradictory recommendations. Certainly faculty members have their own tastes and preferences and their own vested interests. One committee member suggests using a particular scale, whereas a second committee member nominates another scale; one person says to delete a section, whereas another person says to expand it. This is to be expected, and no committee will ever be in total agreement. You need to stay in charge of your own project and negotiate with each faculty member. It is vital to know which suggestions are critical and which are window dressing. There is no point in being obstinate about making minor changes to please someone who possesses a vote on your academic future. At the same time, you need to maintain your integrity on important issues and argue them persuasively, based on facts and logic, not emotional resistance. When committee members have divergent opinions that seem nonnegotiable, it is time to appeal to your chairperson for support and perhaps to turn the dilemma over to the faculty to resolve. Never, however, play faculty members against one another.

The constitution of the committee is significant. Always begin by selecting a chairperson and then consulting with your chair before inviting the other members. All faculty members have a "short list" of colleagues they either enjoy working with or abhor working with. In a general sense, you want committee members who will promote rather than hinder your progress. Beyond this universal guideline, one way to think about the composition of a dissertation or thesis committee is in terms of the roles the participants play. If your study concerns the fears of Asian immigrant children, it makes sense to have at least one committee member representing expertise in each of the major variables: fears, phobias, or anxieties; Asian culture and immigration; and children or developmental issues. If you are fortunate, all of these characteristics may be wrapped up in one or two persons (such as when a study is derived from a faculty mentor's ongoing research program), but it may require three distinct individuals. Be sure to include at least one committee member who has sufficient expertise in the kind of methodology and analysis procedures you anticipate using. Finally, do not forget the important need for social support in the dissertation process. We suggest the inclusion of a committee member who can provide some emotional sustenance during inevitable periods of frustration.

Be mindful of typical committee procedures. Remember that faculty members are inevitably busy people, so you must provide sufficient lead time for them to make responses to drafts and inquiries. It is very reasonable to ask when a response might be forthcoming. Furthermore, you cannot assume that faculty will guard your proposal or dissertation drafts with the same vigilance that you would. Make copies of all documents under all circumstances, including backups of computer files. Our experience, exemplified by a student who lost all existing copies of her dissertation materials in a fire, suggests that backup copies should be stored in a different location. It is truly tragic whenever a manuscript or data are "lost" and there is no surviving record.

Emotional Blocks

We have discovered that technical supervision and consultation with graduate students is not the only kind of support instrumental in facilitating successful completion of the dissertation. The task itself also has a way of stimulating emotional issues that can, if overlooked, stymie the process. It is not unusual for the dissertation process to elicit all kinds of blows to self-esteem. Along the way it is quite common to feel that you will never reach the end of the trail. Some students don't know when to give up on a dead-end idea and switch trails to another topic, whereas other students fail to stay on a trail long enough to negotiate its necessary pitfalls. It is not unusual to question a choice of topic or method and to torture oneself about it. If you are overly compulsive, you will inevitably think that you have left something out, and the dissertation will never feel finished. Students need to maintain a perspective that allows them to know that frustration is predictable and that this too will end. One way of maintaining this perspective is to do the dissertation in small steps by selecting definable targets along the way and by calling on others for emotional support when feelings of failure loom large.

The challenge of completing an acceptable dissertation may also invoke deeply felt beliefs about incompetence and the inability to master this task. In our experience, the dissertation process more often than not stirs up a student's most basic behavioral patterns and emotional vulnerabilities. Here is a sample of the kinds of issues that have been presented by students we know:

- The belief that completing the dissertation and obtaining the doctoral degree will be a sign of disloyalty to parents and family members who never came nearly so far in their own educational pursuits
- The belief that completing the dissertation and obtaining the doctoral degree will bring a greater sense of responsibility and promise of future achievements that seem scary and unattainable
- The belief that completing the dissertation and obtaining the doctoral degree will cost a marriage or relationship due to the threat of living with a "doctor," especially if one is a woman
- The belief that the intelligence it takes to complete a dissertation is way beyond one's capacities
- The belief that one is an impostor, only "pretending" to be capable of completing a dissertation
- The belief that there is no end in sight, that the dissertation will never be accepted as complete
- The belief that one will have to give up moral ideals and sell one's soul to complete the dissertation

This list of beliefs may seem trivial or inappropriate for students at the doctoral level of graduate education. On the contrary, we are convinced that these feelings and attitudes are more common than we usually admit and that they frequently stand in the way of progress on the dissertation. In our program, we use supervision groups that encourage students to share not only their substantive research ideas with one another and with faculty but also their fears and doubts about themselves in the process. We have found that sensitive exploration of these blocks can often forward the process as much as technical support. We have also been gratified to discover that students can generally identify and access significant coping skills that they may never have realized they possessed.

Task Blocks

Writing a dissertation is a time-consuming, fundamentally lonely act that generally takes in the neighborhood of 2 years from start to finish. No matter how secure your social support system, you need to generate great persistence to complete it. Some compulsivity helps, but so does preparatory organization of space and time.

A block that is part emotional and part cognitive is the inability to manage time. It should come as no surprise that our universities are full of ABD's, that is, students who have satisfactorily completed all requirements for the doctoral degree other than the dissertation (All But Dissertation). One of the most common reasons for this state of affairs is the inability to deal with time constraints adequately. To be sure, the dissertation is the singular most time-consuming graduate requirement. Because the completion of courses generally relies on the structure of a graduate program, the indeterminate freedom of the dissertation may be a cause for alarm and paralysis. Here are some tips for arranging your life to conform to the task of completing the dissertation:

1. *Give yourself privacy and quiet.* Arrange a space or area of your house or office that is identified with studying and only studying. This is particularly important in the dissertation process. Make this space sacred so that you engage in other tasks, such as writing bills and talking on the telephone, in other areas. This is a straightforward application of the behavioral principle of stimulus control.

2. *Use the principle of successive approximations to divide it into manageable slices.* Taken as a whole, a dissertation can seem like a forbidding and overwhelming challenge. Tackle the dissertation one step at a time—the Review of the Literature, the research question and Statement of the Problem, and the Method, Results, and Discussion chapters.

3. *Get your thoughts on paper.* Don't allow yourself to obsess and mull over ideas too long without putting those ideas in type. Seeing words on a page or on a computer screen has a way of generating momentum. Don't worry at the outset if your words aren't polished. The important thing is to develop a pattern of producing some output on a regular basis.

4. *Talk your ideas over with others.* Some people, especially extroverted individuals, seem to do their best thinking through discussing ideas with others. Other people prefer to get away by themselves and listen to their own inner voice. In either case, discussing your ideas with friends and colleagues can help you view your work from a fresh perspective and keep you motivated.

5. *Establish a regular weekly schedule that allows for several hours of concentrated dissertation time.* Many of our students recommend reserving some time each day for the dissertation. Your own schedule will, of course, be influenced by your other commitments, but the important thing is the structure and the regularity. A firm schedule will help guide you through the inevitable stages when ideas are not forthcoming, when obstacles arise, or when temptations lure you to greener pastures.

6. *Recognize that even the most productive plow horse needs a break now and then.* Give yourself some time off for enjoyable distractions and do so in a way that reinforces progress. If you find yourself violating your schedule and taking a brief vacation from your dissertation, be gentle and forgiving.

Inevitably, many ordinary life activities will be put on hold during the dissertation. It is crucial to be sensitive to family members because you will no doubt have to negotiate time off from normal responsibilities and contact with them. In our experience, when students graduate with their doctoral degrees, they are most appreciative of the support and tolerance of their family members in dealing with the impact of the dissertation. Moreover, a negative, impatient spouse can sabotage your progress. One way of encouraging ongoing support is to keep one's partner fully informed about the status and content of the dissertation. Otherwise, it is too easy to feel left out and neglected when a significant other is engaged in a scholarly project that may seem arcane, trivial, or simply interminable.

Getting Organized: A Case Study

One of the major tasks of completing a dissertation is maintaining control of the sheer magnitude of the project. You may be testing multiple hypotheses, with different instruments, and using numerous statistical analyses. In this section, we report on how one student managed the project. This student, Helen Barrett, PhD, lives in Alaska and was unable to meet with her committee on a regular basis. Therefore, it was extremely important for her to develop clear and informative presentations of research design and hypothesis-testing procedures. Barrett was interested in the relationship between learning style, adult self-directed learning, and personal computer competency. Her dissertation (Barrett, 1990) involved the testing of 10 hypotheses and a number of subsidiary questions. Data collection required questionnaire and interview strategies, and data analysis included both quantitative and qualitative methods. To make her plans clear to both her committee and herself, Barrett developed two tables, which are reproduced in their entirety here. The first, "Hypotheses, Instruments, and Statistical Analysis," is presented as Table 9.1. Note that the hypotheses are included in their entirety in the left-hand column and form the rows of the table. Barrett used four instruments plus personal interviews to obtain her data. These instruments consisted of a questionnaire that Barrett designed to assess specific aspects of computer use, a Personal Computer Competency Inventory (PCCI), the Kolb Learning Style Inventory (LSI), the Self-Directed Learning Readiness Scale (SDLRS), and personal interviews. Each of these is listed in columns following the hypotheses. By examining the cells formed by crossing the hypothesis with the instruments, one can determine which instruments will be used to examine which hypotheses. The pound sign (#) is used to indicate a specific item number on an instrument. If particular subscales or factor scores derived from an instrument are used, these are indicated in the cells. Following the instruments is a column of variables, which lists the independent and dependent variable for each hypothesis. In the last column, Barrett presented the type of statistical analysis that will be used to examine each hypothesis. By examining this table one can determine exactly how Barrett proposed to test each hypothesis in her research. This was not all that Barrett did to make things simple for her committee. She also developed an "Overview of Research Design," which is presented as Table 9.2.

In Table 9.2, the columns are formed by the concepts of her study (learner characteristics, computer competency, learning style, self-directed learning, and learning strategies). For each major concept, Barrett provided the instrument to be used, the type of data gathered, and the type of scores produced. The remaining space was used to present her proposal for a final synthesis and summary of the findings.

We have not polished these tables to make them acceptable for presentation in this book; they are presented exactly as Barrett constructed them. These tables allowed Barrett, committee members, statistical consultants,

(Text continued on page 216)

212

Table 9.1   Hypotheses and Statistical Analysis

Hypotheses	GQ	PCCI	LSI	SDLR	Variables	Stat Test
H1.1: Competent computer users spend more than 70% of the time learning their computer using self-direct learning strategies	#17				IND = Level of PCC DEP = % of Time SDL	Mean & St. Dev.
H1.2: Competent computer users will have a higher level of self-directed learning readiness than beginning computer users				Total Score	IND = Level of PCC DEP = SDLRS Score	ANOVA
H1.3: Computer users with intrinsic motivation to learn how to use a personal computer have a higher relative level of personal computer competency than those with extrinsic motivation to learn	#3 & 4	Total Score			IND = Source of Motivation DEP = PCCI Score	ANOVA & Chi-Square
H1.4: Computer users with a foundation for learning will have a higher level of personal computer competence	#9, 5, 6, 10, 31, 30, 15, 16, 21	Total Score			IND = Prior Experience, Sources of Assistance, Hours spent, typing speed, user group, PC ownership	ANOVA & Chi-Square

Hypotheses	GQ	PCCI	LSI	SDLR	Variables	Stat Test
H2.1: Computer users with an active learning style will have a higher relative level of personal computer competence than those with a reflective learning style		Total Score	AE-RO		IND = Learning Style DEP = PCCI Score	ANOVA
H2.2: Computer users with an abstract learning style will have a higher relative level of personal computer competence than those with a concrete learning style		Total Score	AC-CE		IND = Learning Style DEP = PCCI Score	ANOVA
Subsidiary Question: What is the relationship between learning style and readiness for self-directed learning?			Four Styles	Total Score	IND = Learning Style DEP = SDLRS Score	ANOVA
H3.1: Computer users with a concrete learning style preference will favor the Graphical User Interface	#33		AC-CE		IND = Learning Style DEP = Interface Preference	Chi-Square
H3.2: Computer users with an abstract learning style preference will favor the text-based user interface	#33		AC-CE		IND = Learning Style DEP = Interface Preference	Chi-Square

(Continued)

Table 9.1 (Continued)

Hypotheses	GQ	PCCI	LSI	SDLR	Variables	Stat Test
H3.3: Competent users of graphical user interface computers will use more types of applications than competent users of text-based systems	#8	No. of Apps			IND = Level Expertise DEP = # of Applications	2-Way ANOVA
H3.4: The type of computer learned has a greater impact on learning strategies than the learners' preferred learning style	#10, 18, 14	Total Score	AC-CE		IND = Learning Style IND = Type of Interface DEP = Strategies	ANOVA Chi-Square

SOURCE: From Barrett (1990). Reprinted with permission of the author.

NOTE: GQ = General Questionnaire; LSI = Learning Styles Inventory; SDLR = Self-Directed Learning Readiness; IND = Independent Variable; DEP = Dependent Variable; PCCI = Personal Computer Competency Inventory.

Table 9.2   Overview of Research Design

Adult Self-Directed Learning, Personal Computer Competency and Learning Style: Models for More Effective Learning Components of Study

	Learner Characteristics	*Personal Computer Competency*	*Learning Style*	*Self-Directed Learning Readiness*	*Learning Strategies*
Instrument	General Questionnaire	PCCI Bersch/Barrett Personal Computer Competency Inventory	LSI Kolb Learning Style Instrument	SDLRS Self-Directed Learning Readiness Scale	Optional Additional Questions
Type of Data Gathered	Quantitative Demographic Data	Quantitative (Single response on list of 60 competencies)	Quantitative (12 questions with forced responses to 4 words/phrases)	Quantitative (58 Likert Scale responses)	Qualitative Responses to open-ended questions
Type of Scores Produced	Single item indicators	Total Score plus ten clusters of computer application skills	Two polarity scores (AE-RO and AC-CE) plus one of four Learning Styles	Total Score plus eight Self-Directed Learning Factors	Analysis of responses by question

Final Synthesis and Summary of Findings:

1. Report findings related to hypotheses.
2. List of questions found to warrant further study.
3. Graphic model of learning process.
4. Suggested methods for "learning how to learn" personal computers.

SOURCE: From *Adult Self-Directed Learning, Personal Computer Competency and Learning Style: Models for More Effective Learning*, by H. D. Barrett, 1990. Unpublished doctoral dissertation, Fielding Graduate University, Santa Barbara, CA. Reprinted with permission of the author.

(Text continued from page 211)

and anyone else with an interest in this research to obtain immediately a picture of the study in question. We offer this example as a model for use in making your own research clear to yourself and to others.

Collecting and Analyzing Data: Depending on Others

It is one thing to control your own behavior and quite something else to manage the behavior of others. There are at least two occasions when helpers or consultants predictably may become involved in the dissertation. One is in setting up the study and collecting the data; the other is in analyzing the data. Many dissertations require the cooperation of agencies and institutions, particularly to access pools of available and suitable participants.

Sometimes it is possible to graft a dissertation onto an ongoing research project of greater scope and magnitude. There is much to be said for this strategy. Much of the best research in any field is collaborative and involves a team of professionals coming together to complete a set of studies. If someone is currently engaged in a large research project, particularly one with grant funding and institutional support, that can be a great advantage. A pool of participants is available and it is often possible to add some additional measures or interventions to those that already constitute the focus of the study. If you choose and have the opportunity to go this route, a number of considerations should be kept in mind:

1. Remember that a doctoral dissertation must be your own project, both in concept and in design, and that you need to retain ownership over it. This means that the data must be available to you to analyze as you see fit and that you must be free to describe whatever conclusions you reach, regardless of anyone's special interest or investment in the project as a whole. Do not rely on vague promises made in passing, particularly by those not in a position to guarantee you the use of a data set or population. Make your needs explicit, and elicit promises regarding your involvement in a project and your use of the data from those authorized to make such promises. You also need to have the freedom to be able to publish the results in your own name.

2. Sometimes the scheduling of someone else's study may not conform to your own needs. We have found that students who collect dissertation or thesis data prior to having a completed, approved proposal do so at considerable risk. Method and procedures need to be in place and agreed on prior to the start of data collection. This may be difficult if you are joining a larger study. It can also be tricky if your need for collecting data is governed by external considerations, such as the availability of schoolchildren at the beginning of

the academic year or the established starting date of a program or group that you need to evaluate. The antidote to this problem is to plan ahead and assume that it will take longer to establish procedures than you imagine. Some very good research studies capitalize on the occurrence of unanticipated events that are ripe for data collection (e.g., a political revolution or ecological disaster), but they rarely result in doctoral dissertations.

3. It should go without saying that you and your committee are the final arbiters of the research questions and procedures of your study. It is not unusual for other people's large-scale projects to use measures or procedures that do not exactly measure what you intend to measure. Be certain that you have the freedom to make methodological changes that are critical to ensuring the quality of your study. If you determine, for example, that the only measure of weight loss available to you is not a sufficient indicator of fitness, the setting for your proposed study may not be right.

A different kind of issue concerns the employment of peers to collect or code data. Many students have had the experience of serving in this role as research assistants. When graduate students use research assistants, however, they may not hold the same authority over them as do professors. In our experience, raters and other assistants often quit or do not reliably follow through on their commitments. It pays to be careful and conscientious in hiring assistants and have backup strategies available if plans go awry. It is also important to train and supervise assistants thoroughly at every step of the process. What seems obvious to you, being totally immersed in your study, may not be so obvious to someone else. A frequent problem is obtaining low interrater reliability on coding data because the raters have not been trained sufficiently.

Finally, whenever you collaborate with faculty or consultants, remember to take and maintain responsibility regarding your own dissertation project. We have witnessed many instances where students, either unwittingly or manipulatively, attempt to shift responsibility to others for problems for which they are responsible. In one prime example, a student had a fixed deadline for completing her dissertation proposal to receive committee authorization to collect data that could only be obtained within a 1-week time period to avoid a 6-month wait for another data collection opportunity. She promised her committee that she would complete her proposal 3 weeks in advance of this date. As the deadline rolled by, she made panicked telephone calls to her committee to move the deadline forward. The committee agreed to extend the deadline by a week. After expressing the need for "just a few more days," the student submitted her proposal 10 days before the collection date. Subsequently, one committee member believed that the student needed to make some changes in her data collection procedures, but there wasn't sufficient time to make the revisions within her window of opportunity. Rather than respecting the extra effort the committee member made to read the draft of her proposal, she summarized the situation by claiming, "Dr. X wouldn't let me collect data." We urge you to avoid this distortion of responsibility attribution in all its numerous forms.

Students also shift blame to consultants, particularly statistical consultants, when things go wrong. Although it is sometimes helpful to rely on an experienced statistician to "crunch your numbers," you should never lose control of your analysis to this person, despite the appeal of discharging this responsibility to someone else and thus making that person accountable. At times it may be proper to use statistical consultants to conduct analyses and assist with the interpretation of results, but this should not be seen as a means of avoiding the need to learn and apply statistics. Take direct responsibility for all phases of the data collection and analysis process and never place yourself in the position of confessing, "I don't know. My consultant was in charge."

Dissertation Orals

The tradition of the final oral defense of the doctoral dissertation is long-standing and likely to engender some anxiety in most doctoral students. The defense ranges from a congenial ritual in which the student publicly presents his or her findings to an assemblage of receptive "colleagues" to a more excruciating examination of the quality of the dissertation and grilling of the candidate by an unsympathetic faculty committee. In our view, no student should be allowed to schedule a final dissertation oral defense if the dissertation is not regarded as complete by the committee. Consequently, part of the function of the defense is a formal "coming out" of the student into the community of scholars, a celebration of the completion of a major scholarly achievement, and a symbolic rite of passage to the awarding of the doctorate. In the best of cases, the oral defense is an opportunity to think about and articulate the implications of your study to your own discipline and to be challenged by your committee to claim your right to sit among them as an acknowledged expert in your field of study.

You can make a number of reasonable preparations to make the experience a positive one. Certainly, being fully familiar with your study is crucial. It is likely that by the time of the oral defense you will be a leading authority on your particular topic. The more familiar you are with the details of your study, including the relevant literature in the area, the more you will appear as the expert. The role that the committee can rightly play is to provide some new lenses through which to view your work because it is likely that by this time you have stood so close to your own study that it may be difficult to gain perspective and appreciate it from other vantage points.

In the best of circumstances, your committee will be aligned with your own goals of presenting your study as a colleague-to-be. Sometimes, unfortunately, the orals become an opportunity for faculty to build up their own egos at your expense. One recommendation for meeting this challenge is to take control of the situation as much as possible. One student we know recounts her attempt to manage her anxiety about the oral defense of her dissertation:

> In order to deal with my anxiety about my dissertation oral exam I decided to become proactive rather than reactive. I arrived at the room for the orals early and rearranged the furniture to suit me. Then I greeted my committee one by one when they entered the room. I started to feel like I had invited them to an event that I was hosting! It really worked in terms of minimizing my anxiety and taking me out of the "victim" position.

Typically, students are asked to spend anywhere from 10 to 45 minutes providing an overview of their study at the outset of the orals. Think carefully about this task beforehand. Try to boil your presentation down to the essentials so that you do not overwhelm your audience with minutiae. Audiovisual tools are almost imperative as aids to help organize and illustrate a presentation. With this in mind, it's time to put away your old slides and overheads and become proficient in PowerPoint or similar computer software programs. Do not plan to chew up your allotted time with a long, drawn-out oral presentation in the hope that there will be no time for questions. Your committee will be suspicious of a presentation that details endless tables and results, without making the theoretical foundation and contribution of the dissertation to the field of study a major focus. Your committee is too smart for time-wasting presentations and will assume that you are insufficiently knowledgeable for meaningful discussion of your work.

The presentation of the summary of the study is followed by questions and comments from the various committee members. On the basis of these comments, which can be benign or intimidating, the committee will determine their recommendations. In the best of circumstances, these rounds of questions can generate lively and enjoyable discussion about the study and the topic that will further establish your credibility as a professional. The more you can frame the final oral defense of the dissertation as an opportunity to present your research publicly, the better the experience is likely to be. The more you take a proactive, nondefensive position, the less likely it is for your committee to humiliate you. Count on being asked a few questions you will not be able to answer. That does not mean the end of the world. It may even be wise to "save something for the committee" so that they can make an acknowledged contribution to the completion of the project.

The most likely outcome of any dissertation orals is a pass with the request for minor revisions. Minor revisions are changes to the dissertation that do not impugn the central thesis, perhaps some additions to the bibliography, some further analyses, or some elaborated discussion. Major changes are more substantive alterations to theory and method and thus are more troublesome. The general antidote to the request for major changes is to keep your committee fully informed about the dissertation throughout the process by inviting them to read every chapter as it comes off the press. The more you request feedback during the 2 years or so of dissertation work, the less likely it is that a committee member will sabotage the entire dissertation at the orals stage. Keep a detailed record of when you send each chapter, to whom you sent it, and when and if they responded. It is not impolite to remind a faculty member that you have not received a response, but allow sufficient time and don't bug your committee with daily mundane questions and requests. Be wary of the committee member who remains on the fringe of your project and does not have time to read your dissertation. This person is likely to ask questions about statistics because asking these sorts of questions does not require knowledge of your field or even the content of your dissertation. Have a good understanding of why you used each statistic for each analysis. Then you will be prepared for questions such as, "Well, Mr. Jones, why did you use an analysis of variance to assess Hypothesis 3?"

There tends to be a significant letdown for students at the conclusion of successfully defending their dissertations. Often this emotional letdown includes not wanting to see the dissertation ever again. We encourage you to respond to the request for changes as soon as possible. Otherwise, completion of the dissertation may drag on interminably.

The doctoral dissertation is likely to be the singular most ambitious research project of most social scientists' careers. As such, it not only has the potential for providing entrée into a field of professional practice and scholarship but also serves as an ongoing source of self-esteem and intellectual achievement. It is a transformative experience. Paradoxically, whereas most students look back on their dissertation experience as grueling, overwhelming, and oftentimes aversive, students also evaluate the experience as confirming, life changing, and an important transition into the world of the professional scholar.

Will You Publish Your Doctoral Dissertation?

Most doctoral dissertations are never published. This is unfortunate because a dissertation is likely to be the single most exhaustive piece of research a young scholar will ever complete. At some universities, it is expected that students will publish their dissertation work as part of the process of professional socialization and integration into an academically based research career; however, for many others the completion of the degree is a stepping-stone into professional practice in which publication is nice but not required for recognition and advancement. On the one hand, publications are the most valuable coinage in the realm of academic career progression, so that should be sufficient motivation for many graduates to seek to publish their dissertations. On the other hand, we maintain that you have an obligation to your discipline to disseminate your findings, which are usually a function of the voluntary participation and collaboration of others, to a larger professional and academic audience whenever possible. As such, we would like to encourage you to publish your work, even if this is the only publication that you ever achieve.

We have found that if a student does not make a concerted effort to publish the results of the dissertation in either book or journal form shortly after the oral defense, it is unlikely that it will ever happen. For all those graduate students who have quickly forgotten their dissertations on the way home from the orals, there are others who have launched their careers by distilling the dissertation into one or more promising publications. The more quickly you can muster the energy and motivation to prepare your dissertation for publication, the greater the chance of doing so. Although not all dissertations are publishable, your key committee members should be good guides to assessing the worthiness of your work for that purpose. Your chair, in particular, will probably have a strong investment in encouraging you to prepare and submit your dissertation for publication. We encourage you to think about the dissertation as part of a collegial process that should be managed jointly and that has a life beyond the final oral defense. In our experience, the following norms govern the attribution of authorship of publications derived from a dissertation in most academic departments:

1. Your chair, in particular, has most likely put a tremendous amount of work into your career and success. It is only right that any publication or presentation arising from that dissertation include his or her name.

2. In academic circles, the order of authors on a publication can be very important. If you want to publish your dissertation after it is complete, then you should be the first author, if and only if you take responsibility for rewriting the dissertation in article form, sending the article to the appropriate journal(s), responding to reviewers' comments, and resubmitting the article as many times as necessary. In other words, you should perform as first author.

3. If you complete the dissertation and then abandon further work toward publication, your chair should have the right to publish the dissertation. Under those circumstances, the order of authorship is determined by who does the work. The faculty member who does the work should be first author and you, the student, second or third, depending on your involvement, if any.

4. Even if you do nothing further after completing the dissertation, your name should be on any publication.

Before you begin to prepare your dissertation for publication, we recommend that you think carefully about where to submit it. By now you should be familiar with the most relevant journals in your area because you will have included studies from those journals in your references. Be sure to consult the journals for guidelines on how to prepare and submit a paper for publication consideration. These instructions differ among journals, both in formatting and in allowable length. Follow the submission instructions meticulously. It is also commonly understood that you may only submit a paper to one journal at a time, so be prepared to have a backup source in mind in case your first submission is rejected. The backup should probably be a journal that is somewhat less competitive than the original one. One likely outcome of a review of your paper is a request for resubmission with revisions. Give yourself enough time to digest the review completely. Then, preferably in consultation with your coauthors, decide how to make the appropriate changes. Provide a thorough response to each of the comments, including a rationale for not following any recommendations that you dispute. If you receive a negative review, don't take the rejection personally. All academic writers have had their papers and studies rejected for publication, including our most famous and noteworthy researchers. Journal editors are usually very helpful in pointing out deficiencies in the study and in the presentation. You may very well be able to draw on their feedback and suggestions to improve the paper, either for resubmission as a revised manuscript to the same journal or as a new submission to a different journal. We strongly recommend that you revise the paper before you submit it to a different publication. After all, the chances are decent that the new publication will use one of the reviewers who previously read your manuscript.

Some academic departments allow or encourage students to write dissertations in a format that is more or less publication ready. In most cases, however, you need to edit and reorganize the dissertation before you submit it for publication. Dissertations tend to be much longer than journal articles. That is especially true for the review of the literature. Whereas dissertations generally include fairly comprehensive literature reviews, published studies usually contain focused reviews that serve as short (at most a few pages) introductions to the study itself. You can obtain a good sense of what to include and what to exclude by skimming your literature review and concentrating on your summary statements and the most essential studies and references.

Daryl Bem (2004) differentiates between the article you planned to write when you designed your study and the article that makes more sense now that you have looked at the results. He strongly advises that you choose the second option and prepare your paper for publication on the basis of the findings that you have now obtained. Many journal articles do not mention specific hypotheses, but they do include one or more clear research questions and a brief overview of the research design prior to a description of the methodology. Most of the material from the Method chapter needs to be included in a published paper. The reader still needs to know exactly what you did to obtain your results. On the other hand, you may not need to include all of the results from your dissertation in a single publication. What is necessary is to examine your data carefully for clear and compelling insights. As Bem (2004) reminds us, no one cares if you predicted these results or not. The findings are much more relevant and important than your prognostications. As long as you do not omit findings that would contradict, minimize, or clarify the findings you cite, you are not obligated to include uninteresting or irrelevant results or to put all of your eggs in one basket, so to speak. Finally, you will no doubt need to trim the Discussion chapter of your dissertation to accommodate the journal format. Just include a clear and thorough accounting of your results and the most pertinent implications and limitations of the study.

It is possible that your dissertation was written for a much more specialized audience than the typical journal article. Thus, Bem (2004) recommends reducing the level of your writing to address the reasonably well-educated person who may not have a sophisticated background in your field of study. Throughout the article, try to write in clear, engaging, and economical prose rather than academic jargon. The reader who wants a more thorough understanding of how to write an empirical journal article is referred to Bem's (2004) wealth of good suggestions for preparing studies for publication. His recommendations, although oriented to the field of psychology, are also relevant for preparing research articles in all social science disciplines.

Finally, we offer some specific suggestions about preparing qualitative dissertations, as opposed to quantitative dissertations, for publication. Due to their lengthy narrative structure, qualitative dissertations may not lend themselves so readily to a severely condensed journal article format. As it turns out, our students who have completed qualitative dissertations are as likely to publish them as book chapters or books as they are to transform them into journal articles. Nonetheless, professional journals in the social sciences are becoming increasingly receptive to the publication of qualitative studies and more and more journals exclusively devoted to qualitative studies are emerging on the scene. To meet stringent publication limitations the newly minted graduate will no doubt have to eliminate much of the textual content and many of the longer quotations from the dissertation. It should still be possible, however, to focus on the research question and maintain the spirit of the dissertation in a significantly shorter form. Fischer (1999) provides useful hints for first-time authors of qualitative reports, and Golden-Biddle and Locke (2005) offer helpful advice on how to transform massive amounts of qualitative data into a framework accessible to a particular audience.

In addition, an article by Elliott, Fischer, and Rennie (1999) sets forth recommended guidelines for assessing published qualitative studies. These recommendations are summarized in Table 9.3. The authors caution that this is a tentative list of guidelines that are sure to evolve over time, and they urge that readers not apply them rigidly. Nonetheless, they are solid suggestions for increasing the likelihood of publishing a qualitative dissertation in a worthy academic or professional journal.

The second list of guidelines found in the table merits some elaboration. *Owning one's perspective* refers to disclosing your values and assumptions that are relevant to the research topic in order help the reader to interpret and understand your conclusions. *Situating the sample* implies including sufficient descriptive data about your participants and the context of your study. *Grounding in examples* means to include enough examples of themes from the data to convey a good understanding of the confluence between the data and their meaning. *Providing credibility checks* suggests the inclusion of methods of demonstrating the credibility of categories, themes, and interpretations. These might include using multiple qualitative analysts, checking your understanding with the respondents, using two or more qualitative approaches, triangulating the interpretation of the data with external sources, and so on. *Coherence* refers to providing an integration (story, narrative, "map," framework) of the disparate strands of textual data. If the purpose of the study is to form a *general* understanding of a phenomenon, then the conclusions must be based on an appropriate range of participants or situations; if the purpose is to understand a *specific* instance or case, then there needs to be enough information to warrant that understanding. Finally, *resonating with the reader* means that your presentation is sufficiently persuasive for the reader to feel that you have represented the topic accurately and have enriched his or her appreciation of it.

Table 9.3   Evolving Guidelines for Publication of Qualitative Research Studies in Psychology and Related Fields

Publishability Guidelines Shared by Both Qualitative and Quantitative Approaches	*Publishability Guidelines Especially Pertinent to Qualitative Research*
1. Explicit scientific context and purpose	1. Owning one's perspective
2. Appropriate methods	2. Situating the sample
3. Respect for participants	3. Grounding in examples
4. Specification of methods	4. Providing credibility checks
5. Appropriate discussion	5. Coherence
6. Clarity of presentation	6. Accomplishing general vs. specific research tasks
7. Contributions to knowledge	7. Resonating with readers

SOURCE: From "Evolving Guidelines for Publication of Qualitative Research Studies in Psychology and Related Fields," by R. Elliott, C. T. Fischer, and D. L. Rennie, 1999, *British Journal of Clinical Psychology*, 38, p. 220. Copyright 1999 by R. Elliott et al. Reproduced with permission from the *British Journal of Clinical Psychology*, © The British Psychological Society.

10

Writing

Jody Veroff

K nowing how to express ideas in written form is an essential skill for the researcher. From the beginning of any research project to its final report, most researchers spend more time writing about their ideas, their understandings of previous theory and research, and their own procedures, findings, and conclusions than they spend actually conducting experiments or performing statistical analyses. It is easy to ignore how much of "science" depends on the communication of ideas in written form. It is also easy to ignore how much the ability to write clear and interesting prose contributes to the success of any research you may undertake. Well-written proposals are more likely to be received positively by funding agencies or dissertation committees, accepted for publication in professional journals, and understood and appreciated by the audiences they reach. Thus, the ultimate impact of any research you undertake is likely to be much enhanced if you can write well about your work.

You can learn a good deal about how to write a research report by referring to books and articles explicitly focused on this topic. I have listed some references in the bibliography at the end of this chapter. These references will teach you conventional approaches to organizing and formatting your work and will help you mirror the characteristic logic and development of research writing. You can also study the writing style and organization of articles in professional journals that publish research reports in areas related to your topic. Modeling these probably will ensure that your report complies sufficiently with that journal's requirements of acceptance.

Unfortunately, many models available in professional journals are masterpieces of indirection, obfuscation, and sheer boredom. Some existing models support the suspicion that the writer has specifically aimed to make the report impossible for the average reader to understand, intending to speak only to an elite audience whose existing understanding of the topic is complete enough to permit them to interpret and translate what has been written. Indeed, this approach to writing about research is so prevalent that one might give it the label "gobbledygook." If you use such writing as your model, you may convince some readers that your work is important and profound because they cannot understand anything you have written, but you will also lose the opportunity to inform and communicate with a readership that is not already in the inner circle.

Most of us at some point have been deeply affected by a scientific article because it helped us understand something we previously could not understand or because it engaged our own thinking and emotions in a way that stimulated our thinking about the topic. If you wish your writing to affect readers in this way, it is important to pay attention to your writing style and to learn to express your ideas with clarity, with energy, and perhaps even with grace. To do this, you need to learn the following skills:

- Write what you mean
- Choose words and ways of putting them together that convey your understandings directly
- Avoid scientific jargon and stylistic "gobbledygook"
- Identify with your potential readers and to try to imagine their process of understanding what you have written

Learning how to write this way seems to me to be no different from learning how to write for any other purpose. Because, for many of us, something about both the realities and myths of "scientific writing" turns our minds to stone or slush and makes us feel awkward, stupid, and convoluted in our very thinking process, it may be easier to learn how to improve our writing in general than to begin with the specific demands of research writing.

Past Experiences With Writing

One way to demystify the process of writing is to retrace your history as "a writer." Remembering your own experiences may help you understand current pleasures you have as a writer as well as negative feelings and writing problems. Although the joys and sorrows of your own past experiences with writing undoubtedly are unique, there are commonalities in human development and similarities in educational structures that typically influence the way most of us learn to write. A brief review of these may help you retrieve some of your own past experiences and may help you understand current feelings and difficulties you may have with writing. Remembering and reappraising these experiences may also suggest ways to change your feelings and take steps to remedy your difficulties.

Learning to Distance Yourself From Writing

Your writing career probably began at a tender age when you learned how to write your name. This is a triumphant accomplishment even when the process is laborious and painful and the final product misshapen and awkward. Writing your name may not seem like "real writing" because it has only to do with learning how to shape letters, but it is the beginning of being able to express yourself on paper, the beginning stage of a new way to communicate with others about your thoughts and feelings. Unfortunately, subsequent education can encourage you to put more distance between your writing and yourself so that you learn to devalue your own voice and may even conclude that it is an inappropriate presence in your writing. You may learn to ignore personal ownership of your writing or any real connection between what you write and who you are or what you think or feel.

This distancing of the self from writing is perhaps inevitable, given the predictable lag between conceptual abilities and the skills required to render thoughts on paper. Stubby little fingers can rarely keep up with the complex ideas that young children may want to express; the spoken vocabularies they command usually are far more extensive and sophisticated than the reading or writing vocabularies they master in the first few years of school. Learning to write "Run, run, run" or "See Betty catch the ball" may be a significant achievement for a first-grade child but one that is essentially mechanical, having little connection with a child's own thoughts or the way he or she talks about the world.

Distancing writing from the self may also be a consequence of typical educational priorities, which tend to focus on the development of essential skills, such as penmanship, spelling, and grammar. Children do, of course, need to master these skills before they can use writing to communicate their ideas in writing, but there is considerable risk that the disconnection between such skill learning and the child's ongoing experience will teach him or her that writing does not have much to do with one's self and the things the child might like to say on paper. Even when writing skills are essentially in place, later school experience may continue to reinforce a separation between the child's own thoughts and feelings and the process of writing. Writing projects are often geared toward teaching children how to use libraries and reference materials and requiring them to demonstrate the facts learned from their "research."

In my school years, students had little choice about topics for writing projects; when your geography class was studying the New England region, you could write about "Principal Products of Lowell, Massachusetts" or a similar topic from a limited list. Although I hope and think that children currently have more choice in the topics they must write about, public libraries are still full of young children straining their eyes over encyclopedias (or more likely, their personal computers—Rudestam & Newton), keeping their place with one hand while they write information with the other. It is easy to imagine that they are writing, just as I did, papers on "The Honey Bee" or "The Mountains of Peru" or "Diphtheria," without much interest in their topic and without much inclination to go beyond recording the information provided in the encyclopedia.

Learning to Think of Writing as a Boring Activity

Using writing projects to augment standard classroom learning or to assess whether children have mastered the skills required to collect information about a topic is a reasonable way to teach children important academic skills. A regrettable conclusion that children may draw, however, is that the purpose of writing is to write down someone else's information about a subject that is not very interesting. Part of their learning may be that writing is a tedious and unrewarding activity to be put off as long as possible. The experience of understanding more about a topic by writing about it and the pleasure of writing about something of personal interest and importance can be rare and unusual for the average child going through school. It is not surprising, then, that so many of us grow up to view writing as burdensome.

Learning to Feel Inadequate as a Writer

In the later years of grade school and on through high school and college, teachers become increasingly evaluative of their students' writing and are particularly alert to errors in grammar, punctuation, and spelling, sometimes to the exclusion of attention to the content or the way ideas have been developed. Most of us can remember the sinking sensation we experienced when writing assignments were returned, covered with red ink and graphically showing how many errors we had made on every page. We searched in vain for any evidence that the teacher liked what we said or the way we said it and found instead that the comments in the margins informed us only of where we had been unclear, illogical, or awkward. Whatever pleasure or excitement we might have felt about the original writing assignment was usually diluted and tarnished. Some of us may remember feeling so stupid and unskilled that we began to be afraid to write papers. Although students with a "natural" gift for writing well and those with more compassionate teachers may escape such aversive experiences, many people respond to less affirming school experiences by learning to be afraid to write. As teachers, especially at the college level, become more concerned about the inability of many students to write at even a minimally acceptable level, they are likely to redouble their efforts to point out errors and will be less inclined to notice or reward the ideas the student has expressed.

This review of common educational experiences around writing has focused on those that foster the following beliefs:

- It is not quite appropriate to write about your own ideas.
- Writing is primarily a boring rehash of other people's ideas.
- What has been written will be read vigilantly by evaluators seeking primarily to find mistakes.

For those of us whose experience was tilted in this way, the surprising thing is that we did not give up on writing altogether once we finished high school or college. It is not surprising if we learned to be afraid to write or to have difficulty in getting ourselves to sit down and write, or to believe we cannot write. Yet most of us continue to write. We write lists of things to do today; we write directions to the baby-sitter or the plumber; we write business letters, letters of complaint, letters of explanation, letters of sympathy and condolence, and occasional letters of thank you. Although the writing of friendly letters is mourned by some as a dying art, some of us still write to our mothers or our children or our friends who live in distant places. If our work requires it, we write progress reports, project proposals, memos, and instructions, all without crippling anxiety or resistance. The old aversive feelings about writing emerge most dramatically when we must write something that someone else will receive and evaluate as "serious" writing. Writing about theory or research may provoke the most intense concern; not only are there conventions and myths about conventions for this kind of writing that limit our freedom of expression, but in addition writing about more abstract topics is generally difficult, especially if we do not fully understand the ideas we are writing about. Although the very process of struggling to write about ideas is often clarifying and can promote deeper comprehension, it is tempting to circumvent this struggle by stringing words, phrases, and clauses together in a way that is sufficiently obscure so that no one will be able to detect our gaps in understanding.

If you are burdened with anxiety about your writing, or by a perpetual reluctance to begin to write, or by a conviction that the demands of writing well require a gift that you do not have, do not despair. If you can think and if you can speak about what you think, it is almost guaranteed that you can learn to write. You are even a good candidate for learning to enjoy writing. The major obstacles that you need to overcome are (a) fear, engendered by past unpleasant experiences associated with writing; (b) boredom, resulting from not caring enough about what you are writing about; (c) perfectionism, which makes you labor too hard over each word you use, worry too much about evaluation, or try to report in full detail everything that has ever been said about your topic; (d) disenfranchisement from your own voice and your own ideas that makes you feel unentitled to express your ideas in a form that others can examine and evaluate; (e) impatience, which allows you to imagine that writing should be effortless, an activity that doesn't require the time and effort ordinarily required to learn to do anything well; and (f) excessive pride, which makes you believe that your public expressions should be wonderful, thus making you unwilling to reveal that sometimes they are not. Additional obstacles may reside in difficulties with spelling, grammar, and sentence structure, but these obstacles usually can be overcome by learning the rules of the grammatical structure of English, by enlisting an editor or a proofreader, by employing word-processing programs designed to pick up such errors, or by using a dictionary and a guide to common grammatical and spelling errors.

Overcoming Obstacles

Overcoming the obstacles created by negative experiences and unrealistic expectations sounds like a formidable challenge that might require a substantial therapeutic intervention to achieve. It is not always easy to lay anxiety to rest or to give up perfectionism or concern about evaluation. Reflections of successful writers on their work suggest that these problems continue to haunt even the best of writers, many of whom suffer from writer's block for extended periods of time and often struggle on a daily basis to keep themselves writing. Most writers emphasize the importance of regular writing and describe strategies they employ to make sure they do this. Many would agree that it is often easier not to begin to write, just as it might be easier not to do the dishes or go jogging or practice the piano. But all skills require regular practice, and most of us are accustomed to imposing sufficient discipline in our lives to attend to the things we consider important. Writers often schedule daily blocks of time they will spend writing or set goals for the number of pages they will complete each day. They take their work as writers seriously enough to organize their lives so that their writing time is at least as sacred as the time they allot to other activities. If you want to learn to write, it is essential to make writing a regular and routine activity that is at least as important to you as brushing your teeth or reading the newspaper. There will be no better way to increase your skill and your comfort.

Getting Started

Making Lists

Resolving to write as a part of your daily routine may not necessarily protect you from the depressing circumstance of staring at a pristine yellow legal pad or the blinking cursor on your computer screen, wondering how in the world to begin. Even when you urgently need to complete a writing project, you may find yourself quite literally at a loss for words. Sometimes it helps to fall back on the kinds of writing most of us do every day. You might, for example, begin by making a list of ideas that seem important to address in your paper. List making is a familiar and comfortable activity that does not have to be any more profound and meaningful than writing a shopping list or a list of things to do today, yet just as these prosaic lists help to organize your thoughts and priorities, a list of ideas that seem important can begin to organize the shape of the piece you want to write. A good list can be played with. You can put the items in order of importance so that your list can remind you of what needs most to be included, just as a list of things to do today reminds you of the priority of paying the electric bill before the lights are turned off. You can also organize a list by establishing which things should be first and last and somewhere in the middle, just as a list of errands might remind you to take the casserole out of the freezer first and buy the ice cream last. A list can help you take into account the way some of the ideas are related to others and need to be clustered together, just as a useful shopping list groups lettuce, apples, and potatoes together, separate from butter, eggs, and milk. Playing with your list of ideas in this way can give you a structure for your writing project that will allow you to get started and to know where you are going.

Clustering

If the linearity of lists stultifies you and you have never been able to make an outline until you have written your piece, a different way of beginning may be more in tune with your thinking style. In her book *Writing the Natural Way,* Gabriele Rico (1983) described a method she believes helps writers to access the natural structuring tendencies of the human brain. She calls this method clustering. It begins with a free associative task that involves writing your topic somewhere in the middle of a piece of paper and then writing words and phrases that come to mind around that central topic, with no conscious attention to their spatial placement. As more apparently random associations are recorded, you can begin to draw lines between ideas that seem connected and gradually fill in the "map" of associated thoughts. Rico contends that at some point a structure emerges that will allow you to write a reasonably well-formed paragraph about your topic that represents your current understanding of your topic, linking and organizing your ideas in a coherent form. I have used this exercise in writing workshops; it does seem to allow most participants to produce a meaningful paragraph in a very short period of time. A few people in each group have found this method so liberating and helpful that they feel their approach to thinking and writing has been virtually transformed. If you are stuck and cannot get yourself to begin to write, you will risk little by trying this method, and you may be lucky and discover that it is uniquely compatible with your way of thinking.

Writing a Letter to a Friend

Another way to trick yourself into beginning is to pretend you are writing to a friend to tell her about your topic and what you have learned about it. Suppose you are interested in exploring whether or not men and women go through different processes in deciding to run for political office. If you were writing about this interest to a friend, you probably would want to tell him or her why you were interested in this topic, why you think it is important, and what hunches you have about differences that might exist. Imagining what you would need to tell your friend to help him or her understand your ideas may help you begin to write and organize your thoughts about the topic without feeling as intimidated as you might if you were imagining your reader to be your dissertation chair or the review committee of a funding agency. Because you may know already what your friend thinks and knows about gender differences or running for political office, you will be able to imagine how your friend might receive and react to what you have written. You can foresee some of the arguments you may have to present to convince your friend that this is an important issue to study.

Beginning as if you were writing to a friend highlights the communicative aspect of writing and reminds you of the importance of your self in the communicative relationship that is created by writing. It encourages you to write about your ideas in simple, direct, and nontechnical language. It also may allow you to make a connection with why you care about your topic. If your "letter to a friend" instead adds fuel to your fear that your topic is so boring that no one could possibly want to read about it, perhaps the exercise will help you decide to find a better topic.

Journalistic Devices

Introductory classes in journalism suggest another trick that may help you get started. Fledgling reporters are instructed to begin every news story with a paragraph that tells the reader *who, what, why, when,* and *where.* (An additional query—*how?*—is a useful addition in writing about research.) Reporters learn to put this essential, bare-bones information in the lead paragraph so that a coherent account of the news event will still remain if the editor decides to cut the remainder of the story. This journalistic device is useful for getting started on any writing project even when you have no reason to fear that your audience will not read beyond your first paragraph. This format may help you get started because it describes a small and delimited task that will help organize your writing and remind you to include the information necessary to tell your reader what your article will be about. It can often become the introductory paragraph of your paper. If you wish, for example, to write about the problem of inner-city violence in adolescents, a good introduction might be this:

(what?) Escalating violence among inner-city adolescents is becoming a major social problem (why?) that exacts an enormous toll in young lives and crime control costs. Understanding the causes of this escalation is, thus, an imperative research agenda. (where?) This study will survey a sample of 15- to 19-year-old adolescents (who?) attending school in Detroit, Michigan, (when?) in the fall of 2006, (how?) using attitude questionnaires to identify their perceptions of the causes of violence in the schools.

The relatively simple task of answering the journalistic questions results in an introduction that states the purpose and approach of the study clearly and directly and prepares the reader for the elaborations that will follow. Your reader can then make a decision about whether or not he or she is sufficiently interested in your topic and your approach to read further.

Writing Stories

If you are a person who likes to tell stories, you might find it useful to write about your topic in story form. The story of how you came to be interested in your topic might be a natural way to begin. Or you might tell the story of how you learned more about your topic. Most of us learned the basic structure of a story when we were very young and know by heart the convention that begins with "Once upon a time" and ends with "and they lived happily ever after." In between the beginning that sets the stage and the ending that brings things to a satisfying conclusion, we know that characters must be introduced and that a problem must be posed that leads to an action that allows for the "happy ending," with enough tension and suspense built in so that the reader cares to keep reading.

You may find it a bit odd to think of writing a research report as if it were a story, but some of the most engaging and interesting examples of scientific writing have qualities similar to a good detective story. The writer describes the "mystery" and tells you how he or she developed "clues," collected the evidence, and ruled out various "wrong" solutions on the way to discovering a convincing answer to the mystery. This device is especially useful in writing about research findings and theories in social science, where the phenomena under consideration are often complex and potential "causes" are both multiple and interactive. Researchers and theorists often begin with a relatively simple hypothesis, such as, for example, that increased stress will be associated with illness. The plot soon thickens, and researchers must attend to other factors that influence this relationship, eventually constructing a "cast of characters" that play a role in how stress affects well-being. Writing the "story" that describes the hunches that have been followed up, the "red herrings" in the case, the new clues that emerge, and the new evidence that must be collected would be an engrossing way to present the literature relevant to this topic, and it might in itself generate new insights.

Each of these devices for getting started provides a way to organize your thoughts and ideas that should allow you to put some words on your pristine piece of paper or your blank computer screen. You may also be able to see where the rest of your writing project will go and the kind of structure it will have because each of these devices creates a purpose for what you are writing:

- To order your ideas
- To recognize the connections between ideas
- To make sense of your ideas in ordinary language
- To persuade someone to follow your way of thinking
- To provide your reader with essential information
- To tell the story of the development of your ideas

If your writing does not initially seem to have a purpose beyond satisfying the requirements of an assignment, these devices may help you generate other purposes that will facilitate the writing process and make it more interesting.

Topic and Passion

If you have any choice at all about topics for your writing, one of the most important things you can do to facilitate your writing is to choose one that you care about and are interested in. Although some advisers warn against choosing topics with high personal relevance on the grounds that your appropriate objectivity will be impaired, this danger is small compared to the problems that arise when you try to write about something entirely divorced from your personal experience, concern, or interest. The energy required to sustain effort, to endure frustration, and to think creatively flows most readily from passion for your topic. This may be a passionate desire to find answers to puzzling questions or a passionate curiosity to learn as much as possible about a topic of interest or a passion to communicate to others the important things you have discovered and learned. Passion not only provides energy that will propel your writing project onward but also helps guarantee that you will interact with the materials you are writing about, testing the ideas and information of others against your own thoughts and ideas and experiences. Thus, what you write will be both more integrative and more likely to generate new insights for yourself and for your readers. Your evident investment in your topic will almost inevitably make what you write interesting to others. The energy derived from your passion and interest will be evident in your writing and will make it exciting for almost any reader.

Sometimes even a randomly chosen topic can inspire interest and passion as you learn more about it. Evidence of growing interest or even passion for a topic exists if you begin to wonder about something you have read or want to argue with its author or become eager to pursue the topic in greater depth. These are exciting moments in intellectual development, and you should not eliminate such possibilities in your search for a topic. Especially when you are writing to fulfill an assignment in a class, you may find it initially difficult to think about anything you care much about. Doing some general reading relevant to the course content before you select a topic for a writing project with special attention to ideas that stimulate questions or connections or curiosity will be useful in identifying a topic sufficiently interesting to sustain your writing momentum.

Even when you care about your topic, you may not be able to generate the kind of passion I have been describing if you limit yourself to reporting what is known about the topic. Such writing often becomes a kind of laundry list of what others have discovered or said about the subject and just as often is both boring to write and boring to read. The "detective mode" usually is more effective in communicating the excitement you feel about your topic. By this I mean the organization of your writing around questions that you have sought to answer and the possible answers that have presented themselves. The difference between writing about a topic and writing about questions could be described as the difference between reviewing what is known about a topic and identifying the relevance of what is known to the questions at hand. Although both approaches communicate essentially the same information, the detective mode engages the writer in interacting with available information and is likely to engage the reader to interact similarly. Whenever you find yourself wondering why something is the way it is or how it works, or who might be affected, or whether it always happens this way or instead depends on something else to set it off, you have more than likely identified a good topic for both research and writing. Your questions will make you care about finding answers and will make it easier for you to write a well-organized and interesting paper.

Authorship and Voice

Much of what I have said about caring and passion is directly related to another important attribute of good writing that I call claiming your authorship. Excluding your self from your writing is a good way to make your writing boring to yourself and to others. The unfortunate tendency to exclude oneself as knower, scholar, interpreter, and discoverer in writing is often learned very early, in ways I already described. Educators, in their eagerness to educate, often emphasize the need for children to demonstrate what they have learned. Children take tests or write papers to demonstrate that they have the requisite knowledge of literature, geography, history, science, and all the other things they might not know if they were not taught. Less often do educators encourage students to think about what they have learned, to share those thoughts, or to write about what they may know from experience or from sources other than standard textbooks and reference materials. It is easy for children to conclude that "received knowledge" (see Belenky et al., 1986) is more true, more valuable, and more rewarded than any other kind of knowing. Received knowledge, by definition, comes from the authority of others. When the measurement of children's learning is their ability to recite the knowledge they have received, it is difficult for them to perceive themselves as entitled to be authors of knowledge.

Scholarly writing about theory and research generally requires the writer to go beyond recording received knowledge. Authors of such writing have almost always thought about issues, reached conclusions on the basis of available evidence, and interacted with their information to organize and integrate it. Yet many theorists and researchers persist in using a style that suggests that it is inappropriate for writers to acknowledge their authorship or involvement with what they have written. Conventions of referring to the self in the third person, never using the word *I*, and predominantly using the passive voice suggest that even a writer who is discussing his or her own discoveries or theories must pretend it was someone else who thought or discovered or concluded. Of course, when writers say "It was discovered that . . . ." or "It is reasonable to conclude that . . . ," we all know that they mean "I discovered this" and "I conclude that," but the language style suggests that the knowledge they are presenting was received from somewhere else and did not really involve the researcher.

I came across an embarrassing example of the extent to which prevailing conventions encourage writers to disown what they have written in this way when I recently reread my doctoral dissertation, written in 1959. Throughout this document, I had disowned not only my authorship but also my gender by referring to my ideas in the masculine third person. Although current emphasis on nonsexist language probably protects young women writing today from such absurd constructions, they were not uncommon in those days, and they provide graphic examples of how this convention of "scientific writing" influences the relationship of the writer to her writing. This kind of depersonalization is motivated not only by a reluctance to claim authority but apparently also by an attempt to demonstrate objectivity by underplaying that there is a real and potentially fallible person who has written about his or her own ideas and conclusions. It serves to reinforce the fears of many that they are not entitled to have ideas or to think about topics or to draw their own conclusions. Claiming authorship requires taking responsibility for what you write; although this may be intimidating, it is also empowering.

Although the stylistic rules of your publisher may require you eventually to disembody yourself in your writing, there is no rule that says you can't begin by openly acknowledging that "I wondered about this, I think these ideas are unsupported by evidence, I surveyed the literature, I designed a study, and I concluded that . . . . " To do so will make you very aware that you are the author of what you write, responsible for what you say, and entitled to communicate your own ideas and understandings. If you must remove the *I* from your writing to satisfy the demands of others, it will be easier to find ways to do this that do not deny your authorship if you have first written more personally. The *Publication Manual of the American Psychological Association* (2004) makes the following observation: "Inappropriately or illogically attributing action in the name of objectivity can be misleading. Writing 'The experimenter instructed the participants' when 'the experimenter' refers to yourself is ambiguous and may give the impression that you did not take part in your own study" (p. 29). Although many journals and advisers continue to insist on the disembodied voice, it is likely that these observations by a major arbiter of style will eventually influence changes in the requirements imposed by journal editors.

Developing a "voice" as a writer depends on a strong sense of self as the possessor of knowledge and ideas who is entitled to speak about these to others. The voices of writers such as Ernest Hemingway, Marcel Proust, Mark Twain, or Sigmund Freud are easily recognized (and can be easily parodied) by readers familiar with their work. If you claim authorship in your writing and practice doing so, your voice will become distinctive in much the same way as is your fingerprint or your way of walking. In this sense, developing your voice not only lends authority to your writing but also tends to make writing a more "natural" process in which ways of expressing ideas or constructing sentences flow more easily without requiring as much conscious and deliberate effort.

No one develops a writing voice overnight, and the steps that might hasten the process are not easy to describe. Peter Elbow struggled to describe voice through a whole chapter in his book *Writing With Power*

(1998), expressing dissatisfaction with people who see it as similar to authenticity, sincerity, or authority:

> Voice is what most people have in their speech but lack in their writing—namely, a sound or texture—the sound of "them." We recognize most of our friends on the phone before they say who they are. A few people get their voice into their writing. When you read a letter or something else they've written, it has the sound of them. (p. 288)

Elbow (1998) contended that conscious work on voice and help from someone else in distinguishing between passages in writing that have voice and those that do not encourages students to do more experimentation in their writing and also to include more about themselves in what they write. In addition to attending to your own thoughts, feeling, and characteristic modes of expression, I believe acquiring a writing voice also depends on developing your sense of entitlement to have ideas and to write about them. Perhaps, however, the development of a sense of entitlement of this sort could be equated with the development of voice.

A part of your voice resides in the kind of words you like to use, the rhythm of your "natural" speech or writing, the way you use metaphor and images to convey your ideas, and the very organization that seems most natural in structuring your thoughts. Sometimes, you can become aware of the absence of your voice by reading aloud what you have written. It is often easier to hear than to see the false notes, the awkward expressions you would never use when speaking, as well as the absence of rhythm and flow. By listening to what you have written, you become the observer of what you have written with an outsider's perspective, and you may become more aware of the dissonance between what you have written and what you intended to communicate.

An exercise that may be useful in alerting you to elements of your voice involves writing about a randomly chosen topic for several minutes with the explicit goal of writing whatever comes to mind and not allowing yourself to stop writing. Such free writing, unmediated by conscious attention to content or "proper" form, can provide helpful insights about your natural style of expression on paper.

An entertaining way to further explore issues of voice involves writing about a given situation from several different perspectives. For example, reviewing a research report of a psychological experiment would be illuminating. In the characteristic mode of objective science, the report would most likely be written from the perspective of a disembodied, anonymous third person who presumably aims to report the facts about the experiment. Try writing about the experiment from the perspective of one of the subjects of the experiment, usually referred to as "S." Then write about the experiment from the perspective of the experimenter, trying to imagine his or her thoughts and feelings while conducting the experiment. Finally, write a description of the experiment from your own perspective as a reader. The differences among your resulting descriptions reflect different voices and can help liberate your own voice. A fringe benefit of this exercise may be new insights about what really happened during the experiment and what interpretations you may want to draw from it.

Concern About Audience and Evaluation

I have stressed the importance of recognizing that writing is a form of communication that involves not only the writer but also the potential reader. It is important to write with some awareness of your potential readers so that you can foresee what they will need to know to understand your ideas. Imagining the needs and interpretive skills of your reader is a way to provide yourself with critical feedback necessary to make sure that your writing communicates what you want to say in the clearest possible fashion. Writing with this kind of awareness of your potential readers is also a good way to retain the kind of liveliness and energy that often characterizes conversation.

There is, however, another kind of awareness of your potential readers that can be a serious obstacle in writing. When you allow yourself to become preoccupied with how the readers of your work will evaluate what you have written, you are likely to stifle the flow of your writing, sometimes to the point of suffocation. If you try to guess what your reader expects or wants you to say, it will be difficult to feel free enough to say what you want to say in a way that honestly reflects your own thinking and ideas. If you focus on trying to impress your readers with how much you know or how elegantly you can write about what you know, you will have lost sight of the real purpose of your writing, which presumably had something to do with ideas you wanted to express. A preoccupying focus on how your writing will be evaluated by its readers may be one cause of writer's block because it encourages you to strive for a "perfect" piece of writing. Because it is impossible to foresee what someone else will see as perfect, you have set yourself an impossible task, and it is not surprising that you cannot go forward. For the extreme perfectionist, no sentence put on paper is quite good enough, and no choice of words exactly captures the idea the writer has in mind. Whenever you find yourself stuck on the first paragraph of a writing project, writing and rewriting your introduction, it may be helpful to ask yourself whose expectations you are trying to meet. Turning off the "editor in your head" may provide you with enough freedom to begin and even to complete a first draft, which will be a more useful basis for corrections and revisions than a page full of false starts.

I can personally attest to the writing problems caused by overconcern with an evaluative audience. In the process of writing this chapter, I have struggled at length and to no particular advantage with both the things I have written and the way I have written them because I imagined it would be highly presumptuous to write about writing if I could not demonstrate that I am a really good writer, qualified to advise other people about their writing. I know that all that I can do is to write what I believe to be true about the challenge of writing, the obstacles that may emerge, and the strategies I have found useful to deal with these; however, my acute awareness that I have exposed myself to public evaluation of my ideas, my writing style, and my logic has continuously impeded my progress and interrupted the flow of my thinking and my writing. It is both consoling and sobering to realize that some members of my audience may actually be relieved to see that a person writing about writing sometimes fails to write clearly or gracefully, but this does not entirely relieve the inhibition caused by overconcern with my audience.

My experience suggests that it is sometimes very difficult to turn off "the editor in your head." The need to do so is signaled when you find yourself struggling for a long time to think of the best way to express an idea or when you realize that you have been working and reworking a passage endlessly without achieving any sense of progress. At such times, it may help to resort temporarily to one or another of the "getting started" strategies I described earlier. Sketching in a passage by listing key ideas that you will return to on another day may allow you to move on. Shifting the focus of your attention from an evaluative audience by pretending you are writing to a friend or are writing a story may reduce your anxiety sufficiently to quiet your concern about all the potential editors out there. Another useful strategy is to conjure up an alternative audience who may benefit in some way if only they have a chance to learn what you know and think about your topic. These tricks will probably afford only partial relief for a severe case of "editor anxiety" but may get you through the worst stage of total paralysis.

Goldberg (1991), in her engaging book about writing, *Writing Down the Bones*, suggested still another strategy. When "the editor is absolutely annoying," Goldberg suggested that you write out your most damning version of what the editor will say about your work in full and gory detail. She observed that "the more clearly you know the editor, the better you can ignore it" (p. 26).

Revision

Despite all of my cautions about not striving for perfection in your writing, I do want to stress the importance of rereading and revising what you have written. It is unlikely that any one of us can execute a first draft of a writing project that:

- Says exactly what we want to say
- Provides all of the information our readers need to understand what we have written
- Does not contain awkward sentences or grammatical constructions
- Cannot be significantly improved upon reconsideration

Reading aloud what you have written is an excellent way to hear the awkward phrases and grammatical errors that inevitably creep into any piece of writing. Because once you have committed your ideas to paper they are apt to seem complete and logical, asking someone else to read what you have written may be a way to get help in identifying places where your development of ideas is confusing or insufficiently supported by evidence even though it seems to make sense to you. It is easy to leave out crucial steps in an argument; we count on readers to follow our thought processes even when these have not been fully stated, and sometimes we expect them to be able to read our minds. A friendly reader can help us see when we have expected our audience to know more than they do and to fill in gaps in our writing that they cannot possibly manage to do. At the other extreme, problems arise from beating an argument to death by repeating essentially the same point in slightly different form. Someone coming fresh to the writing piece is almost always more sensitive than the author to problems of either omission or redundancy.

Douglas Flemons (2001) provided a gold mine of examples of how to improve sentences and paragraphs by thoughtful editing and revision in his chapter "Social Science Papers" (pp. 30–77). This chapter is also extremely valuable because of its clarity in defining the essential parts of a social science paper and at the same time stressing that writers should adapt standard procedures to fit with their own intentions. This is a liberating message and should be encouraging to students who find themselves trying to adapt their own ideas, methodologies, and interpretations to a mold that doesn't quite fit.

In the days before word processing, writing successive drafts of a paper was a time-consuming and laborious task. Writers' wastebaskets overflowed with crumpled sheets of paper containing false starts and discarded passages. Each draft usually involved extensive retyping of the previous draft, and only the most persistent and committed writers could discipline themselves to undertake the multiple drafts that might lead to a final version they found fully acceptable. Composing papers from the start on the computer allows for continuous revision and for free writing of sections that may ultimately fit best many pages later (or that may be deleted with the stroke of a key). This is an extraordinary boon to contemporary writers.

Conclusion

There are many steps between the beginning stages of getting started, choosing a topic, and developing passion and voice and the final stages of revision and completion of the writing project. These are shaped by your writing purpose, your topic, and your audience and cannot easily be addressed in a single chapter about writing. At the end of this chapter, I included a number of references that discuss "how to write" from different perspectives and for different purposes. The following list of "tricks" that summarize what has gone before may also help you keep your momentum from the beginning of your efforts to their successful completion.

Twelve Tricks to Keep You Going When You Write

1. At least in your first draft, use the first person singular to keep you in touch with *your* ideas, *your* reactions, *your* beliefs, and *your* understandings of what other people have written. Enjoy your voice as author. Speak as straightforwardly as you can. Avoid the passive voice whenever possible. If the requirements for publication or whatever dictate some other form, you can always revise later.

2. Write as flamboyantly as you like in your first draft to give voice to your passion. If you like adverbs and adjectives, use them generously.

3. If it makes you nervous to assert your own position, qualify it as often as possible in your first draft. Brave statements seem less dangerous with lots of phrases such as "in my opinion," "I think," and "it seems to me," as well as "probably," "not infrequently," "perhaps," and "in some instances." It is better to get your words on paper than to get hung up by anxiety about whether you have the right or sufficient knowledge or adequate proof to make strong statements.

4. In the beginning, try to forget how your audience might evaluate what you write or how you write it. There will be plenty of time later on to worry about the feedback that editors, publishers, or faculty advisers inevitably will give you. In the beginning, worrying about pleasing evaluating audiences is likely to lead to obsessing about each word you write, and you will often end up trying to impress your evaluators with your erudition, intellect, or elegance of phrase. This wastes a lot of time and energy.

5. Try to write in short sentences, especially in your first draft, so that you don't get tangled up in long, convoluted sentences that can obscure your meaning. Much writing time is wasted trying to straighten out grammatical absurdities that will never exist in the first place if you try to put just one idea in one sentence.

6. Try to find your own comfortable writing style and way of developing ideas. Be respectful of your style. If it is easy and useful for you to outline your ideas and then develop the outline into an essay, do that. If you spend more time making an outline than it would take to write the whole piece, don't let anyone convince you that you should make an outline. If you like to write in the middle of the night, do it. If you need to write around your topic until you finally get to the center of it, do it.

7. Do not be afraid to use the writing of others as a model. This is not a fraudulent act but rather one that acknowledges how much we can learn from master craftspeople. When you come across a piece of writing that seems especially clear, forceful, and enjoyable to read, pay attention to how that writer organizes and communicates ideas.

8. Introduce discipline into your writing task by committing yourself to spend a given number of hours (or minutes) writing or to produce a given amount of written text every day. If it is hard to do this, set your goals low and don't allow yourself to exceed them in the beginning. Set an alarm clock, if necessary, and even if you are in the midst of an interesting idea, stop when the alarm goes off. You will soon find yourself more and more frustrated by having to interrupt your work and more and more eager to extend your writing time just a few more minutes. It is safe to do this, but feel free to go back to your time limits if you find yourself staring at your paper or out the window very long. If you write only a few paragraphs a day, you will probably have six or seven pages to show for your effort at the end of a week. This is much more encouraging to most of us than spending 4 or 5 hours a day with nothing but aimless jottings or a wastebasket full of crumpled paper at the end of each work session.

Later, When Your First Draft Is Finished and
You Are Ready to Revise Your Work

9. Remove all the adverbs and adjectives you so joyously put in your first draft and restore only those that are absolutely necessary to your meaning. If you have been outrageously emotional or have put yourself far out on a limb with your assertions, weed out some of the color and make sure you can defend with evidence what you have said.

10. Eliminate all your qualifying statements and restore only those that are necessary to be honest and to retain your meaning. Now that you are at the end of your project, you will feel braver about what you have written and will not need so much to hide behind disclaimers.

11. If all of your short sentences sound choppy and telegraphic, combine some of your sentences to make a better flow. Be careful when you do this. If you can't combine two sentences without making a ponderous and incomprehensible whole, leave your short sentences alone. It is preferable to suffer a little choppiness than to leave your reader perplexed about what you mean to say. The rhythm that results from varying the length of your sentences can contribute variety and momentum to your writing that will make it more exciting to read.

12. Don't accept any of the foregoing rules or any other rule of writing that can't be broken or doesn't work for you. To paraphrase Julia Child's immortal words about making bread, remember that you are the boss of your writing.

Addendum

Most universities today provide remedial instruction in writing as well as structured opportunities to polish academic writing. In recent years, our colleagues at Fielding Graduate University have created a Virtual Writing Center for our graduate students to improve their writing skills. The exercises they use online (and in face-to-face seminars) include free writing and self-assessment (daily solitary writing on a topic of interest and sharing the writing with peers on an online forum); thesis-statement writing exercises; critical thinking and argumentation; critical summaries of research articles; literature reviews; meaningful question asking; effective expression of ideas; and academic style and grammar. The computer-based learning environment allows for editorial peer review (by posting all writing on a forum accessible to other students) and faculty review and feedback. Our colleague, Sam Osherson (2006), made the savvy comment that scientific writing does not need to be dry and boring. As he put it, many students maintain a "writer-as-cadaver" belief that to be a successful academic scholar and researcher, papers must be stripped of all liveliness and personal enjoyment. In our opinion, the very best research articles (and dissertations) hold the readers' attention through a writing style that reflects the author's interest and attraction to the subject.

Recommended References

American Psychological Association. (1994). *Publication manual of the American Psychological Association* (4th ed.). Washington, DC: Author.

Browne, N., & Keeley, S. (2006). *Asking the right questions: A guide to critical thinking.* Englewood Cliffs, NJ: Prentice-Hall.

Campbell, W. G., & Ballou, S. V. (1993). *Form and style: Theses, reports, term papers* (9th ed.). Boston: Houghton Mifflin.

Elbow, P. (1998). *Writing with power: Techniques for mastering the writing process* (2nd ed.). New York: Oxford University Press.

Flemons, D. (2001). *Writing between the lines: Composition in the social sciences.* New York: Norton.

Flowers, L. (2002). *Problem solving strategies for writing.* New York: International Thomson Publishing.

Goldberg, N. (1991). *Writing down the bones/Wild mind.* New York: Quality Paperback Book Club.

Hall, D., & Berkerts, S. (1997). *Writing well* (9th ed.). Boston: Longman.

Jacobi, E. (1984). *Writing at work: Do's, don'ts, and how-to's.* Rochelle Park, NJ: Hayden.

Lassner, P., Isaacson, H., & Harrington, S. (1995). Peerwriting tutors. In S. Hatcher (Ed.), *Peer programs on the college campus: Theory, training and the voice of the peers* (pp. 311-327). San Jose, CA: Research Publications.

Osherson, S. (2006). *Strengthening your writing voice, while enjoying it more: On teaching writing in graduate school.* Unpublished manuscript, Fielding Graduate University.

Rico, G. L. (1983). *Writing the natural way.* Los Angeles: J. P. Tarcher.

Stark, S. (1999). *Writing to win: The legal writer.* St. Charles, MO: Main Street Books.

Truss, L. (2006). *Eats, shoots and leaves: The zero tolerance approach to punctuation.* London: Gotham.

Zinsser, W. (2006). *On writing well: The classic guide to writing non-fiction* (30th ed.). New York: HarperCollins.

How to Complete Your Dissertation Using Online Data Access and Collection

I n the first edition of this book, we extolled the virtues of personal computer use as a time-saving tool for data analysis, writing, literature searching, and organization but suggested that it might be possible for someone to complete a dissertation without actually using a personal computer. In the second edition, we suggested that no one attempt to complete a dissertation without a personal computer, a host of software, and Internet access. In addition, we described the various software options available for literature review and bibliographic management and quantitative and qualitative analyses and discussed the need for and functions of utilities to safeguard your computer. We have moved much of this earlier information to "Software Guides" that summarize the software designed to facilitate each phase of the dissertation process and provide links to vendors' Web sites. Today's students are sophisticated computer users with experience that typically begins in grade school. However, we don't believe that a chapter describing the role of the personal computer and the Internet is unnecessary, only that its focus should change. Every stage of the research process can now be conducted online. We have reserved this chapter to discuss methods of online data access, analysis, and collection. If the possibility of completing a high quality dissertation without ever leaving your computer seems far-fetched, please read on; our students have completed dissertations in just that manner, and more are doing so all the time.

It is possible, and not unrealistic, to obtain all of the information you need to complete a dissertation directly from the Internet. There are a number of ways to do this, and we discuss each in this chapter. First, recall the difference between primary and secondary data analysis. Primary data analysis refers to the analysis of data collected by the researcher, or by the researcher's trained observers or interviewers. Secondary analysis draws on data collected by other researchers, often for other purposes, or data created by nonresearchers outside the specific context of research. For example, data from the U.S. Census; data collected by the Gallup, Roper, or Field polling organizations; data collected by federally funded research grants; and data from numerous other sources frequently find their way onto the Internet, typically for the explicit purpose of making these data available to researchers. In this chapter, we describe strategies for obtaining access to primary and secondary data via the Internet. We begin, however, with some advice regarding the use of secondary data.

The Pros and Cons of Accessing Secondary Data via the Internet

Conducting secondary analyses of data downloaded from a Web site is becoming commonplace for scientists from all disciplines, not just students engaged in dissertation research. The typical framework for this activity involves first locating the site containing the desired data; second, obtaining the necessary passwords, if any; third, mastering the download format or data extraction system; fourth, downloading the data; and fifth, accessing the downloaded data with statistical software. Secondary data analysis is not a particularly new idea; what is new is the amount of data available and the ease of access to this data. The world's largest archive of computerized social science data is available from the Inter-university Consortium for Political and Social Research (ICPSR) located within the Institute for Social Research at the University of Michigan (http://www .icpsr.umich.edu/). Here you will find information about how to join and download data from their vast database holdings, as well as a list of member institutions, training in quantitative methods to facilitate effective data use, and other data archive material. Hundreds, if not thousands, of dissertations have been completed using data accessed from the ICPSR holdings. The holdings of the U.S. Census can be found at http://www.census.gov/main/www/access.html and instructions for downloading can be found at http://www.census.gov/DES/www/inst .html. We also recommend IPUMS (Integrated Public Use Microdata Series) at the University of Minnesota Population Center (http://www .ipums.umn.edu). Here you will find a national census database dating from 1850 and an international database containing census data from around the world. Along with this ready availability of preexisting data come both great advantages and some serious risks. We first describe our perspective on the advantages of accessing secondary data, and then we add some caveats that should be considered when using secondary data.

First, secondary data are likely to be of much better quality than any graduate student could independently collect. Research is expensive, large-scale survey research is extremely expensive, and large-scale longitudinal survey research is both exorbitantly expensive and impossibly time prohibitive for a graduate student. Yet such data are easily accessible from the Internet. For example, the National Longitudinal Survey of Youth 1997 (NLSY97) is part of the National Longitudinal Surveys (NLS) program, a set of surveys sponsored by the United States Department of Labor, Bureau of Labor Statistics (BLS). These surveys gathered information at multiple points in time on the labor market experiences of diverse groups of men and women. Each of the NLS samples consists of several thousand individuals, some surveyed over several decades (http://www .icpsr.umich.edu/NACJD/). These surveys are available from the National Archive of Criminal Justice Data, accessed through ICPSR. Thus, one of the first advantages of using secondary data is that at virtually every point of the research process the data are of better quality than an individual graduate student could collect.

A second reason for making use of secondary data sources is that the costs of collecting primary data are often greater than the resources of most graduate students, even those with substantial funding. Collecting good quality quantitative data is both expensive and time-consuming. This is why many doctoral dissertations are based on cross-sectional data with small nonrandom samples. This severely limits the ability of these studies to make causal inferences, to generalize to a known population, or to achieve sufficient statistical power. Unfortunately, unless these studies are unique in some other way, they are often not publishable in peer-reviewed journals.

Given these two glowing recommendations for accessing secondary data via the Internet, why wouldn't everyone want to do so? The first reason one might not want to use someone else's data is that the data may not contain the instrumentation the researcher needs to directly address the primary research questions. This results in either changing the questions to "fit" the available instrumentation or trying to create an instrument from parts of someone else's instruments. The problem is that these "derived measures" do not have the record of reliability and validity studies that support the more highly recommended use of an established measure.

The second reason one might not want to use a secondary data source is that working with one can be terribly difficult and frustrating. Despite the archive sites' attempt to make data easy to locate and to provide extensive documentation, the downloading process can be anything but simple. Be prepared to encounter difficulties. Not all archive sites use the same process for downloading or documenting data, and it might be necessary to learn several different methods for doing so. In addition to the potential frustration involved in downloading and accessing a database with your own software, you may also need to struggle with inadequate or inaccurate documentation. You must have access to a complete description of the sampling design, accurate and complete codebooks must be available, and, when all else fails, you must have a resource to contact for help and advice when working with flaws in the available documentation.

A third reason for avoiding secondary data is that your dissertation committee may not approve its use. We find that the reasons for this are twofold. First, the dissertation process is designed to be many things. In addition to representing a new contribution to a field of inquiry, the dissertation is a training vehicle for researchers. Completing a dissertation involves full participation in all phases of the research process, including phases that are likely to be skipped when one uses secondary data, such as developing a sampling design; designing an instrument; collecting, entering, and cleaning data; and building a database. Some dissertation committees believe that because secondary data analysis allows a student to bypass parts of this process, students should not be permitted to use secondary data. Second, some dissertation advisors have had bad experiences with students who have attempted to use secondary data. These derive primarily from the first two reasons for avoiding secondary data cited earlier—lack of a match between the questions the student wants to ask and the questions the data can actually answer and difficulties with downloading and using the data.

In conclusion, we believe that under the right circumstances, using secondary data is a reasonable and acceptable approach; however, the student must do his or her homework first. You cannot assume that the perfect database is easy to find and waiting for you. You must search the available databases, using multiple sites, for the perfect match between your interests and research questions and the available data. We have provided a tip box indicating some of the largest archives of social science data, but it would be impossible to construct a comprehensive list. You might find your ideal database on a site that only contains a few unique holdings. For example, in 1921–1922, during the waning of the eugenics movement and its hereditarian interests, psychologist Lewis Terman launched a study to investigate the maintenance of early intellectual superiority over a 10-year period. This objective was soon extended into the adult years for the purpose of determining the life paths of gifted Californians. So far, 13 waves of data collection have been carried out beginning in 1921–1922 with interviews of parents and the study children and an array of tests and inventories. The first 1922 and 1928 data collections focused on family life and school experience and included interviews and questionnaires involving mothers of children in the study. Fathers were not thought to be important in child rearing, at least compared with mothers, so fathers were not included among the respondents. Various life changes within the Terman sample and new leadership from Robert Sears, Lee Cronbach, Pauline Sears, and Albert Hastorf brought fresh attention to issues of aging, work life and retirement, family, and life evaluation across follow-ups for 1972, 1977, 1982, 1986, and 1991–1992 (from the University of Georgia study description). For a more detailed description of this study and access to the Terman Data Files see http://dataserv.libs.uga.edu/icpsr/8092/8092.html.

A more thorough treatment of secondary analysis, including Web-based data downloads, can be found in *Research Methods in the Social Sciences,* by Chava Frankfort-Nachmias and David Nachmias (2006, Chapter 13). We hope you will give Web-based data collection serious consideration as a primary research approach and not just as a secondary option when traditional methods of data collection fail. If you are just curious, we recommend starting with the general sites at the University of Georgia (http://dataserv.libs.uga.edu/datasite.html) or the University of California San Diego "Data on the Net" site (http://odwin.ucsd .edu/idata/), which contains a searchable listing of 361 Internet sites of numeric social science statistical data, data catalogs, data libraries, social science gateways, addresses, and more.

The Internet as a Primary Data Collection Resource for Quantitative and Qualitative Data

Use of the Internet as a primary data collection resource can occur in a number of ways. First, you may simply wish to use the Internet to access archived records and information. For example, the Proquest (http://www.proquest.com/markets/academic.shtml) database contains all articles from the *New York Times*, searchable by topic or keywords. One of our students is using this database to search for articles describing deaths during the Vietnam War period. Second, you may wish to use the Internet as a source of unobtrusive data in which you monitor online communications that occur in chat rooms, Web logs (blogs), online dating services, and other similar sources of online communications. For example, a number of studies have been published that compare male and female self-descriptions on Internet dating services (e.g., Cornwell & Lundgren, 2001). Third, you may wish to design your own data collection instrument and publish it on the Internet. Only a few years ago this was a major task, best undertaken by an experienced Web page designer. A number of Internet-based survey design and data archiving services have recently appeared that are designed to help you construct an Internet-based survey and receive a complete database in return. This saves much of the drudgery of actually having to enter the data into a database and the costs of mailing, printing, and entering data. In addition, many sites allow online design, which makes the process of designing a survey simple, fast, and intuitive. We provide a tip box in this chapter, taken from an article by Wright (2005), that identifies 20 online survey research companies and provides links, pricing, and services.

Our students have had some experience with the use of online services for survey design and data collection. If you use a Web site service for collecting or analyzing your data, you must vigilantly monitor the process yourself and not rely on the Web site proprietor to do so. For instance, one of our dissertation students was seeking a sample size of 200 to complete a survey. To reach a broad audience, she contracted with a Web-based research company to host her survey so that participants could complete the scales online. To optimize the likelihood of obtaining her required sample size within a reasonable period of time, she offered a $20 fee to any qualified respondent (young women with eating disorders) who completed the survey. One day after she offered the financial inducement, the Web site proprietor informed her that she had 549 completed surveys and several hundred more in process. Both aghast and delighted, she shut down the site immediately, realizing that she now had a terrific sample of participants but owed them almost $11,000 out of her own pocket! She was, of course, ethically obligated to pay all legitimate respondents who completed the task. Her mistake was in not setting a limit to the sample size beforehand, an understandable but costly error. Based on our experience with these and similar problems encountered by our students, we offer the following recommendations:

1. Research the available companies carefully. Services and pricing vary widely. The more expensive sites may offer no more than the less expensive ones offer, or they may offer more than you need.

2. Once online, check every word of every question and all response choice categories against your original instrument. Errors and omissions are common and are your responsibility to locate.

3. Do a trial run with any online survey or experiment because once it is connected to the Internet, small errors can have large consequences. If possible obtain a small "trail" data set to make sure that the download includes everything.

4. Use a stop order to avoid being overwhelmed with data unless collecting additional data is free.

5. Include numerous checks to make certain that those who complete your survey are actually part of your desired population. For example, if you only want to study males, then include instructions at the beginning, indicating that only males are eligible to complete the survey, and then also ask for the respondents' gender later in the survey.

6. Any incentive, monetary or otherwise, is likely to result in multiple responses from the same respondent, or responses from ineligible respondents. Discuss options for preventing this potential problem with the service provider and design your survey in ways to detect cheaters.

7. Remember that a proposal calling for a given number of responses typically doesn't take into consideration ineligible respondents or incomplete data. Plan to eliminate at least 20% or your cases due to incomplete data or unusable responses.

In a recent article, Wright (2005) argued that there are many advantages to online survey research, including access to unique populations, considerably reduced costs, and a significant savings of time. However, Wright (2005) also warned that issues of sampling pose a major problem for online researchers due to the inability to fully specify the sampling frame. We recommend that anyone interested in conducting a Web-based survey read Wright's article, which is available at http://jcmc.indiana.edu/v0110/issue3/wright.html.

There are some important questions to ask before collecting data through the Internet. First, are you comfortable enough with your computer skills to work through the inevitable difficulties that will arise? Second, do you have an extremely clear idea of the population to be sampled and how you can reach this sample through your computer? Third, is your dissertation committee accepting and supportive of your proposed data collection strategy? Given positive answers to these questions you may wish to consider data collection via the Internet. Good resource books include Don Dillman's *Mail and Internet Surveys: The Tailored Design Method* (1999); Dale Nesbary's *Survey Research and the World Wide Web* (1999); and Samuel Best and Brian S. Krueger's *Internet Data Collection* (2004). These books offer a wealth of information on good survey design and how to use the Internet to collect survey data. Finally, *Introduction to Behavioral Research on the Internet,* by Michael Birnbaum (2001), provides helpful guidance for setting up online experiments (as well as surveys).

Internet-Based Data Analysis

A more recent advance in the use of online data archives involves passing the downloading process altogether and analyzing the data while online. A number of data archive sites now offer this option. For example, at both http://webapp.icpsr.umich.edu/GSS/ and http://csa.berkeley .edu:7502 the user may choose to either subset and download a wide variety of data or conduct a wide range of data management and statistical procedures while online. These include recoding and computing variables, cross-tabulation, mean comparisons, and multiple regression analysis. Although these sites are not numerous in number, they represent the next step in access to and statistical manipulation of Internet-based data archives.

A particularly interesting approach to online data analysis has been developed by American Institutes for Research (AIR). AIR Lighthouse (http://lighthouse.air.org/timss/default.asp) empowers users to ask their own questions of complex data sets without specialized research or statistical skills. Users can create custom-run tables, graphs, and other statistics on the Internet. Lighthouse integrates multiple complex surveys, assessments, or other data collections and captures the knowledge of expert statistical analysts. This knowledge database is stored along with the data itself. To the user, the system seems to "know the data" and to choose the right analytic procedures. This knowledge enables the system to hide the technical details and sophisticated statistical procedures from the user, who sees only perfectly tailored answers to his or her queries. Anyone interested in online data analysis should definitely explore this unique and creative approach to statistical analysis.

Data Archives and Libraries

Name of Site	URL	Comments
Center of Demography and Ecology (University of Wisconsin-Madison)	http://www.ssc.wisc.edu/cde/	Boasts "one of the country's finest collections of machine-readable data files in demography"
Cornell Institute for Economic and Social Research (Cornell University)	http://www.ciser.cornell.edu/ASPs/datasource.asp?CATEGORY=2	Direct access to selected data sets available on the Internet and links to dozens of similar sites
Consortium for International Earth Science Information Network (CIESIN)	http://www.ciesin.org/	Data on world population, environment, health, and geography, including several interactive systems to search for data
Council for European Social Science Data Archives	http://www.nsd.uib.no/cessda/index.html	Home page for the Council for European Social Science Data Archives (CESSDA) with search for data available from archives around the world
Data and Program Library Service (University of Wisconsin-Madison)	http://dpls.dacc.wisc.edu/	A collection of social science and cross-disciplinary data files, some (collected at DPLS) available for purchase and/or ftp
Institute for Research in Social Science Data Archive (IRSS) (University of North Carolina)	http://veblen.irss.unc.edu/data_archive/	Public opinion data from the Louis Harris polls, Carolina and Southern Focus Polls, and the National Network of State Polls, including a searchable database to retrieve questions and frequencies with selected data files also available for downloading

(Continued)

Data Archives and Libraries (Continued)

Name of Site	URL	Comments
International Social Survey Programme (ISSP)	http://www.issp.org/homepage.htm	Cross-national collaboration on social science surveys in 34 countries, served by the data archive Zentralarchiv für Empirische Sozialforschung (Universität zu Köln) http://www.gesis.org/ZA/ (in German)
Inter-university Consortium for Political and Social Research (ICPSR)	http://www.icpsr.umich.edu/ ICPSR also co-sponsors the following special topics archives: Health and Medical Care Archive (HMCA) http://www.icpsr.umich.edu/ HMCA/index.html International Archive of Education Data (IAED) http://www.icpsr .umich.edu/IAED/ National Archive of Computerized Data on Aging (NACDA) http://www.icpsr.umich.edu/NACDA/ National Archive of Criminal Justice Data (NACJD) http://www.icpsr.umich .edu/NACJD/ Substance Abuse and Mental Health Data Archive (SAMHDA) http://www.icpsr.umich.edu/SAMHDA/	A vast archive of social science data for research and instruction, training in quantitative methods to facilitate effective data use, a searchable database of archival holdings, as well as direct downloading of data for member institutions
National Archives and Records Administration— Center for Electronic Records	http://www.archives.gov/research/index .html	Information regarding electronic records, including numeric data files, generated by the U.S. Government agencies and available for purchase through the National Archives and Records Administration
National Data Archive of Child Abuse and Neglect	http://www.ndacan.cornell.edu/	Information regarding NDACAN including their mission, publications, and available data sets

Roper Center for Public Opinion Research	http://www.ropercenter.uconn.edu/index.html	An extensive archive of opinion polls including Gallup polls and many others
Social Science and Government Data Library (University of California, Berkeley)	http://goldrush.berkeley.edu/GovData/info/	Interactive access to selected 1990 census data and ftp access to numerous census data files including 1970 Census Fifth Count data
UK Data Archive (University of Essex)	http://www.data-archive.ac.uk/	Approximately 7,000 data sets in the social sciences
Specific Sites for Economic, Social, and Political Data		
The Gallup Organization	http://www.gallup.com/	Public opinion data from the Gallup Organization, including some tables and statistics and articles from their newsletter and other reports
General Social Survey	http://webapp.icpsr.umich.edu/GSS/ http://csa.berkeley.edu:7502/	Information regarding the biennial personal interview survey conducted by the National Opinion Research Center, including a search engine to search the codebook for relevant variables and an extract utility to subset data, as well as other databases and extensive online data analysis options
Federal Election Commission	http://www.fec.gov/	Downloadable data on campaign financing

(Continued)

259

Data Archives and Libraries (Continued)

Name of Site	URL	Comments
Living Standards Measurement Study (LSMS World Bank)	http://www.worldbank.org/html/prdph/lsms/lsmshome.html	Household surveys for numerous countries, with access conditions varying by country
National Election Studies	http://www.umich.edu/~nes/	National surveys of the American electorate, now spanning 5 decades, which provides information on the mission and procedures of the NES and other documentation
Panel Study of Income Dynamics	http://psidonline.isr.umich.edu/	Information regarding the Panel Study of Income Dynamics, a longitudinal study of American families ongoing since 1968, including topics such as employment, income, wealth, housing, and health
Uniform Crime Reports	http://fisher.lib.virginia.edu/collections/stats/crime/	Interactive system for retrieving county-level crime and arrest data
United Kingdom Election Results	http://www.election.demon.co.uk/	Links to election results from British Parliamentary Elections since 1983
HUD USER	http://www.huduser.org/	Data pertaining to housing needs, market conditions, and community development, supplied by the Department of Housing and Urban Development
Statistics about (University of Minnesota)	http://govpubs.lib.umn.edu/stat.phtml	Links to selected statistical tables, publications, and indicators arranged by subject
USDA Economics and Statistics System	http://usda.mannlib.cornell.edu/	Publications and data sets about agriculture available from the statistical units of the USDA: Economic Research Service, National Agricultural Statistics Service, and the World Agricultural Outlook Board.

Government Statistical Agencies		
Bureau of Census	http://www.census.gov/	
Bureau of Economic Analysis	http://www.bea.gov/	
Bureau of Justice Statistics	http://www.ojp.usdoj.gov/bjs/	
Bureau of Labor Statistics	http://www.bls.gov	
Bureau of Transportation Statistics	http://www.bts.gov	
Economic Research Service	http://www.ers.usda.gov	
Energy Information Administration	http://www.eia.doe.gov	
FedStats	http://www.fedstats.gov	
Centers for Medicare and Medicaid Services	http://www.cms.hhs.gov/researchers/statsdata.asp	
IRS, Statistics of Income	http://www.irs.gov/taxstats/article/0,id=117514,00.html	
National Center for Education Statistics	http://www.ed.gov/NCES	
National Center for Health Statistics	http://www.cdc.gov/nchs/default.htm	
National Science Foundation, Division of Science Resources Studies	http://www.nsf.gov/sbe/srs/stats.htm	
Statistics Canada	http://www.statcan.ca	
Statistics Division of the United Nations Dept. for Economic and Social Information and Policy Analysis	http://www.un.org/Depts/unsd	
Data on the Net (University of California San Diego)	http://odwin.ucsd.edu/idata/	Many links to sites with actual data, along with lengthy descriptions of what can be found at each site, searchable by keyword
FedStats	http://www.fedstats.gov/	Links to most U.S. federal government sites providing access to statistical data
Statistical Sources on the Web (University of Michigan)	http://www.lib.umich.edu/govdocs/stats.html	Predominantly links to government-produced data, arranged by subject

Online Services for Survey Design and Data Collection

Company Name/Product	Features	Pricing	Service Limitations
Active Websurvey	Unlimited surveys; software automatically generates HTML codes for survey forms	Information unavailable on Web site	Customer required to purchase software; limited to 9 question formats
Apian Software	Full service Web design and hosting available	$1,195 up to $5,995 depending on number of software users; customer charged for technical support	Customer required to purchase software
CreateSurvey	Standard features; educational discount	$99 a month for unlimited surveys and responses; free email support	Survey housed on company server for a set amount of time
EZSurvey	Unlimited surveys; mobile survey technology available; educational discount	$399 for basic software; additional software is extra; telephone training is $150 an hour	Customer required to purchase software
FormSite	Weekly survey traffic report; multiple language support	$9.95 up to $99.95 per month depending on desired number of response	Survey housed on company server for only a set amount of time; limited number of response per month
HostedSurvey	Standard features; educational discount	Charge is per number of responses; first 250 response are free, then around $20 every 50 responses	Survey housed on company server for only a set amount of time

InfoPoll	Standard features; software can be downloaded for free	Information unavailable on Web site; limited customer support; training available for a fee	Software can be downloaded free, but works best on InfoPoll server; customers appear to be charged for using InfoPoll server
InstantSurvey	Standard features; supports multimedia	Information unavailable on Web site; free 30-day trial	Survey housed on company server for only a set amount of time
KeySurvey	Online focus group feature; unlimited surveys	$670 per year for a basic subscription; free 30-day trial	Survey housed on company server for only a set amount of time; limited to 2000 responses
Perseus	Educational discount; mobile survey technology available	Information unavailable on Web site; free 30-day trial	Survey housed on company server for only a set amount of time
PollPro	Standard features; unlimited surveys	$249 for single user; access to PollPro server is an additional fee	Customer required to purchase software
Quask	Supports multimedia	$199 for basic software; access to Quask server for an additional fee	Customer required to purchase software; more advanced features only come with higher priced software
Ridgecrest	Standard features; educational discount	$54.95 for 30 days	Survey housed on company server for only a set amount of time; limited to 1000 responses for basic package

Online Services for Survey Design and Data Collection (Continued)

SumQuest	Standard features; user guidebook for creating questionnaire available	$495 to purchase software; free unlimited telephone support	Customer required to purchase software
SuperSurvey	Standard features	$149 per week for basic package	Survey housed on company server for only a set amount of time; 2000 response per week limit
SurveyCrafter	Standard features; educational discount	$495 for basic software package; free and unlimited technical support	Customer required to purchase software
SurveyMonkey	Standard features; unlimited surveys	$20 a month for a basic subscription; free email support	Survey housed on company server for a set amount of time; limited to 1000 initial responses
SurveySite	Company helps with all aspects of survey design, data collection, and analysis; online focus group feature	Information unavailable on Web site	Company staff rather than customer create and conduct survey
WebSurveyor	Standard features; unlimited surveys	$1,495 per year for software license	Customer required to purchase software
Zoomerang	Standard features; educational discount	$599 for software	Customer required to purchase software

SOURCE: From "Researching Internet-Based Populations: Advantages and Disadvantages of Online Survey Research, Online Questionnaire Authoring Software Packages, and Web Survey Services," by R. Wright, 2005, *Journal of Computer-Mediated Communication, 10(3)*, article 11, http://jcmc.indiana.edu/vol10/issue3/wright.html. Reprinted with permission.

12

Guidelines for the Presentation of Numbers in the Dissertation

Many dissertations require that the manuscript be typed in the format of the professional association representing the discipline of the dissertation. For example, in a department of psychology, it is likely that the dissertation will present tables and figures and describe these in the text using guidelines presented by the American Psychological Association (APA). This section describes the rules that one is likely to encounter when discussing numbers in text. Numbers may be expressed as words (five) or as figures (5), but when should a word be used as opposed to a figure? This section addresses nine areas of concern as outlined by the *Publication Manual of the American Psychological Association* (American Psychological Association, 2004). We use the guidelines presented by the APA because they are complete, likely to cover a wide range of issues, and not idiosyncratic to the field of psychology.

Expressing Numbers as Figures

General rule: Use figures to express numbers 10 and above and words to express numbers below 10 (American Psychological Association, 2004).

EXAMPLES

Correct	Incorrect
only about 13%	only about thirteen percent
a 22 mm line	a twenty-two millimeter line
four subjects	4 subjects
three out of five groups	3 out of 5 groups

Exceptions:

1. Numbers below 10 that are grouped for comparison with numbers 10 and above, and appear in the same paragraph, are also expressed as figures (American Psychological Association, 2004).

Correct	Incorrect
5 of 32 groups	five of 32 groups five of thirty-two groups
when ranked, the 3rd and 12th	when ranked, the third and twelfth when ranked, the third and 12th
8 of the 30 cases	eight of the 30 cases eight of the thirty cases

2. Numbers that immediately precede a unit of measurement are expressed as figures, regardless of size (American Psychological Association, 2004).

Correct	Incorrect
a 5 mm line	a five millimeter line a five mm line
a mean of 36.22 cm	a mean of thirty-six and twenty-two one hundredths centimeters

3. Numbers that represent statistical or mathematical functions, fractional or decimal quantities, percentages, ratios, and percentiles and quartiles are expressed as figures, regardless of size (American Psychological Association, 2004).

Correct	Incorrect
a mean of 3.54	a mean of three point fifty four
	a mean of three and fifty-four one hundredths
subtracted from 5	subtracted from five
4 3/4 times as many	four and three fourths times as many
0.44	point forty-four
	.44 (must precede a decimal with 0)
a 5 kg weight	a five kilogram weight
scored in the 4th percentile	scored in the fourth percentile

4. Numbers that represent time, dates, ages, sample or population size, scores and points on a scale, exact sums of money, and numerals as numerals are expressed as figures, regardless of size (American Psychological Association, 2004).

Correct	Incorrect
4 persons in each sample	four persons in each sample
seven 9-year-old children	seven nine-year-old children
	7 9-year-old children
in 7 years	in seven years
study began in 1984	study began in nineteen eighty-four
prior to April 1	prior to April first
no group lasted longer than 3.5 hours	no group lasted longer than three and one half hours
a score of 6 or greater	a score of six or greater
each subject was paid $7.50	each subject was paid seven dollars and fifty cents

5. Numbers that denote a specific place in a numbered series, parts of books and tables, and each number in a list of four or more numbers are expressed as figures, regardless of size (American Psychological Association, 2004).

Correct	Incorrect
sample 4	sample four
Figure 1	Figure One
page 60	page sixty
chapters 2, 5, 6, 8, and 23	chapters two, five, six, eight, and 23

Expressing Numbers as Words

General rule: Use words to express numbers below 10 that do not repre-sent precise measurements and that are not grouped for comparison with numbers 10 and above (American Psychological Association, 2004).

EXAMPLES

Correct	Incorrect
about seven or eight	about 7 or 8
one of the first	1 of the first
	1 of the 1st
only two persons	only 2 persons
two surveys	2 surveys
one-way ANOVA	1-way ANOVA
two-tailed F test	2-tailed F test

Exceptions:

1. The numbers *zero* and *one* when the words would be easier to compre-hend than the figures, or when the words do not appear in context with numbers 10 and above, are expressed in words (American Psychological Association, 2004).

Correct	Incorrect
one-on-one session	1 on 1 session
only one subject	only 1 subject
the concept of zero	the concept of 0

2. Any number that begins a sentence, title, or heading should be expressed in words. (Whenever possible, reword the sentence to avoid beginning with a number [American Psychological Association, 2004].)

Correct	Incorrect
Five studies support	5 studies support
Twenty-six percent of . . .	26% of . . .
	Twenty-six % of . . .

3. Common fractions are expressed as words (American Psychological Association, 2004).

Correct	Incorrect
one half the sample	1/2 the sample
	1 half the sample
exactly one fifth	exactly 1/5

4. Honor universally accepted usage (American Psychological Association, 2004).

Correct	Incorrect
the Twelve Apostles	the 12 Apostles
the Ten Commandments	the 10 Commandments
the Fourth of July	the 4th of July

Combining Figures and Words to Express Numbers

General rule: Use a combination of figures and words to express rounded large numbers and back-to-back modifiers (American Psychological Association, 2004).

EXAMPLES: Rounded large numbers

Correct	Incorrect
About 3 thousand	About 3,000
	About three thousand
A net loss of $1 billion	A net loss of one-billion dollars
	a net lost of $1,000,000

EXAMPLES: Back-to-back modifiers

Correct	Incorrect
3 one-way interactions	three one-way interactions
2 two dollar bills	2 $2.00 bills
	2 2 dollar bills

Ordinal Numbers

General rule: Treat ordinal numbers (except percentiles and quartiles) as you would cardinal numbers (American Psychological Association, 2004).

EXAMPLES

Correct	Incorrect
the first sample	the 1st sample
the 11th grade	the eleventh grade
the 2nd and 12th	the second and 12th
	the second and twelfth
the second	the 2nd
the 12th	the twelfth

Decimal Fractions

General rule: Place the decimal point on the line, not above the line. Use a zero before the decimal point when numbers are less than 1 (American Psychological Association, 2004).

EXAMPLES

Correct	Incorrect
0.45 mm	point forty-five millimeters
	.45 mm
a 0.2 s interval	a .2 second interval

Exception: Do not use a zero before a decimal fraction when the number cannot be greater than 1, as in correlations, probability values, proportions, and levels of statistical significance (American Psychological Association, 2004).

$$r = .44, p < .01.$$

Arabic or Roman Numerals

General rule: Use Arabic, not Roman, numerals, whenever possible (American Psychological Association, 2004).
Exception: If Roman numerals are part of an established terminology, do not change to Arabic numbers, for example, "Type II error" (American Psychological Association, 2004).

Commas

General rule: Use commas between groups of three digits in most figures of 1,000 or more (American Psychological Association, 2004).

Exceptions:

Page numbers	page 2134
Binary digits	001101010
Serial numbers	571606999
Degrees of temperature	2349° F
Acoustic frequency designations	3000 Hz
Degrees of freedom	$F(35, 1100)$
Numbers to the right of a decimal point	6,750.0748

Plurals of Numbers

General rule: To form the plurals of numbers, whether expressed as figures or as words, add "s" or "es" alone, without an apostrophe (American Psychological Association, 2004).

EXAMPLES

Correct	Incorrect
the early 1960s	the early 1960's
from the 30s and 40s	from the 30's and 40's

APA Requirements for Statistical and Mathematical Copy

1. *Your Responsibilities.* You are responsible for selecting the correct statistical method and the accuracy of all supporting data. Raw data should be retained for 5 years following publication (American Psychological Association, 2004).

2. *Should References for Statistical Analyses Be Presented?* Statistics in common use are not referenced. Less common statistics not commonly found in textbooks should be referenced. When a statistic is used in a unique or controversial manner, or when the statistic is itself the focus of the research, references should be given (American Psychological Association, 2004).

3. *Presenting Inferential Statistics in Text.* Give the symbol, degrees of freedom, value, and probability level. In addition, give the mean or other descriptive statistic to clarify the nature of the effect (American Psychological Association, 2004).

EXAMPLES: F and t tests

$F(2, 34) = 67.22, p < .001$

$t(35) = 3.71, p < .001$

EXAMPLES: Chi-square statistics

$\chi^2(4, N = 78) = 11.15, p < .05$

4. *Should Symbols or Word Terms Be Used in the Text?* Use the term, not the symbol (American Psychological Association, 2004).

EXAMPLES

Correct	Incorrect
The means were	The *M*s were
	The *X*s were
The standard deviations were	The *SD*s were

5. *How Do I Express the Number of Subjects?* Use an uppercase *N* to designate the number of members in the total sample and a lowercase *n* to designate the number of members in a limited portion of the total sample (American Psychological Association, 2004).

EXAMPLES
- a total sample of $N = 130$
- $n = 50$ in each group

6. *How Do I Express Percentages?* Use the symbol for percent only when it is preceded by a numeral. Use the word *percentage* when a number is not given (American Psychological Association, 2004).

EXAMPLES
- 21% of the sample
- the percentage of the sample

Exception: In table and figure headings and legends, use the % symbol to conserve space (American Psychological Association, 2004).

This completes our discussion of the presentation of numbers in text, but the details of APA and other formats include considerably more than just this set of rules. In addition, APA has an excellent guide to assist students with the use of the APA publication manual, *Mastering APA Style: Student's Workbook and Training Guide Fifth Edition* (Gelfand & Walker, 2002). This reference includes instruction and exercises covering references and citations, tables, statistical and mathematical copy, and other topics.

Finally, it is advisable to begin using your discipline's style at the very beginning of the dissertation process. This gives you considerable time to master the intricacies of the style and prevents you from having to "fix" hundreds of pages of text at the very end.

13

Informed Consent and Other Ethical Concerns

A s a graduate student and budding professional, one of your primary responsibilities is always to act in an ethical manner, which includes having your research reviewed for its adherence to ethical standards by an independent review committee. All universities have ethical standards for conducting research with human beings, and most have formally established research ethics committees and institutionalized procedures to guarantee that informed consent is obtained prior to initiating all research. It is the student's responsibility to become knowledgeable about the university's requirements, obtain the necessary documentation, and follow the university's guidelines. This should be done prior to collecting data, as early as possible after the research procedures are established. One important reason for meeting these expectations in a timely fashion is that you will be required to obtain an authorizing signature from the institutional review board (IRB) at your university and quite possibly the review board(s) at the site(s) where you will conduct your research. This must be completed prior to conducting your research and may take many months.

The criteria commonly proposed for determining whether or not a specific research study is ethical are grounded in norms and values reinforced by the scientific community. The following five norms are particularly noteworthy (Sieber, 1992):

1. *Validity of Research.* It is disrespectful to use people for invalid research. Invalid research yields knowledge that is apt to be erroneous, misleading, and socially harmful.

275

2. *Competency of the Researcher.* It is disrespectful to use people for research conducted by incompetent investigators. Such research does not produce good outcomes.

3. *Beneficence of Research.* It is disrespectful of people to put them in situations associated with unusual or unnecessary risk or to conduct research on a population that will not benefit from the knowledge derived from the research. Although research may involve risks, beneficence implies maximizing benefits over risks.

4. *Special Populations.* It is disrespectful to subject vulnerable people to conditions to which they cannot object.

5. *Informed Consent.* It is disrespectful to compromise people's autonomy by not allowing them to decide for themselves whether they see value in participating in a research study and whether they are willing to tolerate the associated risks.

The two main ethical issues that pertain to using subjects in social science research are the need for fully informed consent to participate and the need to emerge from the experience unharmed. Ultimately, the value of a study is determined by balancing the potential benefits, in terms of generalizable knowledge, with the costs and potential risks. A recurrent problem is the failure of students to reflect conscientiously on how particular participants are likely to experience the study. One cannot cavalierly assume that experimental manipulations, interviews, questionnaires, or even feedback of results will not be upsetting, distressing, or in some other way costly to some participants. It is permissible for research to carry some risk, but it is imperative to anticipate such risks beforehand.

Not all studies may require written informed consent agreements; however, this is not a decision that the researcher makes independently. All studies should be reviewed, regardless of the researcher's belief regarding the lack of potential harm. Examples of methodologies that typically do not require informed consent include secondary analyses of data, archival research, and the systematic observation of publicly observable data, such as shoppers in a suburban mall. In these cases, an institutional review may permit, and a researcher may request, an "expedited review" under the likelihood that the study will be determined as representing "minimal risk." There is some lack of clarity and need for judgment about the standard of minimal risk. For example, the criterion of minimal risk could pertain to research involving brief questionnaires that do not address questions likely to be disturbing to the participants. Questions regarding favored sports or preferred television programs are probably not disturbing; questions regarding childhood victimization, current mental status, and alcohol or drug abuse probably are. One way to think through the potential impact of your research procedures is to reverse roles and imagine what it would be like to be a participant in your study. What concerns would you have regarding confidentiality? What information about the study would be important for you to know? Would you feel free to decline to participate if others in your selected group did participate?

Perhaps the most controversial type of research design is one that employs concealment or deception. Famous representatives include Solomon Asch's (1955) conformity studies and Stanley Milgram's (1963) studies of obedience to authority. One question is whether more straightforward, alternative procedures are available and whether the deception is justified by the theoretical or applied value of the study. Full disclosure also needs to be given to participants as soon as possible after the data have been obtained (see following debriefing). Over the course of time, the biggest drawback to the use of concealment or deception is probably the gradual erosion of public trust in the research enterprise.

Field studies may also raise important ethical concerns when the investigator deviously manipulates variables in the environment or when a research component is covertly introduced into an everyday situation, such as gathering data from unwitting employees in the course of their work. An often-cited body of work is of Piliavin and Piliavin's studies of bystander intervention. In one 1972 study, the behavior of passengers was observed when an experimenter, posing as a "victim" with a cane, "collapsed" in a moving subway car. To experimentally manipulate the "cost" of helping, in half of the conditions the victim "bled" from the mouth and in half he did not bleed. The researchers assumed that the presence of blood increased the cost of helping because the sight of blood should arouse feelings of fear and revulsion in the typical bystander. The researchers staged approximately 42 of these incidents, each lasting approximately 3 minutes (the time between station stops). Problems encountered during the experiment included discovery and harassment by transit authority police, potentially dangerous actions on the part of real bystanders (e.g., attempting to pull the emergency cord to stop the train), and passenger panic during some of the blood trials. Clearly, such a study would not be permitted today; however, these studies illustrate the extent to which researchers are likely to go without some outside guidance from noninterested parties.

The rule here is to seek informed consent whenever there is more than minimal risk of harm to the participants. Informed consent is an active process. As the researcher, you must be convinced that the participants fully understand the project and the risks (and potential benefits) involved. Thus, in some cases it may not be sufficient to gain written informed consent when the participants are not fully informed.

The American Psychological Association (APA) has a clearly stated set of guidelines for research with human participants. The National Institutes of Health provide an excellent description of research ethics guidelines, available online at www.nihtraining.com/ohsrsite/guide lines/GrayBooklet82404.pdf. We reproduce the APA guidelines in their entirety in the box at the end of this chapter. Other disciplines may oper- ate with somewhat different standards, but this is a relatively complete list that well represents the ethical concerns voiced by researchers in the social sciences. The APA guidelines form the foundation for obtaining informed consent according to the 11 points discussed in the next section.

The Elements of Informed Consent

Tell the Participant Who Is Conducting the Study

This is usually the student; however, other persons, such as friends, spouses, or paid employees, may also be used to collect data. Include the institutional affiliation of the researcher, as well as the supervisor of the dissertation or thesis, and provide contact information.

Why Was the Particular Person Singled Out for Participation?

Answer the "Why me?" question. For example, "You have been selected to participate in this project because you have recently experienced the birth of your first child. We are particularly interested in your experience of. . . . " Sometimes not all potential participants are chosen to be included in the study. If this is the case, you need to sensitively communicate inclu- sion and exclusion criteria to those who were not selected.

What Is the Time Commitment?

Let the participant know about how long it will take to complete his or her involvement. For example, "Pretesting with these instruments indicates that it takes approximately 45 minutes to complete all forms."

Are There Any Benefits to Be Expected?

Be reasonable, but don't oversell the study. Typically, there are few or no advantages to participating in most research, although greater self-awareness, monetary remuneration, or an enhanced sense of altruism might apply. The researcher can hope that a potential participant will feel good about helping someone collect data or learn more about himself or herself, but this is not a particular benefit.

Are There Any Potential Risks, and How Have These Been Managed?

Let the participants know what the potential risks are. This includes any possible emotional, psychological, physical, social, economic, or political difficulties or harm that might ensue from participating. What will you offer participants who experience difficulties attributable to participating in your study? For example, "Some people may experience negative emotions when discussing parental alcoholism. If you would like to discuss these with someone, please feel free to call the study director (or resource) listed below. " In the case of studies with no foreseeable risks, state "there are no known risks associated with participation in this research."

Explain the Study and Offer to Answer Questions

This should be done in lay language that is easily understood by your subject population. If you cannot share the purpose of the study fully because it would compromise the integrity of the research, describe what the participant is expected to do and provide the purpose during the debriefing, a discussion following the completion of the study during which the purpose of the research is fully disclosed. Offer to answer questions about the study at that time.

Explain that Participation Is Always Voluntary

Although you have a right to use procedures that research has shown to improve response rates, potential research participants should not be subtly pressured to participate by your assumption of social status or the scientific establishment to lend more authority to the project. Moreover, the participant has a right to withdraw from the study at any time with or without a reason.

When conducting research in any setting where the participant is likely to experience pressure to participate, it is important to make this point explicit. For example, "Your participation in this research is not required and will have no effect on your grade in this course. You may choose to withdraw from the research at any time without penalty." In some settings, a person may be apprehensive that his or her social standing, job security, or friendships would be affected by participating or by not participating. In these situations, it is of particular importance that decisions to participate, to decline to participate, and to withdraw be confidential. If an agreement has been made to provide data from your study to a sponsoring agency from which participants are selected, it is important to include this information in your informed consent letter and to guarantee that demographic information that might lead to identification of a participant, such as birth date, not be included.

Provide the Participants With a Copy of the Informed Consent Form

The participant should be given a copy of the "informed consent form" (if relevant) and asked to sign another copy for the researcher. For example, "If you would like to participate in this study, please sign one copy of the attached consent form and return it in the enclosed envelope. Keep the other copy for your records."

Advise the Participant of Payment

Will the subject receive compensation for participation? Let the subject know what payment he or she can expect, if any. Payment or incentives cannot be so great as to be coercive in the sense that the participant is induced into the project by the payment.

Explain the Limits of Confidentiality to the Participant

Confidentiality refers to the treatment of information that a participant has disclosed in a relationship of trust, with the expectation that it will not be divulged to others without permission in ways that are inconsistent with the understanding of the original disclosure. Confidentiality is different from anonymity. *Anonymity* means that no one, including the researcher, will know the participant's identity, whereas confidentiality means that the participant's identity will be preserved, at all costs, by the researcher. For example, if your data are transcribed or analyzed by a third party, how can you guarantee confidentiality? If local laws require disclosure of specific events (e.g., abuse), this exception must be noted in the informed consent document. In addition, HIPAA (Health Insurance Portability and Accountability Act) requirements allow for the disclosure of information that in the past may have been kept confidential. (The official central governmental hub for all HIPAA issues including rules, standards, and implementation is http://www.hhs.gov/ocr/hipaa/.) This exception must also be noted. Typically, summary statistics based on data will be public. In funded research the data may also be public, but identifying information is removed, and there is too little relevant information available to identify specific individuals.

Inform the Participant About Debriefing

If there is to be a debriefing, let the participant know how you will do it. Typically, all participants deserve to have the opportunity to learn about the results of the study. You may choose to describe the purpose of the study in more detail at the end, as in a study that involves deception, or you may offer to send a summary of the results to those who wish to receive it. For example, "If you would like to receive a summary of the results of this research, please write your name and address in the space provided at the end of the questionnaire." (In this case, the respondent would yield anonymity, but his or her confidentiality may be preserved.) Feedback in the debriefing should be in lay language and general enough to be informative without being harmful. In general, summarized, aggregate data rather than individualized test results should be given to participants.

We have included in this chapter a sample letter of invitation (see Table 13.1) to participate in a dissertation study and a sample informed consent form from Joe Ferguson's dissertation proposal (see Table 13.2). We have also included a more generic informed consent form that allows you to fill in the blanks, that is, if the form meets the requirements of your particular institutional IRB (see Table 13.3). Note that some groups are simply not able to provide informed consent on their own. These include (but are not limited to) persons less than 18 years of age, the mentally challenged, and the psychologically disabled. In these situations, the participant's parent or legal guardian should sign the informed consent form. Finally, Table 13.4 presents a list of questions to guide you in determining whether or not you have attended to all relevant ethics principles in administering your study.

Table 13.1   Sample Letter of Invitation to Participate in a Research Project

---

CHILDHOOD TRAUMA AND PERSONALITY

I am currently involved in a research project addressing clinical issues related to childhood trauma and personality. The project examines the relationship of certain childhood experiences to specific heightened abilities. The study is performed as a partial fulfillment of the requirements for my PhD degree in clinical psychology at the University of the North Pole under the supervision of Dr. Chilly Scholar.

Your participation in this project will provide useful information on this topic. You qualify for participation if you are between the ages of 18 and 65 years. You will be asked to complete five (5) brief true-false instruments that will take about 30 minutes. You will also be asked to fill out a background questionnaire and a childhood history survey that will take approximately 20 to 30 minutes.

Participation in this study is strictly voluntary. You may withdraw from the study at any point without penalty. Participation is not associated with your class grade. All data from this project are confidential and will be used for research purposes only. Data from questionnaires and instruments are anonymous. Names of participants will not be connected to information and scores.

Although there are no foreseeable risks to the participant, the childhood history survey contains detailed questions regarding family violence and abuse. If you feel questions of this type would upset you, please feel free to decline from participation at any point in this project.

Thank you for your assistance.

(Signature)
Name of researcher
Telephone number

Bias-Free Writing

We conclude this chapter with a brief discussion of ethical issues in scholarly writing. Throughout the dissertation process, it is important to avoid language and materials that are oppressive or discriminatory to any group of people. Questionnaires and measures should be checked scrupulously to be certain that they do not imply that it is "normal" or "right" to belong to a specific ethnic group, have a particular sexual preference, or engage in a particular lifestyle. Writers need to stay current with language that is sensitive to diverse groups because what was acceptable terminology yesterday may not be acceptable today.

Table 13.2   Informed Consent to Participate in Research

This study is concerned with the way in which men enrolled in the Domestic Abuse Counseling Center (DACC) treatment program think about the future. The results of this research may help to improve programs like the one you are enrolled in. This study is being conducted by Joe Ferguson, under the supervision of Anthony Greene PhD, in partial fulfillment of his requirements for the PhD in clinical psychology from Fielding Graduate University.

Please read this form carefully and sign it if you choose to participate in this research study. *Your participation is entirely voluntary and you should feel free NOT to complete this form or the enclosed materials if you do not want to. You may withdraw from the study at any time even if you choose to participate. If you do not participate, there will be no penalty of any kind, and it will not affect your status in the DACC program.* **If you do not want to participate in this study, please read the enclosed article while others complete their surveys and then return the forms in the envelope that they came in,** *keeping the article and one unsigned copy of the informed consent for yourself.*

The study involves the completion of 4 short questionnaires plus a short form indicating your age, ethnicity, marital status, number of children, education, employment, family income, and number of weeks completed in the DACC program so far. It should take 20 to 30 minutes to complete all study materials. The information you provide will be kept strictly confidential and anonymous. *The questionnaires will not include your name and no personally identifying information will be recorded anywhere except on this informed consent form.* This informed consent form will be separated from the other study materials immediately following this group session and stored for a period of 3 years, after which they will be destroyed. The only use that will be made of the personal information on this form will be to select a winner of the *optional* $100 lottery for research participants, and to mail a summary of results when this research project is completed if you request one. No individual results will be recorded or reported. The $100 lottery prize will be mailed to a participant selected at random after the study is completed at the address you may choose to provide below. There is no other financial reward for participation in this study.

There is no risk to you perceived in this research study and you may develop some personal awareness as a result of your participation in this research. If you become uncomfortable at any time you are free to withdraw from the study, and you can call the DACC hotline for support any time at XX. The results of this research will be published in the researcher's dissertation and possibly in journals or books.

If you have any questions about any aspect of this study please speak to Joe Ferguson before signing this form. Feel free to contact Joe Ferguson at any time by phone at XX, or by mail at XX. You may also contact Dr. Anthony Greene at XX or Dr. Kjell Rudestam at XX.

Two copies of this informed consent form have been provided. If you choose to participate in this study, please sign both, indicating you have read, understood, and agreed to participate in this research. Whether you choose to

(Continued)

Table 13.2 (Continued)

---

participate or not, please return one copy of the informed consent in the envelope along with the other research materials and keep the other copy for yourself.

The Institutional Review Board of Fielding Graduate University retains access to all signed informed consent forms.

I certify that I am over 18 years of age, and that I agree to the terms and conditions above.

NAME OF PARTICIPANT (please print)

SIGNATURE OF PARTICIPANT   DATE

Provide your mailing address below *only if* you want to enter the $100 participant lottery or if you want to receive a summary of the results from this study after it is completed.

❑   Check here to enter the optional $100 lottery for participants
❑   Check here to receive a summary of research results

STREET ADDRESS

CITY, STATE, ZIP

SOURCE: Ferguson, 2006. Reprinted with permission of the author.

Here are a few guidelines to keep in mind to eliminate bias:

1. Substitute gender-neutral words and phrases for gender-biased words. A common mistake is the inadvertent use of sexist terms that are deeply entrenched in our culture, such as *chairman* instead of *chairperson, mothering* instead of *parenting,* and *mankind* instead of *humankind.*

2. Use designations in parallel fashion to refer to men and women equally: "5 men and 14 women," *not* "5 men and 14 females."

3. Do not assume that certain professions are gender related (e.g., "the scientist . . . he") and avoid sexual stereotyping (e.g., "a bright and beautiful female professor").

Table 13.3   Sample Informed Consent Form

Include the words "Informed Consent" (Letter, Form, etc.) at the top. Everything in *italics* would be deleted from a final version.

You have been asked to participate in a research study conducted by _____, a doctoral student in the School of _____ at _____. This study is supervised by _____. This research involves the study of _____ and is part of _____'s doctoral dissertation. You are being asked to participate in this study because you _____. *(Note: If someone has given you this person's name, explain that here. Indicate that the nominator will not be advised whether or not the nominee chose or chose not to participate.)*

The study involves _____, to be arranged at your convenience. This will last approximately _____ minutes. *(Note: If you are asking the participant to do several things, include each of them in this way.)* The total time involved in participation will be approximately _____.

The information you provide will be kept strictly confidential. The informed consent forms and other identifying information will be kept separate from the data. All materials will be kept _____ *(state where and how)*. *(Note: If using recordings, add)* "The tape recordings will be listened to only by the researcher *(and include anyone else, such as the dissertation chair)*, and possibly a confidential research assistant, who has signed the attached Professional Assistance Confidentiality Agreement." *(Note: If using any kind of assistant, include a statement here.)* Any records that would identify you as a participant in this study, such as informed consent forms, will be destroyed by _____ approximately ____ years after the study is completed.

You will be asked to provide a different name for any quotes that might be included in the final research report. If any direct quotes will be used, permission will be sought from you first.

The results of this research will be published in my dissertation and possibly in subsequent journals or books.

You may develop greater personal awareness of _____ as a result of your participation in this research. The risks to you are considered *(minimal, moderate, significant)*; there is *(no likelihood, a small chance, a possible chance, a probability)* that you may experience some emotional discomfort during or after your participation. Should you experience such discomfort, please contact _____.

You may withdraw from this study at any time, either during or after your participation, without negative consequences. Should you withdraw, your data will be eliminated from the study and will be destroyed. *(Note: Sometimes it is impossible to do this, e.g., for focus group participants. If that is so, make sure to say so.)*

(Continued)

Table 13.3 (Continued)

No compensation will be provided for participation. *(Note: If you are providing compensation or an incentive, describe it in this section, and how and when it will be provided.)*

You may request a copy of the summary of the final results by indicating your interest at the end of this form.

If you have any questions about any aspect of this study or your involvement, please tell the Researcher before signing this form. You may also contact the supervising faculty if you have questions or concerns about your participation in this study. The supervising faculty has provided contact information at the bottom of this form.

Two copies of this informed consent form have been provided. Please sign both, indicating you have read, understood, and agree to participate in this research. Return one to the researcher and keep the other for your files. The Institutional Review Board of _____ retains access to all signed informed consent forms.

_____
NAME OF PARTICIPANT (please print)

_____
SIGNATURE OF PARTICIPANT

_____
DATE

FACULTY ADVISOR'S NAME HERE   RESEARCHER'S NAME HERE
RESEARCHER'S ADDRESS LINE
RESEARCHER'S TELEPHONE HERE

Yes, please send a summary of the study results to:

_____
NAME (please print)

_____
STREET ADDRESS

_____
CITY, STATE, ZIP

Table 13.4   The Five C's of Research Ethics Principles

1. Confidentiality
   - How are you going to keep the identities of your participants, organizations, and other named entities confidential? Will you use numbers, code, or pseudonyms? How will you disguise the location and types of organizations?
   - How will you prevent other members of a group or organization from knowing who was a participant and who was not? If you use referrals or nominations, will you identify the nominators? Why?
   - How will you keep the names of anyone or any organizations mentioned in an interview or journal or focus group confidential?
   - If you are using groups, how will you keep the information discussed in the group confidential? Will it matter if the group members are able to identify each other?
   - How will you store the data and when will they be destroyed?

2. Coercion
   - How will you contact volunteers and obtain their consent?
   - How will your position or personal relationship with them affect their participation and how will you guard against feelings of coercion?
   - How will you make sure that the supervisors/teachers/therapists of your participants (if relevant) do not exert any pressure on them to participate?
   - How will you ensure that the supervisors/teachers/therapists will not know who participated and who did not (if this is a consideration)?
   - How will you make it clear that participants can withdraw from the study or withdraw all or some of the data they have generated?

3. Consent
   - Do you tell your participants everything about what is expected of them, including what they must do, what the time commitment is, what the procedures are, and so forth? If not, why not?
   - Do you tell the participants what the study is about? If not, why not?
   - Do you identify yourself, the name of your faculty supervisor, and your institution on the informed consent form?
   - Do you tell members of any group who may be excluded why their data or their participation is unnecessary?
   - Do you make clear that participants have the right to withdraw any or all of the data they have generated without adverse consequences for any employment, therapy, educational services, etc. to which they are entitled?
   - Do you make clear what the risks and benefits of the research are for the participant?

(Continued)

Table 13.4 (Continued)

---

4. Care
    - Do you describe the risks and benefits of your research fairly?
    - What will you do if someone experiences distress as a result of participating in your research?
    - Do you make it clear that you will be available to answer questions?
    - Have you considered the effects of any personal questions you intend to ask and do you warn your participants that there will be personal materials involved in the research?

5. Communication
    - How will you check out the accuracy of your transcripts and quotes (if applicable)?
    - How will you inform your participants about the outcome of your study?
    - Did you make a copy of the informed consent form available to the participant?

SOURCE: "The Five C's: Principles to Keep in Mind," in Research Ethics Committee, The Fielding Institute, *Fielding Institute Research Ethics Procedures* (1999). Reprinted with permission from Fielding Graduate Institute.

4. Avoid gender-biased pronouns (e.g., "A consultant may not always be able to see *his* clients"). A few nonsexist alternatives to this pervasive problem are to:
    a. Add the other gender: *"his or her* clients."* This alternative should be used only occasionally because it can become very cumbersome. It is, however, preferable to awkward constructions such as *s/he, him/her,* or *he(she).*
    b. Use the plural form: "Consultants . . . *their* clients."
    c. Delete the adjective: "to see clients."
    d. Rephrase the sentence to eliminate the pronoun: "Clients may not always be seen by their consultants."
    e. Replace the masculine or feminine pronouns with *one* or *you.*

5. Do not identify people by race or ethnic group unless it is relevant. If it is relevant, try to ascertain the currently most acceptable terms and use them.

6. Avoid language that suggests evaluation or reinforces stereotypes. For example, referring to a group as "culturally deprived" is evaluative, and remarking that the "Afro-American students, *not surprisingly,* won the athletic events" reinforces a stereotype.

7. Don't make unsupported assumptions about various age groups (e.g., that the elderly are less intellectually able or are remarkable for continuing to work energetically).

Ethical Principles of Psychologist and Code of Conduct (2002)

8. Research and Publication

8.01 Institutional Approval

When institutional approval is required, psychologists provide accurate information about their research proposals and obtain approval prior to conducting the research. They conduct the research in accordance with the approved research protocol.

8.02 Informed Consent to Research

(a) When obtaining informed consent as required in Standard 3.10, Informed Consent, psychologists inform participants about (1) the purpose of the research, expected duration, and procedures; (2) their right to decline to participate and to withdraw from the research once participation has begun; (3) the foreseeable consequences of declining or withdrawing; (4) reasonably foreseeable factors that may be expected to influence their willingness to participate such as potential risks, discomfort, or adverse effects; (5) any prospective research benefits; (6) limits of confidentiality; (7) incentives for participation; and (8) whom to contact for questions about the research and research participants' rights. They provide opportunity for the prospective participants to ask questions and receive answers. (See also Standards 8.03, Informed Consent for Recording Voices and Images in Research; 8.05, Dispensing With Informed Consent for Research; and 8.07, Deception in Research.)

(b) Psychologists conducting intervention research involving the use of experimental treatments clarify to participants at the outset of the research (1) the experimental nature of the treatment; (2) the services that will or will not be available to the control group(s) if appropriate; (3) the means by which assignment to treatment and control groups will be made; (4) available treatment alternatives if an individual does not wish to participate in the research or wishes to withdraw once a study has begun; and (5) compensation for or monetary costs of participating including, if appropriate, whether reimbursement from the participant or a third-party payor will be sought. (See also Standard 8.02a, Informed Consent to Research.)

8.03 Informed Consent for Recording Voices and Images in Research

Psychologists obtain informed consent from research participants prior to recording their voices or images for data collection unless (1) the research consists solely of naturalistic observations in public places, and it is not anticipated that the recording will be used in a manner that could cause personal identification or harm, or (2) the research design includes deception, and consent for the use of the recording is obtained during debriefing. (See also Standard 8.07, Deception in Research.)

8.04 Client/Patient, Student, and Subordinate Research Participants

(a) When psychologists conduct research with clients/patients, students, or subordinates as participants, psychologists take steps to protect the prospective participants from adverse consequences of declining or withdrawing from participation.

(Continued)

Ethical Principles of Psychologist and Code of Conduct (2002) (Continued)

(b) When research participation is a course requirement or an opportunity for extra credit, the prospective participant is given the choice of equitable alternative activities.

8.05 Dispensing With Informed Consent for Research

Psychologists may dispense with informed consent only (1) where research would not reasonably be assumed to create distress or harm and involves (a) the study of normal educational practices, curricula, or classroom management methods conducted in educational settings; (b) only anonymous questionnaires, naturalistic observations, or archival research for which disclosure of responses would not place participants at risk of criminal or civil liability or damage their financial standing, employability, or reputation, and confidentiality is protected; or (c) the study of factors related to job or organization effectiveness conducted in organizational settings for which there is no risk to participants' employability, and confidentiality is protected or (2) where otherwise permitted by law or federal or institutional regulations.

8.06 Offering Inducements for Research Participation

(a) Psychologists make reasonable efforts to avoid offering excessive or inappropriate financial or other inducements for research participation when such inducements are likely to coerce participation.

(b) When offering professional services as an inducement for research participation, psychologists clarify the nature of the services, as well as the risks, obligations, and limitations. (See also Standard 6.05, Barter With Clients/Patients.)

8.07 Deception in Research

(a) Psychologists do not conduct a study involving deception unless they have determined that the use of deceptive techniques is justified by the study's significant prospective scientific, educational, or applied value and that effective nondeceptive alternative procedures are not feasible.

(b) Psychologists do not deceive prospective participants about research that is reasonably expected to cause physical pain or severe emotional distress.

(c) Psychologists explain any deception that is an integral feature of the design and conduct of an experiment to participants as early as is feasible, preferably at the conclusion of their participation, but no later than at the conclusion of the data collection, and permit participants to withdraw their data. (See also Standard 8.08, Debriefing.)

8.08 Debriefing

(a) Psychologists provide a prompt opportunity for participants to obtain appropriate information about the nature, results, and conclusions of the research, and they take reasonable steps to correct any misconceptions that participants may have of which the psychologists are aware.

(b) If scientific or humane values justify delaying or withholding this information, psychologists take reasonable measures to reduce the risk of harm.

(c) When psychologists become aware that research procedures have harmed a participant, they take reasonable steps to minimize the harm.

8.09 Humane Care and Use of Animals in Research

(a) Psychologists acquire, care for, use, and dispose of animals in compliance with current federal, state, and local laws and regulations, and with professional standards.

(b) Psychologists trained in research methods and experienced in the care of laboratory animals supervise all procedures involving animals and are responsible for ensuring appropriate consideration of their comfort, health, and humane treatment.

(c) Psychologists ensure that all individuals under their supervision who are using animals have received instruction in research methods and in the care, maintenance, and handling of the species being used, to the extent appropriate to their role. (See also Standard 2.05, Delegation of Work to Others.)

(d) Psychologists make reasonable efforts to minimize the discomfort, infection, illness, and pain of animal subjects.

(e) Psychologists use a procedure subjecting animals to pain, stress, or privation only when an alternative procedure is unavailable and the goal is justified by its prospective scientific, educational, or applied value.

(f) Psychologists perform surgical procedures under appropriate anesthesia and follow techniques to avoid infection and minimize pain during and after surgery.

(g) When it is appropriate that an animal's life be terminated, psychologists proceed rapidly, with an effort to minimize pain and in accordance with accepted procedures.

8.10 Reporting Research Results

(a) Psychologists do not fabricate data. (See also Standard 5.01a, Avoidance of False or Deceptive Statements.)

(b) If psychologists discover significant errors in their published data, they take reasonable steps to correct such errors in a correction, retraction, erratum, or other appropriate publication means.

8.11 Plagiarism

Psychologists do not present portions of another's work or data as their own, even if the other work or data source is cited occasionally.

8.12 Publication Credit

(a) Psychologists take responsibility and credit, including authorship credit, only for work they have actually performed or to which they have substantially contributed. (See also Standard 8.12b, Publication Credit.)

(b) Principal authorship and other publication credits accurately reflect the relative scientific or professional contributions of the individuals involved, regardless of their relative status. Mere possession of an institutional position, such as department chair, does not justify authorship credit. Minor contributions to the research or to the writing for publications are acknowledged appropriately, such as in footnotes or in an introductory statement.

(c) Except under exceptional circumstances, a student is listed as principal author on any multiple-authored article that is substantially based on the student's doctoral dissertation. Faculty advisors discuss publication credit with students as

(Continued)

Ethical Principles of Psychologist and Code of Conduct (2002) (Continued)

early as feasible and throughout the research and publication process as appropriate. (See also Standard 8.12b, Publication Credit.)

8.13 Duplicate Publication of Data

Psychologists do not publish, as original data, data that have been previously published. This does not preclude republishing data when they are accompanied by proper acknowledgment.

8.14 Sharing Research Data for Verification

(a) After research results are published, psychologists do not withhold the data on which their conclusions are based from other competent professionals who seek to verify the substantive claims through reanalysis and who intend to use such data only for that purpose, provided that the confidentiality of the participants can be protected and unless legal rights concerning proprietary data preclude their release. This does not preclude psychologists from requiring that such individuals or groups be responsible for costs associated with the provision of such information.

(b) Psychologists who request data from other psychologists to verify the substantive claims through reanalysis may use shared data only for the declared purpose. Requesting psychologists obtain prior written agreement for all other uses of the data.

8.15 Reviewers

Psychologists who review material submitted for presentation, publication, grant, or research proposal review respect the confidentiality of and the proprietary rights in such information of those who submitted it.

SOURCE: Copyright © 2002 by the American Psychological Association. Adapted with permission.

References

American Psychological Association. (2004). *Publication manual of the American Psychological Association* (5th ed.). Washington, DC: American Psychological Association.

Armstrong, D. G. (1994). *The dreams of the blind and their implications for contemporary theories of dreaming.* Unpublished doctoral dissertation, Fielding Graduate University, Santa Barbara, CA.

Asch, S. E. (1955). Opinions and social pressure. *Scientific American, 193,* 31-35.

Atkinson, P., & Hammersley, M. (1994). Ethnography and participant observation. In N. K. Denzin & Y. S. Lincoln (Eds.), *Handbook of qualitative research* (pp. 249-261). Thousand Oaks, CA: Sage.

Bailey, P. A. (1992). *A phenomenological study of the psychological transition from being a mother of dependent daughters to being a mother of adult daughters.* Unpublished doctoral dissertation, Fielding Graduate University, Santa Barbara, CA.

Baron, R. M., & Kenny, D. A. (1986). The moderator-mediator variable distinction in social psychological research: Conceptual, strategic, and statistical considerations. *Journal of Personality and Social Psychology, 51,* 1173-1182.

Barrett, H. D. (1990). *Adult self-directed learning, personal computer competency and learning style: Models for more effective learning.* Unpublished doctoral dissertation, Fielding Graduate University, Santa Barbara, CA.

Becker, C. (1986). Interviewing in human science research. *Methods, 1,* 101-124.

Belenky, M., Clinchy, B., Goldberger, N., & Tarule, J. (1986). *Women's ways of knowing: The development of self, voice and mind.* New York: Basic Books.

Bem, D. J. (2004). Writing the empirical journal article. In J. M. Darley, M. P. Zanna, & H. L. Roediger (Eds.), *The complete academic: A career guide* (2nd ed., pp. 185-219). Washington, DC: American Psychological Association.

Best, S., & Krueger, B. S. (2004). *Internet data collection.* Thousand Oaks, CA: Sage.

Bevan, W. (1991). Contemporary psychology: A tour inside the onion. *American Psychologist, 46,* 475-483.

Birnbaum, M. H. (2001). *Behavioral research on the Internet.* Upper Saddle River, NJ: Prentice-Hall.

Bower, D. (2006). *Overt narcissism, covert narcissism, and self-concept clarity: Predictors of juvenile aggression.* Unpublished doctoral dissertation, Fielding Graduate University, Santa Barbara, CA.

Butler, A. (2006). *Voices from the valley: People of color discuss the intersection of race, class, and privilege in a predominantly white college town.* Unpublished doctoral dissertation, Fielding Graduate University, Santa Barbara, CA.

Caddell, D. P. (1989). *Moral education in the college environment.* Unpublished master's thesis, California State University, Fullerton.

Campbell, D. T., & Stanley, J. T. (2005). *Experimental and quasi-experimental designs for research.* Boston: Houghton Mifflin.

Charmaz, K. (2005). Grounded theory in the 21st century: Applications for advancing social justice studies. In N. K. Denzin & Y. S. Lincoln (Eds.), *The Sage handbook of qualitative research* (3rd ed., pp. 507-535). Thousand Oaks, CA: Sage.

Chase, S. E. (2005). Narrative inquiry: Multiple lenses, approaches, voices. In N. K. Denzin & Y. S. Lincoln (Eds.), *The Sage handbook of qualitative research* (3rd ed., pp. 651-679). Thousand Oaks, CA: Sage.

Christensen, G. (2005). *Conflict at the governance level in friends' schools: Discovering the potential for growth.* Unpublished doctoral dissertation, Fielding Graduate University, Santa Barbara, CA.

Clark, V. (1997). *Hidden textures: Memories of unanticipated mortal danger.* Unpublished doctoral dissertation, Fielding Graduate University, Santa Barbara, CA.

Cohen, J. (1988). *Statistical power analysis for the behavioral sciences* (2nd ed.). New York: Academic Press.

Cohen, J. (1990). Things I have learned so far. *American Psychologist, 45,* 1304-1312.

Colaizzi, P. R. (1973). *Reflections and research in psychology.* Dubuque, IA: Kendall/ Hunt.

Connell, D. (1992). *The relationship between Siddah meditation and stress in psychotherapists: A transpersonal perspective.* Unpublished doctoral dissertation, Fielding Graduate University, Santa Barbara, CA.

Cook, T. D., & Campbell, D. T. (1979). *Quasi-experimentation: Design and analysis issues for field settings.* Chicago: Rand McNally.

Cornwell, B., & Lundgren, D. C. (2001). Love on the Internet: Involvement and misrepresentation in romantic relationships in cyberspace vs. realspace. *Computer in Human Behavior, 17,* 197-211.

Cowles, M. (2000). *Statistics in psychology: An historical perspective.* (2nd ed.). Mahwah, NJ: Lawrence Erlbaum.

Crane, C. (2005). *A neuropsychological and familial study of developmental synesthesia.* Unpublished doctoral dissertation, Fielding Graduate University, Santa Barbara, CA.

Creswell, J. W. (1998). *Qualitative inquiry and research design: Choosing among five traditions.* Thousand Oaks, CA: Sage.

Creswell, J. W. (2003). *Research design: Qualitative, quantitative and mixed methods approaches* (2nd ed.). Thousand Oaks, CA: Sage.

Cronbach, L. J. (1975). Beyond the two disciplines of scientific psychology. *American Psychologist, 30,* 116-127.

Crotty, M. (1998). *The foundations of social research.* Thousand Oaks, CA: Sage.

Csikszentmihalyi, M. (1991). *Flow: The psychology of optimal experience.* New York: Harper.

Davenport, L. (1991). *Adaptation to dyslexia: Acceptance of the diagnosis in relation to coping efforts and educational plans.* Unpublished doctoral dissertation, Fielding Graduate University, Santa Barbara, CA.

Demoville, D. B. (1999). *The dynamics of organizational alignment.* Unpublished doctoral dissertation, Fielding Graduate University, Santa Barbara, CA.

Denzin, N., & Lincoln, Y. (1998). *Collecting and interpreting qualitative materials.* Thousand Oaks, CA: Sage.

Diamond, J. (2005). *Collapse: How societies choose to fail or succeed.* New York: Penguin.

Dillman, D. (1999). *Mail and Internet surveys: The tailored design method.* New York: Wiley.

Dong, L. (2005). *The impact of ethnic identity and self-esteem on Southeast and East Asian juvenile delinquents.* Unpublished doctoral dissertation, Fielding Graduate University, Santa Barbara, CA.

Dumas, C. (1989). *Daughters in family-owned business: An applied systems perspective.* Unpublished doctoral dissertation, Fielding Graduate University, Santa Barbara, CA.

Einhorn, J. (1993). *Help-seeking interactions in women's friendships: A relational perspective.* Unpublished doctoral dissertation, Fielding Graduate University, Santa Barbara, CA.

Elbow, P. (1998). *Writing with power. Techniques for mastering the writing process* (2nd ed.). New York: Oxford University Press.

Elliott, J. (1997). *Bridging of differences in dialogic democracy.* Unpublished doctoral dissertation, Fielding Graduate University, Santa Barbara, CA.

Elliott, R., Fischer, C. T., & Rennie, D. L. (1999). Evolving guidelines for publication of qualitative research studies in psychology and related fields. *British Journal of Clinical Psychology, 38,* 215-229.

Erickson, B. (2003). *A psychobiography of Richard Price: Co-founder of Esalen Institute.* Unpublished doctoral dissertation, Fielding Graduate University, Santa Barbara, CA.

Ewing, N. R. (1992). *Psychodevelopmental influences in augmentation mammoplasty.* Unpublished doctoral dissertation, Fielding Graduate University, Santa Barbara, CA.

Ferguson, J. (2006). *Time perspective and impulsivity among intimate partner violence offenders.* Unpublished doctoral dissertation, Fielding Graduate University, Santa Barbara, CA.

Feyerabend, P. K. (1981). *Philosophical papers: Vol. 2. Problems of empiricism.* Cambridge, UK: Cambridge University Press.

Fischer, C. T. (1999). Designing qualitative research reports for publication. In M. Kopola & L. Suzuki (Eds.), *Using qualitative methods in psychology* (pp. 105-122). Thousand Oaks, CA: Sage.

Flemons, D. (2001). *Writing between the lines.* New York: W. W. Norton.

Flick, U. (2002). *An introduction to qualitative research.* Thousand Oaks, CA: Sage.

Frankfort-Nachmias, C. (2006). *Research methods in the social sciences.* New York: Worth.

Frazier, P. A., Tix, A. P., & Barron, K. E. (2004). Testing moderator and mediator effects in counseling psychology research. *Journal of Counseling Psychology, 51*(1), 115-134.

Freud, S. (1997). *Dora: An analysis of a case of hysteria.* New York: Touchstone.

Gelfand, H., & Walker, C. J. (2002). *Mastering APA style: Student's workbook and training guide* (5th ed.). Washington, DC: American Psychological Association.

Gergen, K. J. (2001). Psychological science in a postmodern context. *American Psychologist, 56,* 803-813.

Gergen, M. (1988). Toward a feminist metatheory and methodology in the social sciences. In M. M. Gergen (Ed.), *Feminist thought and the structure of knowledge* (pp. 87-104). New York: New York University Press.

Gigerenzer, G. (1991). From tools to theory: A heuristic of discovery in cognitive psychology. *Psychological Review, 98,* 254-267.

Gilbert, M. K. (2007). *Attachment anxiety and avoidance, negative affectivity, alexithymia, and body image disturbance as predictors of binge eating in women.* Unpublished doctoral dissertation, Fielding Graduate University, Santa Barbara, CA.

Giorgi, A. (1985). *Phenomenology and psychological research.* New York: Harper & Row.

Glaser, B. G. (1998). *Doing grounded theory: Issues and discussions.* Mill Valley, CA: Sociology Press.

Glaser, B. G., & Strauss, A. L. (1967). *The discovery of grounded theory: Strategies for qualitative research.* Chicago: Aldine/Atherton.

Glass, G. V. (1976). Primary, secondary, and meta-analysis of research. *Educational Researcher, 5*(10), 3-8.

Glover, L. (1994). *The relevance of personal theory in psychotherapy.* Unpublished doctoral dissertation, Fielding Graduate University, Santa Barbara, CA.

Goffman, E. (1961). *Asylums.* Garden City, NY: Anchor.

Goldberg, E. (2003). *Diabetes self-care autonomy in young children within the home and school environments.* Unpublished doctoral dissertation, Fielding Graduate University, Santa Barbara, CA.

Goldberg, N. (1991). *Writing down the bones/Wild mind.* New York: Quality Paperback Book Club.

Golden-Biddle, K., & Locke, K. D. (2005). *Composing qualitative research.* Thousand Oaks, CA: Sage.

Goodwin, C. (2006). *The impact of disclosure on the supervisory relationship.* Unpublished doctoral dissertation, Fielding Graduate University, Santa Barbara, CA.

Greenwood, D. J., & Levin, M. (2006). *Introduction to action research* (2nd ed.). Thousand Oaks, CA: Sage.

Gubrium, J. F., & Holstein, J. A. (1997). *The new language of qualitative method.* New York: Oxford University Press.

Hamilton, L. C. (1990). *Modern data analysis.* New York: Wadsworth.

Hardwick, C. (1990). *Object relations and reality testing in adult children of alcoholics: An exploratory and descriptive study.* Unpublished doctoral dissertation, Fielding Graduate University, Santa Barbara, CA.

Haring, E. (2006). *Between-worlds tension: A grounded theory of repatriate sensemaking.* Unpublished doctoral dissertation, Fielding Graduate University, Santa Barbara, CA.

Harlow, L. L., Mulaik, S. A., & Steiger, J. H. (Eds.). (1997). *What if there were no significance tests?* Mahwah, NJ: Lawrence Erlbaum.

Hedges, V. (2003). *Latinos surviving the educational system: A grounded theory on enhancing identity.* Unpublished doctoral dissertation, Fielding Graduate University, Santa Barbara, CA.

Hein, S. F., & Austin, W. J. (2001). Empirical and hermeneutic approaches to phenomenological research in psychology: A comparison. *Psychological Methods, 6*(1), 3-17.

Herr, K., & Anderson, G. L. (2005). *Action research dissertation.* Thousand Oaks, CA: Sage.

Holtz, P. (2003). *The self- and interactive regulation and coordination of vocal rhythms, interpretive accuracy, and progress in brief psychodynamic psychotherapy.* Unpublished doctoral dissertation, Fielding Graduate University, Santa Barbara, CA.

Hoshmand, L. T. (1989). Alternate research paradigms: A review and teaching proposal. *Counseling Psychologist, 17,* 3-79.

Human and Organization Development Program of Fielding Graduate University. (1998). *Inquiry and research knowledge area study guide of the Human and Organization Development Program of Fielding Graduate University.* Santa Barbara, CA: Fielding Graduate University.

Humphrey, D. (2003). *Adopted women who give birth: Loss, reparation, and the self-object functions.* Unpublished doctoral dissertation, Fielding Graduate University, Santa Barbara, CA.

Husserl, E. (1970). *Crisis of European sciences and transcendental phenomenology.* Evanston: Northwestern University Press.

Jersild, D. (2006). *The experience of agency in women: Narratives of women whose mothers achieved occupational success and recognition.* Unpublished doctoral dissertation, Fielding Graduate University, Santa Barbara, CA.

Jones, S. H. (2005). Autoethnography: Making the personal political. In N. K. Denzin & Y. S. Lincoln (Eds.), *The Sage handbook of qualitative research* (3rd ed., pp. 763-792). Thousand Oaks, CA: Sage.

Josselson, R., & Lieblich, A. (2003). A framework for narrative research proposals in psychology. In R. Josselson, A. Lieblich, & D. P. McAdams (Eds.), *Up close and personal: The teaching and learning of narrative research* (pp. 259-274). Washington, DC: American Psychological Association.

Katz, S. R. (1995). *The experience of chronic vulvar pain: Psychosocial dimensions and the sense of self.* Unpublished doctoral dissertation, Fielding Graduate University, Santa Barbara, CA.

Kazdin, A. E. (1982). Single case experimental designs in clinical research and practice. *New Directions for Methodology of Social and Behavioral Science, 13,* 33-47.

Kazdin, A. E. (2002). *Research design in clinical psychology* (3rd ed.). New York: Harper & Row.

Keen, E. (1975). *A primer in phenomenological psychology.* Lanham, MD: University Press of America.

Kennedy, C. H. (2004). Recent innovations in single case designs. *Journal of Behavioral Education, 13,* 209-211.

Kerlinger, F. N. (1977). *Foundations of behavioral research* (3rd ed.). New York: Holt, Rinehart & Winston.

Kerlinger, F. N., & Lee, H. B. (1999). *Behavioral research: A conceptual approach.* New York: Holt, Rinehart & Winston.

Knight, C. (2005). *Humanistic psychotherapy training: Significant experiences contributing to perceived competency development of exceptional humanistic psychotherapists.* Unpublished doctoral dissertation, Fielding Graduate University, Santa Barbara, CA.

Krebs, C. (2005). *Organic constuctionism and living process theory: A unified constructionist epistemology and theory of knowledge.* Unpublished doctoral dissertation, Fielding Graduate University, Santa Barbara, CA.

Kuhn, T. (1962). *The structure of scientific revolutions.* Chicago: University of Chicago Press.

Kvale, S. (1996). *Interviews: An introduction to qualitative research interviewing.* Thousand Oaks, CA: Sage.

LaPelle, N. (1997). *Thriving on performance evaluations in organizations.* Unpublished doctoral dissertation, Fielding Graduate University, Santa Barbara, CA.

Leon, J. M. (1991). *Family and peer relations of delinquent juvenile gang members and non-gang members.* Unpublished doctoral dissertation, United States International University, San Diego, CA.

Lewin, K. (1948). *Resolving social conflict.* New York: Harper.

Lewis, O. (1961). *The children of Sanchez: Autobiography of a Mexican family.* New York: Random House.

Liebow, E. (1968). *Tally's corner.* New York: Back Bay Books.

Lincoln, Y. S., & Guba, E. G. (1985). *Naturalistic inquiry.* Beverly Hills, CA: Sage.

Lincoln, Y. S., & Guba, E. G. (2000). Paradigmatic controversies, contradictions, and emerging confluences. In N. K. Denzin & Y. S. Lincoln (Eds.), *The Sage handbook of qualitative research* (2nd. ed., pp. 163-189). Thousand Oaks, CA: Sage.

Locke, L. F., Spirduso, W. W., & Silverman, S. J. (1999). *Proposals that work: A guide for planning dissertations and grant proposals.* Newbury Park, CA: Sage.

Lynch-Ransom, J. (2003). *Bricks and cliques: Unity and division as Internet organizational culture in an established company—An ethnographic study.* Unpublished doctoral dissertation, Fielding Graduate University, Santa Barbara, CA.

Lynd, R. S., & Lynd, H. M. (1929). *Middletown: A study in modern American culture.* New York: Harcourt Brace Jovanovich.

Macdonald, S. (1990). *Empathy, personal maturity, and emotional articulation.* Unpublished doctoral dissertation, Fielding Graduate University, Santa Barbara, CA.

MacDougall, S. (2005). *Calling on spirit: An interpretive ethnography of PeerSpirit circles as transformative process.* Unpublished doctoral dissertation, Fielding Graduate University, Santa Barbara, CA.

MacNulty, W. (2004). *Self-schemas, forgiveness, gratitude, physical health, and subjective well-being.* Unpublished doctoral dissertation, Fielding Graduate University, Santa Barbara, CA.

Mahoney, M. J. (1990). *Human change processes.* New York: Basic Books.

Marshall, C., & Rossman, G. B. (2006). *Designing qualitative research* (4th ed.). Thousand Oaks, CA: Sage.

McAdams, D. P., Josselson, R., & Lieblich, A. (Eds.). (2001). *Turns in the road: Narrative studies of lives in transition.* Washington, DC: American Psychological Association.

Mead, G. H. (1934). *Mind, self and society.* Chicago: Chicago University Press.

Mertens, D. M. (2005). *Research and evaluation in education and psychology* (2nd ed.). Thousand Oaks, CA: Sage.

Miles, M. B., & Huberman, A. M. (1994). *Qualitative data analysis: A sourcebook of new methods.* Beverly Hills, CA: Sage.

Milgram, S. (1963). Behavioral study of obedience. *Journal of Abnormal and Social Psychology, 67,* 371-378.

Mishler, E. G. (1990). Validation in inquiry-guided research: The role of exemplars in narrative studies. *Harvard Educational Review, 60*, 415-442.

Mishler, E. G. (1991). *Research interviewing: Control and narrative.* Cambridge, MA: Harvard University Press.

Moore, E. (1995). *Creating organizational cultures: An ethnographic study.* Unpublished doctoral dissertation, Fielding Graduate University, Santa Barbara, CA.

Moos, R. H. (1985, August). *Work as a human context.* Lecture presented at the American Psychological Association annual convention, Los Angeles.

Morgan, D. (1998). Practical strategies for combining qualitative and quantitative methods: Applications to health research. *Qualitative Health Research, 8*(3), 362-376.

Morse, J. M. (1994). *Critical issues in qualitative research methods.* Thousand Oaks, CA: Sage.

Morse, J. M. (1998). Designing funded qualitative research. In N. K. Denzin & Y. S. Lincoln (Eds.), *Strategies of qualitative inquiry* (pp. 220-235). Thousand Oaks, CA: Sage.

Moustakas, C. (1994*). Phenomenological research methods.* Thousand Oaks, CA: Sage.

National Opinion Research Center. (2003). *General social survey.* Chicago: Author.

Neighbors, J. (1991). *Factors influencing psychologists' attitudes towards education and training.* Unpublished doctoral dissertation, United States International University, San Diego, CA.

Neimeyer, R. A. (1993). An appraisal of constructivist psychotherapies. *Journal of Consulting and Clinical Psychology, 61*(2), 221-234.

Nelson, D. (2000). *How personal relationships influence response to trauma: A study of mothers of medically fragile infants.* Unpublished doctoral dissertation, Fielding Graduate University, Santa Barbara, CA.

Nesbary, D. (1999). *Survey research and the World Wide Web.* Boston: Allyn & Bacon.

New, N. (1989). *Professional identity and gender: Impact on private practice management procedures.* Unpublished doctoral dissertation, United States International University, San Diego, CA.

Newton, R. R., & Rudestam, K. E. (1999). *Your statistical consultant: Answers to your data analysis questions.* Thousand Oaks, CA: Sage.

Newton, S. G. (1991). *The incidence of depression, substance abuse, and eating disorders in the families of anorexic probands.* Unpublished doctoral dissertation, Fielding Graduate University, Santa Barbara, CA.

Nobles, D. (2002). *The war on drugs: Metaphor and public policy imprementation.* Unpublished doctoral dissertation, Fielding Graduate University, Santa Barbara, CA.

Osherson, S. (2006). *Strengthening your writing voice while enjoying it more: On teaching writing in graduate school.* Unpublished paper, Fielding Graduate University, Santa Barbara, CA.

Packer, M. J. (1985). Hermeneutic inquiry in the study of human conduct. *American Psychologist, 40*, 1081-1093.

Patterson, G. R., DeBaryshe, B. D., & Ramsey, E. (1989). A developmental perspective on antisocial behavior. *American Psychologist, 44*, 329-335.

Peplau, L. A., & Conrad, E. (1989). Beyond nonsexist research: The perils of feminist methods in psychology. *Psychology of Women Quarterly, 13*, 379-400.

Piliavin, J. A., & Piliavin, I. M. (1972). Effect of blood on reactions to a victim. *Journal of Personality and Social Psychology, 23,* 353-361.

Polkinghorne, D. E. (1983). *Methodology for the human sciences: Systems of inquiry.* Albany: State University of New York Press.

Polkinghorne, D. E. (1989). Phenomenological research methods. In R. Valle & S. Halling (Eds.), *Existential-phenomenological perspectives in psychology* (pp. 3-16). New York: Plenum.

Popper, K. (1965). *Conjectures and refutations: The growth of scientific knowledge.* New York: Harper & Row.

Quittner, A. L., Glueckauf, R. L., & Jackson, D. N. (1990). Chronic parenting stress: Moderating versus mediating effects of social support. *Journal of Personality and Social Psychology, 5,* 1266-1278.

Rainaldi, L. (2004). *Incorporating women: A theory of female sexuality informed by psychoanalysis and biological science.* Unpublished doctoral dissertation, Fielding Graduate University, Santa Barbara, CA.

Rennie, D. (1998). Grounded theory methodology: The pressing need for a coherent logic of justification. *Theory and Psychology, 8,* 101-119.

Richards, L. (2005). *Handling qualitative data: A practical guide.* Thousand Oaks, CA: Sage.

Richards, N. (1991). *School-based assessment of students at risk for drug abuse.* Unpublished doctoral dissertation, United States International University, San Diego, CA.

Rico, G. L. (1983). *Writing the natural way.* Los Angeles: J. P. Tarcher.

Riessman, C. K. (1990). *Divorce talk: Women and men make sense of personal relationships.* New Brunswick, NJ: Rutgers University Press.

Rogers, S. J., Parcel, T. L., & Menaghan, E. G. (1991). The effects of maternal working conditions and mastery on child behavior problems: Studying the intergenerational transmission of social control. *Journal of Health and Social Behavior, 32*(2), 145-164.

Rubin, H. J., & Rubin, I. S. (2004). *Qualitative interviewing: The art of hearing data* (2nd ed.). Thousand Oaks, CA: Sage.

Sangster, M. J. (1991). *Judgment and decision making under conditions of uncertainty.* Unpublished doctoral dissertation, Fielding Graduate University, Santa Barbara, CA.

Schaefer, J. A., & Moos, R. H. (1998). The context for personal growth: Life crises, individual and social resources, and coping. In R. Tedeschi, C. Park, & L. Calhoun (Eds.), *Post traumatic growth: Theory and research in the aftermath of crisis* (pp. 99-125). New York: Lawrence Erlbaum.

Schecter, E. (2004). *Women-loving women loving men: Sexual fluidity and sexual identity in midlife lesbians.* Unpublished doctoral dissertation, Fielding Graduate University, Santa Barbara, CA.

Schutz, W. C. (1966). *FIRO: A three dimensional theory of interpersonal behavior.* Palo Alto, CA: Science and Behavior Books.

Shapiro, J. J., & Nicholsen, S. (1986). *Guidelines for writing papers.* Santa Barbara, CA: Fielding Graduate University.

Sherman, S. (1995). *Living with asthma: An exploration of meaning.* Unpublished doctoral dissertation, Fielding Graduate University, Santa Barbara, CA.

Sieber, J. E. (1992). *Planning ethically responsible research: a guide for students and internal review boards.* Thousand Oaks, CA: Sage.

Silverman, D. (2005). *Doing qualitative research: Theory, method, and practice.* Thousand Oaks, CA: Sage.

Silverman, D. (2006). *Interpreting qualitative data: Methods for analyzing talk, text, and interaction.* (3rd ed.). Thousand Oaks, CA: Sage.

Slanger, E. (1991). *A model of physical risk-taking.* Unpublished doctoral dissertation, Fielding Graduate University, Santa Barbara, CA.

Slanger, E., & Rudestam, K. E. (1997). Motivation and disinhibition in high-risk sports: Sensation seeking and self-efficacy. *Journal of Research in Personality, 31,* 355-374.

Smith, M. B. (1991, August). *Human science—Really!* Invited symposium address presented at the American Psychological Association annual convention, San Francisco.

Smith, P. (1998). *Centeredness and the lived experience of family/divorce mediators as facilitators of dispute resolutions and as leader/advocates.* Unpublished doctoral dissertation, Fielding Graduate University, Santa Barbara, CA.

Stake, R. E. (2000). *Case studies.* In N. Denzin & Y. Lincoln (Eds.), *Handbook of qualitative research* (2nd ed., pp. 435-454). Thousand Oaks, CA: Sage.

Stake, R. E. (2005). Qualitative case studies. In N. K. Denzin & Y. S. Lincoln (Eds.), *The Sage handbook of qualitative research* (3rd ed., pp. 443-466). Thousand Oaks, CA: Sage.

Stevick, E. L. (1971). An empirical investigation of the experience of anger. In A. Giorgi, W. F. Fischer, & E. Von Eckartsberg (Eds.), *Duquesne studies in phenomenological psychology* (Vol. 1, pp. 132-138). Pittsburgh, PA: Duquesne University Press.

Stewart, L. M. (2006). Percieved stress, self-efficacy and depression, hopelessness, and suicidal ideation in a group of incarcerated women. Unpublished doctoral dissertation proposal, Fielding Graduate University, Santa Barbara, CA.

Strauss, A., & Corbin, J. (1998). *Basics of qualitative research: Grounded theory procedures and techniques* (2nd ed.). Thousand Oaks, CA: Sage.

Stringer, E. T. (1999). *Action research: A handbook for practitioners* (2nd ed.). Thousand Oaks, CA: Sage.

Sutherland, E. (1924). *Principles of criminology.* Philadelphia: W. B. Saunders.

Tabachnick, B. G., & Fidell, L. S. (2006). *Using multivariate statistics* (5th ed.). Boston: Allyn & Bacon.

Tal, I. (2004). *Exploring the meaning of becoming a woman in a non-Western culture: A narrative analysis of first menstruation stories of Ethiopian Jewish women.* Unpublished doctoral dissertation, Fielding Graduate University, Santa Barbara, CA.

Tashakkori, A., & Teddlie, C. (1998). *Mixed methodology: Combining qualitative and quantitative approaches.* Thousand Oaks, CA: Sage.

Toulmin, S. (1972). *Human understanding: The collective use and evolution of concepts.* Princeton, NJ: Princeton University Press.

Truss, L. T. (2003). *Eats, shoots and leaves.* New York: Penguin.

Turner, V. (1988). *The anthropology of performance.* New York: Performing Arts Journal Publications.

van Kaam, A. (1966). Application of the phenomenological method. In A. van Kaam (Ed.), *Existential foundations of psychology* (pp. 294-329). Lanham, MD: University Press of America.

Veroff, J. (1993). *Common differences between quantitative and qualitative methods.* Unpublished manuscript, Fielding Graduate University, Santa Barbara, CA.

Wardell, W. (1985). *The reunion of the male prison inmate with his family.* Unpublished doctoral dissertation, Fielding Graduate University, Santa Barbara, CA.

Wegmann, M. F. (1992). *Information processing deficits of the authoritarian mind.* Unpublished doctoral dissertation, Fielding Graduate University, Santa Barbara, CA.

Weiss, R. S. (1994). *Learning from strangers.* New York: Free Press.

Whyte, W. F. (1955). *Street corner society: The social structure of an Italian slum.* Chicago: University of Chicago Press.

Williams, H. (2006). *Our bodies, our wisdom: Engaging Black men who experience same-sex desire in Afrocentric ritual, embodied epistemology, and collaborative inquiry.* Unpublished doctoral dissertation, Fielding Graduate University, Santa Barbara, CA.

Williams, R. L. (1989). *Finding voice: The transition from individualism to social advocacy.* Unpublished doctoral dissertation, Fielding Graduate University, Santa Barbara, CA.

Winograd, T., & Flores, F. (1986). *Understanding computers and cognition: A new foundation for design.* Norwood, NJ: Ablex.

Witt, J. (1997). *Learning to learn: Action research in community college administration.* Unpublished doctoral dissertation, Fielding Graduate University, Santa Barbara, CA.

Wolcott, H. F. (1994). *Transforming qualitative data: Description, analysis, and interpretation.* Thousand Oaks, CA: Sage.

Woodard, C. (2001). *Hardiness and the concept of courage.* Unpublished doctoral dissertation, Fielding Graduate University, Santa Barbara, CA.

Wright, K. B. (2005). Researching Internet based populations: Advantages and disadvantages of online survey research, online questionnaire authoring packages, and Web survey services. *Journal of Computer-Mediated Communication, 10*(3). Retrieved October 2, 2006, from http://jcmc.indiana.edu/vol10/issue3/wright.html.

Yin, R. K. (2002). *Case study research* (3rd ed). Thousand Oaks, CA: Sage.

Zemansky, T. (2005). *The risen phoenix: Positive transformation within the context of long-term recovery in alcoholics anonymous.* Unpublished doctoral dissertation, Fielding Graduate University, Santa Barbara, CA.

Name Index

Anderson, G., 57
Armstrong, D., 91, 183
Asch, S., 277
Atkinson, P., 41
Austin, W., 49

Bailey, P., 106
Barron, K., 13
Baron, R., 13
Barrett, H., 211, 214, 215
Barry, C., 180
Becker, C., 64
Belenky, M., 44, 239
Bem, D., 223, 224
Best, S., 256
Bevan, W., 26, 58
Birnbaum, M., 256
Bower, D., 126
Butler, A., 184
Bybee, D., 172

Caddell, D., 90, 91
Campbell, D., 28, 30, 89
Charmaz, K., 43
Chase, S., 44, 45, 187, 189
Christensen, G., 53
Clark, V., 40
Clinchy, B., 44
Cohen, J., 31–32, 131
Colaizzi, P., 183
Connell, D., 104
Conrad, E., 35
Cook, T., 28
Corbin, J., 43, 107, 108, 185
Cornwell, B., 254
Crane, C., 91

Creswell, J., 52, 54, 107, 184
Cronbach, L., 30
Crotty, M., 35, 36, 38, 39, 42, 43, 48
Csikszentmihalyi, M., 53

Davenport, L., 75
DeBaryshe, B., 15, 16
Demoville, D., 55
Denzin, N., 36
Dillman, D., 256
Dong, L., 78
Dumas, C., 189, 190, 191, 192, 193

Einhorn, J., 186, 187
Elbow, P., 240, 241
Elliott, J., 49
Elliott, R., 224, 225
Erickson, B., 51
Erikson, E., 49
Ewing, N., 74

Ferguson, J., 165, 281, 284
Feyerabend, P., 35
Fidell, L., 163
Fischer, C., 224, 225
Flemons, D., 244
Flick, U., 113
Flores, F., 48
Frankfort-Nachmias, C., 253
Frazier, P., 13
Freud, S., 51

Gelfand, H., 273
Gergen, K., 35
Gergen, M., 52
Gigerenzer, G., 31

Gilbert, M., 97
Giorgi, A., 40, 183
Glaser, B., 43, 107, 185
Glass, G., 56
Glover, L., 55
Glueckauf, R., 13
Goffman, E., 41
Goldberg, E., 75, 76
Goldberg, N., 244
Goldberger, N., 44
Golden-Biddle, K., 224
Goodwin, C., 92
Greenwood, D., 56
Guba, E., 39, 106, 111, 112
Gubrium, J., 39

Hamilton, L., 34
Hammersley, M., 41
Hardwick, C., 96
Haring, E., 189, 190
Harlow, L., 131
Hedges, V., 43
Hein, S., 49
Herr, K., 57
Holstein, J., 39
Holtz, P., 51
Hoshmand, L., 41, 48
Huberman, A., 46, 112, 177, 191
Humphrey, D., 45
Husserl, E., 39

Jackson, D., 13
Jersild, D., 79, 80, 91
Jones, S., 42
Josselson, R., 71, 79, 106, 108, 111

Katz, S., 76, 107, 187
Kazdin, A., 28, 50
Keen, E., 183
Kennedy, C., 50
Kenny, D., 13
Kerlinger, F., 6, 27, 28, 89
Knight, C., 44
Kramer, S., 84
Krebs, C., 55
Krueger, B., 256

Kuhn, T., 24, 64
Kvale, S., 111

LaPelle, N., 77, 78, 110
Lee, H., 6, 28, 89
Leon, J., 191
Levin, M., 56
Lewin, K., 57
Lewis, O., 44
Lieblich, A., 71, 79, 106, 108, 111
Liebow, E., 41
Lincoln, Y., 36, 39, 106, 111, 112
Locke, K., 224
Locke, L., 74
Lundgren, D., 254
Lynch-Ransom, J., 79
Lynd, H., 51
Lynd, R., 51

Macdonald, S., 89
MacDougall, S., 42
MacNulty, W., 16, 17
Mahoney, M., 48
Marshall, C., 112
McAdams, D., 79
Mead, G., 42, 43
Menaghan, E., 147
Mertens, D., 42
Miles, M., 46, 112, 177, 191
Milgram, S., 277
Mishler, E., 111, 113
Moore, E., 108
Moos, R, 16, 17
Morgan, D., 52
Morse, J., 77, 79, 113
Moustakas, C., 40, 76, 182, 183
Mulaik, S., 131

Nachmias, D., 253
Neighbors, J., 165
Neimeyer, R., 35, 54
Nelson, D., 53
Nesbary, D., 256
New, N., 90
Newton, R., 56, 94, 119, 131, 145, 149, 163
Newton, S., 101

Nicholsen, S., 62, 63
Nobles, D., 53

Osherson, S., 247

Packer, M., 49
Parcel, T., 147
Patterson, G., 15, 16
Peplau, L., 35
Piliavin, I., 277
Piliavin, J., 277
Polkinghorne, D., 39, 47
Popper, K., 35

Quittner, A., 13

Rainaldi, L., 55
Ramsey, E., 15, 16
Rennie, D., 43, 71, 110, 224, 225
Richards, L., 112, 177, 182
Richards, N., 146
Rico, G., 234
Riessman, D., 45
Rogers, S., 147
Rossman, G., 112
Rubin, H., 111
Rubin, I., 111
Rudestam, K., 56, 94, 100, 119,
    131, 145, 149, 163

Sangster, M., 89, 145
Schaefer, J., 16
Schecter, E., 45
Schutz, W., 24
Shapiro, J., 62, 63
Sherman, S., 41
Sieber, J., 275
Silverman, D., 112, 114, 177
Silverman, S., 74
Slanger, E., 53, 100
Smith, M., 58
Smith, P., 48, 77

Spirduso, W., 74
Stake, R., 49, 50
Stanley, J., 30, 89
Steiger, J., 131
Stevick, E., 183
Stewart, L., 104
Strauss, A., 43, 107, 108, 185
Stringer, E., 80
Sullivan, C., 172
Sutherland, C., 172
Sutherland, E., 24

Tabachnick, B., 163
Tal, I., 188, 200
Tarule, J., 44
Tashakkori, A., 51, 52
Teddlie, C., 51, 52
Tix, A., 13
Toulmin, S., 35
Truss, L., 63
Turner, V., 45

van Kaam, A., 40, 182
Veroff, J., 36, 227

Walker, C., 273
Wardell, W., 40
Wegmann, M., 200
Weiss, R., 111
Whyte, W., 51
Williams, H., 80
Williams, R., 192, 194
Winograd, T., 48
Witt, J., 58
Wolcott, H., 184
Woodard, C., 98
Wright, K., 92, 254, 255
Wright, R., 264

Yin, R., 50

Zemansky, T., 91

Subject Index

Abstracts, 199–201
Action research, 56–58, 80
Alpha levels, 93–94
American Psychological Association guidelines for human participants, 278, 289f–292f
Analysis of covariance, 34f
Analysis of variance (ANOVA), 30, 150, 154–157
Anonymity, 280
ANOVA test, 30, 150, 154–157
APA style:
 for figures, 127–128, 169–170, 172
 habit of using, 81
 numbers and, 265–273
 for tables, 127–130, 172
 in text vs. bibliography, 84
Appendices, 97, 102–103
Applied studies, 3–4, 6–7
Archival data, 100–102, 250–253, 256f–261f
Audit trail, 114
Axiologic level of knowledge, 24
Axial Coding, 185
Axiology, 24

Backup copies, 207
Barrett, Helen, 210–216
Bevan, William, 26
Bias in writing, 282, 284, 288
Bibliographic management software, 85
Bivariate tables:
 continuously distributed variables, 146–148
 cross-tabulations, 141–145
 means and standard deviations, 145–146, 147f

Blocks. *See* Emotional blocks; Task blocks
Brainstorming, 18–20
Bystander intervention studies, 277

Case studies, 49–51
Categorizing, 186–187
Causal relationships, 28–30
Cell frequencies, 142
Census data, 250–251, 261f
Children of Sanchez (Lewis), 44
Chi-square test, 149, 151, 167
Citations, 81, 84–85
Close-ups, 68–70
Clustering, 234
Coding, in Grounded Theory Approach, 185
Committees, 206–207, 218–220, 222, 252
Comparison groups as control, 34f
Concept, 6–7, 11, 18, 22, 44–45, 72–73, 100
Conceptual framework, 5–6
Conclusions chapter, 199, 202n
Confidence intervals, 152–153
Confidentiality, 103, 277, 280–281, ethics, and, 285–292
Constant comparative method, 185–186
Construct, defined, 22n
Constructivism, 35
Control, of variables, 27–34, 37–38, 67–68
Conversational analysis, 39
Copyrighted scales, use of, 98
Correlational paradigms, 30–31
Correlation coefficients, 31–32

Correlation matrix, 147, 149, 159–160, 163–164
Correlational study, 29
Criterion, 13, 107

Cronbach, Lee, 253
Cross-sectional design, 29, 88–89, 251
Cross-tabulations, 141–145

Data:
    archival, 100–102, 250–253, 256f–261f
    backup copies, 207
    coding, 139–140, 182–187, 217
    primary vs. secondary, 250
    qualitative vs. quantitative methods, 36
    secondary, 250–253
    Internet sources, 257–261
Data analysis:
    dependence on others for, 216–218
    exploratory, 119
    internet, using for, 256
    meta-analysis and, 56
    preparation for, 132–133
    presentation of. See Results chapter in qualitative studies; Results chapter in quantitative studies
    primary vs. secondary, 250
    process of in qualitative studies, 182–183, 185, 186–188
    proposals and, 103–105
    in qualitative studies, 111–112
    research question type and, 149–151
    in research wheel, 5
    software for, 174–175, 177–181
Data collection:
    archival data, 100–102, 250–253, 256f–261f
    case studies and, 51
    formatting the variables for, 132–133
    incentives for, 254–255
    instrument modification and, 99–100
    internet, using for, 91–92, 253–256, 262f–264f
    in mixed models, 52–54
    in qualitative studies, 111

research design and, 46–47
in research wheel, 5
saturation and, 107–108, 185
secondary data and, 250–253
theoretical dissertations and, 54–55
transcription programs for, 178
working with others for, 216–218
Debriefing, 115, 281
Deception, 277, 281, 289–290
Deductive, 7, 36, 41, 43, 46
Delimitations in research design, 105
Demographic data sheets, 100
Description of sample section, 118–119
Descriptive statistics, defined, 27
Design. See Research design
Design statements, 88–89
Detective mode, 238
Deviant case analysis, 114, 186
Diamond, Jared, 28
Directional hypotheses, 74
Disclosure, 280–281
Discriminate sampling, 108
Discussion chapter, 195–199
    elements of, 195
    negative results, 198
    oversights in, 197–198
    qualitative dissertation in, 199
    student suggestions, 202
    summary and conclusions, 199
Dissertation barriers:
    depending upon others, 216
    emotional blocks, 208
    task blocks, 209
Dissertation Abstracts, 199
Dissertation approaches
    action research, 56–58
    case studies, 49–51
    hermeneutics, 47–49
    meta-analysis, 56
    mixed models, 51–54
    theoretical dissertations, 54–55
    See also Qualitative methods; Quantitative methods; Research design; Theoretical dissertations

Dissertation Orals, 218
Duquesne University, 40
Dust bowl empiricism, 72–73

EDA (exploratory data analysis), 119
Effect size, 131, 153
Emic perspective, 42
Emotional blocks, 208–209, 230–232
Empirical level of knowledge, 24
Empirical observation, 5, 28–29
Empirical phenomenology, 40
Empiricism, 24
Epistemic level of knowledge, 24
Epistemology, 24–26
Ethics:
  anonymity, 280
  APA guide to, 278, 289f–292f
  bias-free writing, 282
  checklist for, 287f–288f
  confidentiality, 285–292
  criteria for, 275–276
  debriefing, 115
  deception, 277, 281, 289–290
  disclosure, 280–281
  five "Cs" of research ethics, 287
  gender neutral words, 284
  human subjects committees, 103
  informed consent examples,
    283f–284f, 285f–286f
  letter of invitation, 282f
  minimal risk, 278
  procedures for meeting
    standards for, 275
Ethnographic inquiry, 41–42, 79,
  108–109, 184
Ethnomethodology, 39
Etic perspective, 42
Experimental control. See also
  Control
Experimental design, 28–30
  posttest only design, 30
  pretest, posttest, control group
    design, 29
Exploratory data analysis (EDA), 119
Exploratory study, 50
Ex post facto research designs, 28–29
External validity, 113

Fielding Graduate University, 247–248
Field study, 38, 53
Figures. See Statistical presentation
Freimuth, Marilyn, 23–25
Frequency distribution, 34f, 132

Genograms, 192f
Gobbledygook, 228
Grammar:
  disconnection from writing and,
    229–230, 239–240
  importance of, 62–63
  learning of, 230–231
  numbers and, 265–273
  tips for, 82–83
Graphs. See Figures
Grounded theory:
  data coding and, 184–187
  interviews in, 110
  overview of, 42–44
  results chapter in, 189, 190f
  sample size and, 107–108
  Statement of the Problem and, 77–79
GSS (National Opinion Research
  Center General Social Survey),
  100, 134–141

Handlon, Joseph, 68–70
Hastorf, Albert, 253
Health Insurance Portability and
  Accountability Act (HIPAA), 281
Hermeneutics, 47–49
Heuristic research, defined, 40
Hierarchical regression, 34f
Hierarchy of knowledge, 23–25
HIPAA (Health Insurance Portability
  and Accountability Act), 281
Homogeneous sampling, 107
How Many Subjects? Statistical Power
  Analysis in Research (Kraemer), 93
Human subjects committee, 103
Hyper TRANSCRIBE, 178
Hypotheses:
  alternative, 120, 173
  defined, 24
  directional, 74
  inductive analysis and, 185–186

null, 74, 93, 130–131
  as positive assertions, 74
  research, 73, 94, 120, 173
  research questions and, 74–75
  in research wheel, 5
  in Statement of the Problem
    chapters, 72–76
  statistical, 172–173
  testing, 4, 25, 94, 130–131,
    151–152, 211

ICPSR (Inter-university Consortium
    for Political and Social Research),
    250, 258f
Idea file, 22
Inductive analysis, 185–186, 196
Inferential statistics, 27, 148–153
Informed consent:
  APA guide to, 289f–290f
  elements of, 278–281
  as ethical criteria, 276
  example forms for, 283f–284f,
    285f–286f
  need for, 276–277
  in procedures section, 103
  when needed, 278
Institute for Social Research, 250
Institutional review boards
    (IRB), 275
Instrumentation section, 95–102,
    109–111
Instrument development, 98–99
  copyrighted, 96
  See also Scales
Integrated Public Use Microdata
    Series (IPUMS), 251
Internal validity, 113
Internet:
  data analysis and, 256
  for data collection, 91–92,
    253–256, 262f–264f
  for participant recruitment,
    91–92
  secondary data and, 250–253
Internet Data Collection (Best &
    Krueger), 256
Interrater reliability, 217

Inter-university Consortium for
    Political and Social Research
    (ICPSR), 250, 258f
Interviewing, 44–45, 47, 109–111
Introduction sections, 61–62, 235–236
Introduction to Behavioral Research on
    the Internet (Birnbaum), 256
IPUMS (Integrated Public Use
    Microdata Series), 251
IRB (Institutional review boards), 275

Jargon, 228
Journal publication, 221–225,
    227–228
Jung, Carl, 49

Kinsey report, 13
Knowledge, approach to generating,
    25–26
Knowledge by acquaintance, 7
Knowledge by description, 7
Knowledge hierarchy, 23–25

Letters of invitation, 282f
Letter-writing, 234–235
Levels of Emotional Awareness Scale
    (LEAS), 97
Libraries, use of, 84–85
Life histories, 44–45
Literature reviews:
  as argument for dissertation,
    62–64
  contradictions in, 11
  critiquing of studies, 66–68
  depth of treatment and, 68–70
  as dialogue with reader, 63
  discussion chapters and, 196–197
  introduction section for, 61–62
  maintaining authority in, 64–66
  oral defense and, 218–219
  proposals and, 20–21
  publication of dissertation and, 223
  purpose of, 62
  qualitative dissertations and, 71–72
  selectivity of, 65–66
  Statement of the Problem,
    connecting with, 72

theoretical dissertations and, 54–55
tips for, 82
topic selection and, 9
Logical positivism, 26, 35
Long, Judy Stevens, 83
Longitudinal Survey of Youth 1997
(NLSY97), 251
Long shots, 68–70

Mail and Internet Surveys: The
Tailored Design Method
(Dillman), 256
Marginal frequencies, 142
*Mastering APA Style: Student's
Workbook and Training Guide Fifth
Edition* (Gelfand & Walker), 273
Matching, 30, 34
MAX Maps, 178, 181f
Measures. *See* Instrumentation section;
specific instruments
Medium shots, 68–70
Member checks, 114
Meta-analysis, 56
Method chapter in qualitative
dissertations:
data analysis and, 111–112
data collection and, 111
instrumentation section of,
109–111
sampling and sample size,
106–109
validity and reliability, 112–115
Method chapter in quantitative
dissertations:
data analysis and, 103–105
design statement in, 88–89
instrumentation section of, 95–102
procedures section, 102–103
sample size and, 92–95
sections of, 88
subjects section of, 89–95
Methodological control, 27.
See also Control
Methodologies, 38
Methods. *See* Qualitative methods;
Quantitative methods; Research
design

Missing values, 132–134, 137, 139
Mixed models, 51–54
Mnemonics, 129
Moderator variable, 13, 19, 104
Models, 13–18, 24
Modern Data Analysis (Hamilton), 34
*Modern Statistical Methods:
Substantially Improving Power
and Accuracy* (Wilcox), 93
MRA (multiple regression analysis),
149, 157–164
Multiple correlation (R), 158
Multiple regression, 30–31
Multiple regression analysis
(MRA), 149, 157–164

N (sample size), 142. *See also*
Sample size
Narrative inquiry, 44–45, 79–80
National Archive of Criminal Justice
Data, 251
National Institutes of Health, 278
National Longitudinal Surveys
(NLS), 251
National Opinion Research
Center General Social Survey
(GSS), 100, 134–141
Naturalistic research, 41, 112
Naturalistic Inquiry (Lincoln and
Guba), 112
Nested design, 52–53
New York Times, 254
NLS (National Longitudinal
Surveys), 251
NLSY97 (Longitudinal Survey
of Youth 1997), 251
Nonrandom sampling, 90–92
Notes for tables, 129–131
nQuery Advisor (program), 93
Null hypotheses, 74, 93
Null-hypothesis-significance-test
approach, 130–131
Numbers in dissertations, rules
for, 128–129, 265–273

Observational study, 109
One-tailed test, 130, 148, 173

Open coding, 187
Operationalize, 15, 22, 67, 73–74,
    76, 97
Oral defense, 218–221
Oral histories, 44–45
*Organic Constructionism and Living
    Process Theory: A Unified
    Constructionist Epistemology and
    Theory of Knowledge* (Krebs), 55
Organizational skills, 210–216

p values, 32, 122–124, 130–131, 157–159
    reporting of, 122–123
    See also Probability values
Paradigm, 24
Participants:
    impact of research on, 275–277
    informed consent and, 278–281
    letter of invitation for, 282f
    pilot tests for, 96, 115
    See also Subjects, Subjects section
Path analysis, 107
Peer review, 115
Percentage difference, 144–145
Perkins, David, 121–124, 170n
Phenomenology:
    data coding and, 183
    hermeneutics and, 48–49
    interviews in, 109–110
    overview of, 39–41
    sampling and sample size, 106–107
    Statement of the Problem and,
        76–80
Pilot tests, 96, 115
Plan-act-observe-reflect cycle, 57
Plan of inquiry. *See* Method chapter in
    qualitative dissertations
Power analyses, 93–95
Precision matching, 34f
Predictors, 13
Pretest-posttest control group
    design, 29–30
Price, Richard, 51
Primary source materials,
    importance of, 64
Probability values, reporting of,
    122–123

Problems with dissertation:
    committee selection, 206–207
    dependence on others for data,
        216–218
    emotional blocks and, 208–209,
        230–232
    oral defense and, 218–221
    organizational skills, 210–216
    time management, 209–210
Procedures section, 102–103
Proposals:
    as contract, 4–5
    data analysis and, 103–105
    elements of, 5
    introduction section for, 61–62
    issues to consider, 20–21
    limitations of research section, 105
    qualitative research and, 46–47
Propositions in research wheel, 5
Proquest, 254
*Publication Manual of the American
    Psychological Association*
    (2004), 81, 122, 240, 265. *See also*
    Numbers, rules for
Publication of dissertations,
    10, 221–225

Qualitative methods:
    case studies and, 49–51
    constructivism and, 35–36
    dissertation and, 47
    ethnographic inquiry, 41–42
    grounded theory, 42–44
    literature reviews and, 71–72
    mixed models, 51–54
    narrative inquiry, 44–45
    phenomenology, 39–41
    prison behavior example, 46–47
    proposals and, 46–47
    publication of dissertation and,
        224–225
    quantitative methods vs., 36–38
    Statement of the Problem
        and, 76–80
Quantitative methods:
    applied limitations of, 28
    control vs. meaningfulness, 32

correlational paradigms, 30–31
descriptive vs. inferential
   statistics, 27
experimental designs and, 30
ex post facto design, 28–29
logical positivism and, 26
mixed models, 51–54
multiple regression and, 30–31
publication of dissertation and, 224
qualitative methods vs., 36–38
randomization and, 27, 30, 34f
random sampling as, 27
single-subject designs, 50
stem-and-leaf design, 32, 33f–34f
t test and, 30
Quasi-experimental research
   designs, 28–29
Questionnaires, 31, 52, 91
   bias free writing, 282
   ethics, 290
   informed consent, 282
   minimal risk, 276
Quotations in literature reviews, 65

Randomization, 27, 30, 34f
Random sampling, 27, 90–92
Rationalism, 24
References, 81, 84–85
Reflexivity, 45, 114
Release forms, 103
Reliability, 96, 113
Research articles, critiquing of,
   66–68
Research design:
   case studies and, 49–51
   causal relationships and, 30
   control methods, 34f
   deception and, 277
   design statements, 88–89
   ex post facto, 28–29
   hermeneutics and, 47–49
   limitations in, 105
   literature reviews and, 66–68
   meta-analysis as, 56
   mixed models, 51–54
   pretest-posttest control group,
      29–30

selection of, 26, 39
social science discipline and, 25–26
statistics and, 31–32
See also Qualitative methods;
   Quantitative methods
Research Methods in the Social Sciences
   (Frankfort-Nachmias and
   Nachmias), 253
Research problem, wording of, 61–62
Research questions:
   brainstorming for, 18–20
   data analysis and, 149–151
   deduction and, 7
   hypotheses and, 74–75
   as relationship between multiple
      variables, 11–13
   in research wheel, 5
   results section organization and, 120
   as snapshot, 15
   types of, 149–151
   visual models of, 16–18
Research wheels, 5–8, 196
Russell, Bertrand, 7–8
Results chapter in qualitative studies
   data coding and, 182–187
   introduction section for, 188
   organization of, 188–189
   results presentation, 189–194
   software for data analysis, 177–181
   type of study and, 183–185
Results chapter in quantitative
   studies:
   data coding and, 182
   description of sample section,
      118–119
   organization of, 117–118
   research questions and, 120
   Statement Type I, 121
   Statement Type II, 122
   Statement Type III, 122–123
   Statement Type IV, 123–124
   subheadings in, 119–120
   See also Statistical presentation
Reviews of the literature. *See*
   Literature reviews
Revisions, 244–245, 247
Rolett, Barry, 28

Sample Power (program), 93
Sample size, 92–95, 106–109, 142
Sampling design, 90–92, 106–109
Saturation, 107–108, 185
Scatter plots, 146
Scales:
   copyrighted, 96
   describing in tables, 128, 165
   measurement, 96–99
   online administration of, 254
   selection of, 95
   See also Instruments
Sears, Pauline, 253
Sears, Robert, 253
Secondary data, 250–253
Selective coding, 187
Self-schema model, 16–17
Single-subject designs, 50
Snowball technique, 91
Social constructivism, 35
Software programs, 174–175,
   177–181, 219, 254
Source materials, primary, 64
Statement of the Problem chapters
   contents of, 72–73
   hypotheses in, 72–76
   literature reviews, connecting
      with, 72
   qualitative dissertations and,
      71–72
   in qualitative studies, 76–80
Statement Type I, 121
Statement Type II, 122
Statement Type III, 122–123
Statement Type IV, 123–124
*Statistical Power Analysis for the
   Behavioral Sciences* (Cohen), 93
Statistical presentation:
   ANOVA and, 154–157
   APA style and, 272–273
   bivariate tables. *See* Bivariate tables
   confidence intervals in, 152–153
   determination of, 171–172
   figures, 127, 168–170, 190f, 191–194
   multiple regression analysis and,
      149, 157–164

research question type and, 149–151
   streamlining tables, 165–168
   summaries, examples of, 124–126
   univariate tables, 134–141
Statistical significance, effect size
   and, 131
Statistics, 27, 31–32, 124–126. *See also*
   Statistical presentation
Stem-and-leaf designs, 32, 33f–34f
Street Corner Society (Whyte), 51
Structure, 96
Student suggestions, 22, 81, 115, 202
Subjects:
   expressing number of, 273
   describing, in sample, 89–90
   power, and 93–95
   statistical significance, and 131
   See also Participants
Subjects section, 89–95
   See also Participants
Summary chapter, 199, 202n
Supervision groups, 209
*Survey Research and the World
   Wide Web* (Nesbary), 256
Symbolic interaction, 42–43

t tests, 30, 94
Tables:
   need for, 126–127
   parts of, 128–131, 133–134
   in qualitative studies, 191, 193f
   See also Statistical presentation
Task blocks, 209–216
Terman, Lewis, 253
Terman Data Files, 253
Texts, study of, 47–49
Theoretical dissertations, 54–55
Theoretical level of knowledge, 24
Theoretical saturation, 107–108
Theoretical studies, applied
   studies vs., 6–7
Theories, 24
Thick description, 113
Three-level hierarchy of
   knowledge, 23–25
Time management, 209–210

Titles, 129, 201–202
Topic selection:
    applied vs. theoretical, 6–7
    emotional blocks and, 208
    exploration of field and, 9
    guidelines for appropriateness,
        10–11
    instrument design as, 98–99
    research question development and,
        11–13
    writing dissertation and, 237–238
    See also Research questions
Transcription, 178
Trephining, 25
Triangulation, 114–115
Two-tailed test, 130
Type II errors, 93

Unitizing, 185, 186
Univariate tables, 134–141
University of Minnesota Population
    Center, 251
U.S. Census, 250–251, 261f

Validity, 96, 112–113, 275
Variables:
    continuously distributed, 146–148
    defined, 22n
    dependent, 13, 142–143
    formatting of, 132–133
    independent, 13, 142–143
    mediating, 13–15
    moderator, 13–15
    operationalization of, 73–74
    research questions and, 11–13
    sample size and, 94–95
    table placement of, 142–143

Venn diagrams, 69–70
Virtual Writing Center, 247–248
Visuals, 16–18
Voice (writing), 238–242

Websites. See Internet
Women's Ways of Knowing
    (Belenky et. al.), 44
Writer's block, 232–233, 242–243
Writing:
    authorship and voice, 238–242
    bias and, 282, 284, 288
    detective mode in, 238
    grammar. See Grammar
    journal publication and, 227–228
    numbers and, 128–129, 265–273
    past experience and, 228–232
    publication of dissertation
        and, 224
    reader response and, 242–244
    revision, 244–245, 247
    skills needed, 228
    topic selection and, 237–238
    tricks for, 245–247
    writer's block and, 232–233,
        242–243
    writing exercises, 233–237,
        241–242, 243
Writing Down the Bones
    (Goldberg), 244
Writing the Natural Way (Rico), 234
Writing With Power (Elbow), 240–241

Young Man Luther (Erikson), 49
Your Statistical Consultant: Answers
    to Your Data Analysis Questions
    (Newton), 94

About the Authors

Kjell Erik Rudestam, PhD, is Associate Dean of Academic Affairs at Fielding Graduate University in Santa Barbara, California. He was previously professor of psychology at York University, Toronto. He received his PhD in psychology from the University of Oregon. He is author of *Methods of Self-Change, Experiential Groups in Theory and Practice, Treating the Multi-Problem Family* (with Mark Frankel); *Your Statistical Consultant: Answers to Your Data Analysis Questions* (with Rae Newton); *Handbook of Online Learning* (with Judith Schoenholtz-Read); and *Encyclopaedia of Distributed Learning* (with Anna DiStefano and Robert Silverman), as well as numerous articles in professional journals. His research interests are in the areas of psychotherapy and change processes, suicide, and family and organizational systems. He is a licensed clinical psychologist, Fellow of the American Psychological Association, and Diplomate of the American Board of Examiners in Professional Psychology (Clinical).

Rae R. Newton, PhD, is Professor Emeritus at California State University Fullerton, Department of Sociology. He currently serves as a consulting faculty member at Fielding Graduate University in Santa Barbara, California, and is coprincipal investigator, with Dr. Alan Litrownik, on a 20-year longitudinal study of the etiology and impact of child maltreatment, funded by the National Center on Child Abuse and Neglect. His research with Dr. Litrownik and other collaborators has helped shape researchers' understanding of the long-term consequences of removal and reunification from abusive, violent, and neglectful environments.